Modern Critical Views

Chinua Achebe
Henry Adams
Aeschylus
S. Y. Agnon
Edward Albee
Raphael Alberti
Louisa May Alcott
A. R. Ammons
Sherwood Anderson
Aristophanes
Matthew Arnold
Antonin Artaud
John Ashbery
Margaret Atwood
W. H. Auden
Jane Austen
Isaac Babel
Sir Francis Bacon
James Baldwin
Honoré de Balzac
John Barth
Donald Barthelme
Charles Baudelaire
Simone de Beauvoir
Samuel Beckett
Saul Bellow
Thomas Berger
John Berryman
The Bible
Elizabeth Bishop
William Blake
Giovanni Boccaccio
Heinrich Böll
Jorge Luis Borges
Elizabeth Bowen
Bertolt Brecht
The Brontës
Charles Brockden Brown
Sterling Brown
Robert Browning
Martin Buber
John Bunyan
Anthony Burgess
Kenneth Burke
Robert Burns
William Burroughs
George Gordon, Lord
   Byron
Pedro Calderón de la Barca
Italo Calvino
Albert Camus
Canadian Poetry: Modern
   and Contemporary
Canadian Poetry through
   E. J. Pratt
Thomas Carlyle
Alejo Carpentier
Lewis Carroll
Willa Cather
Louis-Ferdinand Céline
Miguel de Cervantes

Geoffrey Chaucer
John Cheever
Anton Chekhov
Kate Chopin
Chrétien de Troyes
Agatha Christie
Samuel Taylor Coleridge
Colette
William Congreve & the
   Restoration Dramatists
Joseph Conrad
Contemporary Poets
James Fenimore Cooper
Pierre Corneille
Julio Cortázar
Hart Crane
Stephen Crane
e. e. cummings
Dante
Robertson Davies
Daniel Defoe
Philip K. Dick
Charles Dickens
James Dickey
Emily Dickinson
Denis Diderot
Isak Dinesen
E. L. Doctorow
John Donne & the
   Seventeenth-Century
   Metaphysical Poets
John Dos Passos
Fyodor Dostoevsky
Frederick Douglass
Theodore Dreiser
John Dryden
W. E. B. Du Bois
Lawrence Durrell
George Eliot
T. S. Eliot
Elizabethan Dramatists
Ralph Ellison
Ralph Waldo Emerson
Euripides
William Faulkner
Henry Fielding
F. Scott Fitzgerald
Gustave Flaubert
E. M. Forster
John Fowles
Sigmund Freud
Robert Frost
Northrop Frye
Carlos Fuentes
William Gaddis
André Gide
W. S. Gilbert
Allen Ginsberg
J. W. von Goethe
Nikolai Gogol
William Golding

Oliver Goldsmith
Mary Gordon
Günther Grass
Robert Graves
Graham Greene
Thomas Hardy
Nathaniel Hawthorne
William Hazlitt
H. D.
Seamus Heaney
Lillian Hellman
Ernest Hemingway
Hermann Hesse
Geoffrey Hill
Friedrich Hölderlin
Homer
A. D. Hope
Gerard Manley Hopkins
Horace
A. E. Housman
William Dean Howells
Langston Hughes
Ted Hughes
Victor Hugo
Zora Neale Hurston
Aldous Huxley
Henrik Ibsen
Eugene Ionesco
Washington Irving
Henry James
Dr. Samuel Johnson and
   James Boswell
Ben Jonson
James Joyce
Carl Gustav Jung
Franz Kafka
Yasonari Kawabata
John Keats
Søren Kierkegaard
Rudyard Kipling
Melanie Klein
Heinrich von Kleist
Philip Larkin
D. H. Lawrence
John le Carré
Ursula K. Le Guin
Giacomo Leopardi
Doris Lessing
Sinclair Lewis
Jack London
Frederico García Lorca
Robert Lowell
Malcolm Lowry
Norman Mailer
Bernard Malamud
Stéphane Mallarmé
Thomas Malory
André Malraux
Thomas Mann
Katherine Mansfield
Christopher Marlowe

Continued at back of book

Modern Critical Views

PERCY BYSSHE SHELLEY

Modern Critical Views

PERCY BYSSHE SHELLEY

Edited with an introduction by

Harold Bloom

Sterling Professor of the Humanities
Yale University

1985
CHELSEA HOUSE PUBLISHERS
New York

THE COVER:
The cover illustration represents Shelley's vision of the autumnal leaves coming down as a harbinger of societal revolution and apocalyptic transformation in his "Ode to the West Wind." The leaves are emblematic of the words of his own poetry, which he calls "dead thoughts," meaning, among much else, his celebrated insight that the mind in creation is like a fading coal.—H.B.

Cover illustration by Michael Garland

Copyright © 1985 by Chelsea House Publishers,
a division of Chelsea House Educational Communications, Inc.
   345 Whitney Avenue, New Haven, CT 06511
   95 Madison Avenue, New York, NY 10016
   5068B West Chester Pike, Edgemont, PA 19028

Printed and bound in the United States of America

10 9 8 7 6 5 4 3

Library of Congress Cataloging in Publication Data

Shelley, modern critical views.
      Bibliography: p.
      Includes index.
      Contents: Introduction to Shelley / Harold Bloom—
Scepticism and Platonism / C.E. Pulos—The role
of Asia in Prometheus unbound / Frederick A. Pottle—
[etc.]
      1. Shelley Percy Bysshe, 1792–1822—Criticism and inter-
pretation—Addresses, essays, lectures. I. Bloom, Harold.
PR5438.S46   1984   821'.7   84–27400
ISBN 0–87754–609–6

Contents

Introduction......*Harold Bloom* 1

Scepticism and Platonism......*C. E. Pulos* 31

The Role of Asia in the Dramatic Action
    of Shelley's *Prometheus Unbound*
    Frederick A. Pottle.................................. 47

Orpheus and the West Wind......*James Rieger*............ 57

The Cenci: The Tragic Resolution......*Stuart Curran*....... 73

Shelley and His Precursors......*Harold Bloom*............ 91

Epipsychidion......*Leslie Brisman* 113

Shelley Disfigured: *The Triumph of Life*......*Paul de Man* ... 121

Adonais......*Jean Hall* 145

Shelley's *Defence of Poetry* in Our Time......*Paul Fry* 159

Shelley's Last Lyrics......*William Keach*................. 185

Chronology 217

Contributors 219

Bibliography 221

Acknowledgments 225

Index 227

Editor's Note

This volume gathers together a representative selection of the best criticism of Shelley written during the last thirty years. It begins with the editor's "Introduction" to a volume of Shelley's poetry, published about half-way through the period, and reflecting the debate of the 1950's and early 1960's as to Shelley's aesthetic eminence. This debate passed away with the Age of Eliot and the New Criticism that he inspired (F. R. Leavis, Allen Tate, W. H. Auden were the principal anti-Shelleyans), but it prepared the way for a more advanced criticism of Shelley.

The essay by C. E. Pulos begins the chronologically arranged sequence of this book, an apt starting-point because Pulos pioneered in demonstrating Shelley's skepticism and empiricism, in opposition to the mistaken scholarly tradition that emphasized Shelley's supposed Platonism as being other than skeptical. Frederick A. Pottle's masterly reading of *Prometheus Unbound* complements Pulos by setting Shelley's cognitive skepticism against his heart's pervasive desires, in a dialectical interplay that never ceased in Shelley's work.

James Rieger's account of Shelley's esotericism is balanced by Stuart Curran's analysis of the poet's more formal relation to the tradition of tragic drama. This is followed by the editor's revisionary essay on Shelley's anxious inheritance from poetic tradition, and from Wordsworth in particular.

The readings of *Epipsychidion* by Leslie Brisman, of *The Triumph of Life* by the late Paul de Man, of *Adonais* by Jean Hall and of Shelley's final lyrics by William Keach are all distinguished attempts at applying four very different modes of contemporary criticism to Shelley's major poems. Paul Fry's exegesis of the "Defence of Poetry" is the most profound reading that Shelley's superb critical rhapsody has received.

Introduction

*Mesdames, one might believe that Shelley lies
Less in the stars than in their earthy wake,
Since the radiant disclosures that you make
Are of an eternal vista, manqué and gold
And brown, an Italy of the mind, a place
Of fear before the disorder of the strange,
A time in which the poet's politics
Will rule in a poets' world.*
— WALLACE STEVENS

I

Percy Bysshe Shelley, one of the greatest lyrical poets in Western tradition, has been dead for more than a hundred and forty years, and critics have abounded, from his own day to ours, to insist that his poetry died with him. Until recently, it was fashionable to apologize for Shelley's poetry, if one liked it at all. Each reader of poetry, however vain, can speak only for himself, and there will be only description and praise in this introduction, for after many years of reading Shelley's poems, I find nothing in them that needs apology. Shelley is a unique poet, one of the most original in the language, and he is in many ways *the* poet proper, as much so as any in the language. His poetry is autonomous, finely wrought, in the highest degree imaginative, and has the spiritual form of vision stripped of all veils and ideological coverings, the vision many readers justly seek in poetry, despite the admonitions of a multitude of church-wardenly critics.

The essential Shelley is so fine a poet that one can feel absurd in urging his claims upon a reader:

> I am the eye with which the Universe
>   Beholds itself and knows itself divine;
> All harmony of instrument or verse,
>   All prophecy, all medicine is mine,
>   All light of art or nature—to my song
> Victory and praise in its own right belong.

That is Apollo singing, in the "Hymn" that Shelley had the sublime audacity to write for him, with the realization that, like Keats, he was a rebirth of Apollo. When, in *The Triumph of Life*, Rousseau serves as Virgil to Shelley's Dante, he is made to speak lines as brilliantly and bitterly condensed as poetry in English affords:

> And if the spark with which Heaven lit my spirit
> Had been with purer nutriment supplied,
>
> Corruption would not now thus much inherit
> Of what was once Rousseau—nor this disguise
> Stain that which ought to have disdained to wear it.

The urbane lyricism of the "Hymn of Apollo," and the harshly self-conscious, internalized dramatic quality of *The Triumph of Life* are both central to Shelley. Most central is the prophetic intensity, as much a result of displaced Protestantism as it is in Blake or in Wordsworth, but seeming more an Orphic than Hebraic phenomenon when it appears in Shelley. Religious poet as he primarily was, what Shelley prophesied was one restored Man who transcended men, gods, the natural world, and even the poetic faculty. Shelley chants the apotheosis, not of the poet, but of desire itself:

> Man, oh, not men! a chain of linked thought,
> Of love and might to be divided not,
> Compelling the elements with adamantine stress;
>   As the sun rules, even with a tyrant's gaze,
>   The unquiet republic of the maze
> Of planets, struggling fierce towards heaven's free wilderness.
>
>   Man, one harmonious soul of many a soul,
>   Whose nature is its own divine control,
> Where all things flow to all, as rivers to the sea. . . .

The rhapsodic intensity, the cumulative drive and yet firm control of those last three lines in particular, as the high song of humanistic celebration approaches its goal—that seems to me what is crucial in Shelley, and its presence throughout much of his work constitutes his special excellence as a poet.

Lyrical poetry at its most intense frequently moves toward direct address between one human consciousness and another, in which the "I" of the poet directly invokes the personal "Thou" of the reader. Shelley is an intense lyricist as Alexander Pope is an intense satirist; even as Pope assimilates every literary form he touches to satire, so Shelley converts forms as diverse as drama, prose essay, romance, satire, epyllion, into lyric. To an extent he himself scarcely realized, Shelley's genius desired a transformation of all experience, natural and literary, into the condition of lyric. More than all other poets, Shelley's compulsion is to present life as a direct confrontation of equal realities. This compulsion seeks absolute intensity, and courts straining and breaking in consequence. When expressed as love, it must manifest itself as mutual destruction:

> In one another's substance finding food,
> Like flames too pure and light and unimbued
> To nourish their bright lives with baser prey,
> Which point to Heaven and cannot pass away:
> One Heaven, one Hell, one immortality,
> And one annihilation.

Shelley is the poet of these flames, and he is equally the poet of a particular shadow, which falls perpetually between all such flames, a shadow of ruin that tracks every imaginative flight of fire:

> O, Thou, who plumed with strong desire
> Wouldst float above the earth, beware!
> A Shadow tracks thy flight of fire—
> Night is coming!

By the time Shelley had reached his final phase, of which the great monuments are *Adonais* and *The Triumph of Life,* he had become altogether the poet of this shadow of ruin, and had ceased to celebrate the possibilities of imaginative relationship. In giving himself, at last, over to the dark side of his own vision, he resolved (or perhaps merely evaded, judgment being so difficult here) a conflict within his self and poetry that had been present from the start. Though it has become a commonplace of recent criticism and scholarship to affirm otherwise, I do not think that Shelley changed very much, as a poet, during the last (and most important) six years of his life, from the summer of 1816 until the summer of 1822. The two poems of self-discovery, of mature poetic incarnation, written in 1816, "Mont Blanc" and the "Hymn to Intellectual Beauty," reveal the two contrary aspects of Shelley's vision that his entire sequence of major poems reveals. The head and the heart, each totally honest in encountering reality, yield rival reports as to the name and nature of reality. The head, in "Mont Blanc," learns, like Blake, that there is no natural religion. There is a Power, a secret strength of things, but it hides its true shape or its shapelessness behind or beneath a dread mountain, and it shows itself only as an indifference, or even pragmatically a malevolence, towards the well-being of men. But the Power speaks forth, through a poet's act of confrontation with it which is the very act of writing his poem, and the Power, rightly interpreted, can be used to repeal the large code of fraud, institutional and historical Christianity, and the equally massive code of woe, the laws of the nation-states of Europe in the age of Castlereagh and Metternich. In the "Hymn to Intellectual Beauty" a very different Power is invoked, but with a deliberate and even austere tenuousness. A shadow, itself invisible, of an unseen Power, sweeps through our dull dense world, momentarily awakening both nature and man to a sense of love and beauty, a sense just beyond the normal range of apprehension. But the shadow departs, for all its benevolence, and despite the poet's prayers for its more habitual sway. The heart's responses have not failed, but the shadow that is antithetically a radiance will not come to stay. The mind, searching for what would suffice, encountered an icy remoteness, but dared to affirm the triumph of its imaginings over the solitude and vacancy of an inadvertent nature. The emotions, visited by delight, felt the desolation of powerlessness, but dared to hope for a fuller visitation. Both odes suffer from the evident straining of their creator to reach a finality, but both survive in their creator's tough honesty and gathering sense of form.

"Mont Blanc" is a poem of the age of Shelley's father-in-law, William Godwin, while the "Hymn to Intellectual Beauty" belongs to the age of Wordsworth, Shelley's lost leader in the realms of emotion. Godwin became a kind of lost leader for Shelley also, but less on the intellectual than on the personal level. The scholarly criticism of Shelley is full of sand traps, and one of the deepest is the prevalent notion that Shelley underwent an intellectual metamorphosis from being the disciple of Godwin and the French philosophical materialists to being a Platonist or Neoplatonist, an all but mystical idealist. The man Shelley may have undergone such a transformation, though the evidence for it is equivocal; the poet Shelley did not. He started as a split being, and ended as one, but his awareness of the division in his consciousness grew deeper, and produced finally the infernal vision of *The Triumph of Life*.

II

But even supposing that a man should raise a dead body to life before our eyes, and on this fact rest his claim to being considered the son of God;—the Humane Society restores drowned persons, and because it makes no mystery of the method it employs, its members are not mistaken for the sons of God. All that we have a right to infer from our ignorance of the cause of any event is that we do not know it. . . .

(Shelley, *Notes On Queen Mab*)

The deepest characteristic of Shelley's poetic mind is its skepticism. Shelley's intellectual agnosticism was more fundamental than either his troubled materialism or his desperate idealism. Had the poet turned his doubt against all entities but his own poetry, while sparing that, he would have anticipated certain later developments in the history of literature, but his own work would have lost one of its most precious qualities, a unique sensitivity to its own limitations. This sensitivity can be traced from the very beginnings of Shelley's mature style, and may indeed have made possible the achievement of that style.

Shelley was anything but a born poet, as even a brief glance at his apprentice work will demonstrate. Blake at fourteen was a great lyric poet; Shelley at twenty-two was still a bad one. He found himself, as a stylist, in the autumn of 1815, when he composed the astonishing *Alastor*, a blank verse rhapsodic narrative of a destructive and subjective quest. *Alastor*, though it has been out of fashion for a long time, is nevertheless a great and appalling work, at once a dead end and a prophecy that Shelley finally could not evade.

Shelley's starting point as a serious poet was Wordsworth, and *Alastor* is a stepchild of *The Excursion*, a poem frigid in itself, but profoundly influential, if only antithetically, on Shelley, Byron, Keats, and many later poets. The figure of the Solitary, in *The Excursion*, is the central instance of the most fundamental of Romantic archetypes, the man alienated from others and himself by excessive self-consciousness. Whatever its poetic lapses, *The Excursion* is our most extensive statement of the Romantic mythology of the Self, and the young Shelley quarried in it for imaginatively inescapable reasons, as Byron and Keats did also. Though the poet-hero of *Alastor* is not precisely an innocent sufferer, he shares the torment of Wordsworth's Solitary, and like him:

> sees
> Too clearly; feels too vividly; and longs
> To realize the vision, with intense
> And over-constant yearning—there—there lies
> The excess, by which the balance is destroyed.

Alastor, whatever Shelley's intentions, is primarily a poem about the destructive power of the imagination. For Shelley, every increase in imagination ought to have been an increase in hope, but generally the strength of imagination in Shelley fosters an answering strength of despair. In the spring of 1815 Shelley, on mistaken medical advice, confidently expected a rapid death of consumption. By autumn this expectation was put by, but the recent imagining of his own death lingers on in *Alastor*, which on one level is the poet's elegy for himself.

Most critical accounts of *Alastor* concern themselves with the apparent problem of disparities between the poem's eloquent Preface and the poem itself, but I cannot see that such disparities exist. The poem is an extremely subtle internalization of the quest-theme of romance, and the price demanded for the internalization is first, the death-in-life of what Yeats called "enforced self-realization," and at last, death itself. The *Alastor* or avenging daemon of the title is the dark double of the poet-hero, the spirit of solitude that shadows him even as he quests after his emanative portion, the soul out of his soul that Shelley later called the epipsyche. Shelley's poet longs to realize a vision, and this intense and overconstant yearning destroys natural existence, for nature cannot contain the infinite energy demanded by the vision. Wordsworthian nature, and not the poet-hero, is the equivocal element in *Alastor*, the problem the reader needs to, but cannot, resolve. For this nature is a mirror-world, like that in Blake's "The Crystal Cabinet," or in much of Keats's *Endymion*. Its pyramids and domes are sepulchers for the imagination, and all its appearances are illusive, phantasmagoric, and serve only to thwart the poet's vision, and drive him on more fearfully upon his doomed and self-destructive quest. *Alastor* prophesies *The Triumph of Life*, and in the mocking light of the later poem the earlier work appears also to have been a dance of death.

The summer of 1816, with its wonderful products, "Mont Blanc" and the "Hymn to Intellectual Beauty," was for Shelley, as I have indicated, a rediscovery of the poetic self, a way out of the impasse of *Alastor*. The revolutionary epic, first called *Laon and Cyntha*, and then *The Revolt of Islam*, was Shelley's first major attempt to give his newly directed energies adequate scope, but the attempt proved abortive, and the poem's main distinction is that it is Shelley's longest. Shelley's gifts were neither for narrative nor for straightforward allegory, and the *terza rima* fragment, *Prince Athanase*, written late in 1817, a few months after *The Revolt of Islam* was finished, shows the poet back upon his true way, the study of the isolated imagination. Whatever the dangers of the subjective mode of *Alastor*, it remained always Shelley's genuine center, and his finest poems were to emerge from it. *Prince Athanase* is only a fragment, or fragments, but its first part at least retains something of the power for us that it held for the young Browning and the young Yeats. Athanase, from a Peacockian perspective, is quite like the delightfully absurd Scythrop of *Nightmare Abbey*, but if we will grant him his mask's validity we do find in him one of the archetypes of the imagination, the introspective, prematurely old poet, turning his vision outward to the world from his lonely tower of meditation:

His soul had wedded Wisdom, and her dower
Is love and justice, clothed in which he sate
Apart from men, as in a lonely tower,

Pitying the tumult of their dark estate.

There is a touch of Byron's Manfred, and of Byron himself, in Athanase, and Byron is the dominant element in Shelley's next enduring poem, the conversational *Julian and Maddalo*, composed in Italy in the autumn of 1818, after the poets had been reunited. The middle portion of *Julian and Maddalo*, probably based upon legends of Tasso's madness, is an excrescence, but the earlier part of the poem, and its closing lines, introduce another Shelley, a master of the urbane, middle style, the poet of the "Letter to Maria Gisborne," the "Hymn to Mercury," of parts of *The Witch of Atlas* and *The Sensitive Plant*, and of such beautifully con-trolled love lyrics as "To Jane: The Invitation" and "Lines Written in the Bay of Lerici." Donald Davie, who as a critic is essentially an anti-Shelleyan of the school of Dr. Leavis, and is himself a poet in a mode antithetical to Shelley's, has written an impressive tribute to Shelley's achievement as a master of the urbane style. What I find most remarkable in this mastery is that Shelley carried it over into his major achievement, the great lyrical drama, *Prometheus Unbound*, a work written almost entirely in the high style, on the precarious level of the sublime, where urbanity traditionally has no place. The astonishingly original tone of *Prometheus Unbound* is not always successfully maintained, but for the most part it is, and one aspect of its triumph is that critics should find it so difficult a tone to characterize. The urbane conversationalist, the relent-lessly direct and emotionally uninhibited lyricist, and the elevated prophet of a great age to come join together in the poet of *Prometheus Unbound*, a climactic work which is at once celebratory and ironic, profoundly idealis-tic and as profoundly skeptical, passionately knowing its truths and as passionately agnostic towards all truth. More than any other of Shelley's poems, *Prometheus Unbound* has been viewed as self-contradictory or at least as containing unresolved mental conflicts, so that a consideration of Shelley's ideology may be appropriate prior to a discussion of the poem.

The clue to the apparent contradictions in Shelley's thought is his profound skepticism, which has been ably expounded by C. E. Pulos in his study, *The Deep Truth*. There the poet's eclecticism is seen as centering on the point "where his empiricism terminates and his idealism begins." This point is the skeptic's position, and is where Shelley judged Montaigne, Hume, and his own older contemporary, the metaphysician Sir William Drummond, to have stood. From this position, Shelley was able to reject both the French materialistic philosophy he had embraced in his youth and the Christianity that he had never ceased to call a despotism. Yet the skeptic's position, though it powerfully organized Shelley's revolutionary polemicism, gave no personal comfort, but took the poet to what he himself called "the verge where words abandon us, and what wonder if we grow dizzy to look down the dark abyss of how little we know." That abyss is Demogorgon's, in *Prometheus Unbound*, and its secrets are not revealed by him, for "a voice is wanting, the deep truth is imageless," and Demogorgon is a shapeless darkness. Yeats, sensing the imminence of his apocalypse, sees a vast image, a beast advancing before the gathering darkness. Shelley senses the great change that the Revolution has heralded, but confronts as apocalyptic harbinger only a fabulous and formless darkness, the only honest vision available to even the most apocalyptic of skeptics. Shelley is the most Humean poet in the language, oddly as his temperament accords with Hume's, and it is Hume, not Berkeley or Plato, whose view of reality informs *Prometheus Unbound* and the poems that came after it. Even Necessity, the dread and supposedly Godwinian governing demon of Shelley's early *Queen Mab*, is more of a Humean than a Holbachian notion, for Shelley's Necessity is "conditional, tentative and philosophically ironical," as Pulos points out. It is also a Necessity highly advantageous to a poet, for a power both sightless and unseen is a power removed from dogma and from philosophy, a power that only the poet's imagination can find the means to approach. Shelley is the unacknowledged ancestor of Wallace Stevens' conception of poetry as the Supreme Fiction, and *Prometheus Unbound* is the most capable imagining, outside of Blake and Wordsworth, that the Romantic quest for a Supreme Fiction has achieved.

The fatal aesthetic error, in reading *Prometheus Unbound* or any other substantial work by Shelley, is to start with the assumption that one is about to read Platonic poetry. I mean this in either sense, that is, either poetry deeply influenced by or expressing Platonic doctrine, or in John Crowe Ransom's special sense, a poetry discoursing in things that are at any point legitimately to be translated into ideas. Shelley's skeptical and provisional idealism is *not* Plato's, and Shelley's major poems are mythopoeic, and not translatable into any terms but their own highly original ones. Shelley has been much victimized in our time by two rival and equally pernicious critical fashions, one that seeks to "rescue" visionary poetry by reading it as versified Plotinus and Porphyry, and another that condemns visionary poetry from Spenser through Hart Crane as being a will-driven allegorization of an idealistic scientism vainly seeking to rival the whole of experimental science from Bacon to the present day. The first kind of criticism, from which Blake and Yeats have suffered as much as Shelley, simply misreads the entire argument against nature that visionary poetry complexly conducts. The second kind, as pervasively American as the first is British, merely underestimates the considerable powers of mind that Shelley and other poets of his tradition possessed.

Shelley admired Plato as a poet, a view he derived from Montaigne, as Pulos surmises, and he appears also to have followed Montaigne in considering Plato to be a kind of skeptic. Nothing is further from Shelley's mind and art than the Platonic view of knowledge, and nothing is further from Shelley's tentative myths than the dogmatic myths of Plato. It is one of the genuine oddities of critical history that a tough-minded Humean poet, though plagued also by an idealistic and psuedo-Platonic heart, should have acquired the reputation of having sought beauty or truth in any Platonic way or sense whatsoever. No Platonist would have doubted immortality as darkly as Shelley did, or indeed would have so recurrently doubted the very existence of anything transcendent.

The most obvious and absolute difference between Plato and Shelley is in their rival attitudes toward aesthetic experience. Shelley resembles Wordsworth or Ruskin in valuing so highly certain ecstatic moments of aesthetic contemplation precisely because the moments are fleeting, because they occupy, as Blake said, the pulsation of an artery. For Shelley these are not moments to be put aside when the enduring light of the Ideas is found; Shelley never encounters such a light, not even in *Adonais*, where Keats appears to have found a kindred light in death. There is no ladder to climb in Shelley's poetry, any more than there is in Blake's. There are more imaginative states-of-being and less imaginative ones, but no hierarchy to bridge the abyss between them.

III

It is no longer sufficient to say, like all poets, that mirrors resemble the water. Neither is it sufficient to consider that hypothesis as absolute and to suppose . . . that mirrors exhale a fresh wind or that thirsty birds drink them, leaving empty frames. We must go beyond such things. That capricious desire of a mind which becomes compulsory reality must be manifested—an individual must be shown who inserts himself into the glass and remains in its illusory land (where there are figurations and colors but these are impaired by immobile silence) and feels the shame of being nothing more than an image obliterated by nights and permitted existence by glimmers of light.

(Jorge Luis Borges)

It has been my experience, as a teacher of Shelley, that few recent students enjoy *Prometheus Unbound* at a first reading, and few fail to admire it greatly at a second or later reading. *Prometheus Unbound* is a remarkably subtle and difficult poem. That a work of such length needs to be read with all the care and concentration a trained reader brings to a difficult and condensed lyric is perhaps unfortunate, yet Shelley himself affirmed that his major poem had been written only for highly adept readers, and that he hoped for only a few of these. *Prometheus Unbound* is not as obviously difficult as Blake's *The Four Zoas*, but it presents problems comparable to that work. Blake has the advantage of having made a commonplace understanding of his major poems impossible, while Shelley retains familiar (and largely misleading) mythological names like Prometheus and Jupiter. The problems of interpretation in Shelley's lyrical drama are as formidable as English poetry affords, and are perhaps finally quite unresolvable.

It seems clear that Shelley intended his poem to be a millennial rather than an apocalyptic work. The vision in Act III is of a redeemed nature, but not of an ultimate reality, whereas the vision in the great afterthought of Act IV does concern an uncovered universe. In Act IV the imagination of Shelley breaks away from the poet's apparent intention, and visualizes a world in which the veil of phenomenal reality has been rent, a world like that of the Revelation of St. John, or Night the Ninth of *The Four Zoas*. The audacity of Shelley gives us a vision of the last things without the sanction of religious or mythological tradition. Blake does the same, but Blake is systematic where Shelley risks everything on one sustained imagining.

I think that a fresh reader of *Prometheus Unbound* is best prepared if he starts with Milton in mind. This holds true also for *The Prelude*, for Blake's epics, for Keats's *Hyperion* fragments, and even for Byron's *Don Juan*, since Milton is both the Romantic starting point and the Romantic adversary. Shelley is as conscious of this as Blake or any of the others; the Preface to *Prometheus Unbound* refers to that demigod, "the sacred Milton," and commends him for having been "a bold inquirer into morals and religion." Searching out an archetype for his Prometheus, Shelley finds him in Milton's Satan, "the Hero of *Paradise Lost*," but a flawed, an imperfect hero, of whom Prometheus will be a more nearly perfect descendant. Shelley's poem is almost an echo chamber for *Paradise Lost*, but all the echoes are deliberate, and all of them are so stationed as to "correct" the imaginative errors of *Paradise Lost*. Almost as much as Blake's "brief epic," *Milton*, Shelley's *Prometheus Unbound* is a courageous attempt to save Milton from himself, and for the later poet. Most modern scholarly critics of Milton sneer at the Blakean or Shelleyan temerity, but no modern critic of Milton is as illuminating as Blake and Shelley are, and none knows better than they did how omnipotent an opponent they lovingly faced, or how ultimately hopeless the contest was.

Paraphrase is an ignoble mode of criticism, but it can be a surprisingly revealing one (of the critic as well as the work of course) and it is particularly appropriate to *Prometheus Unbound*, since the pattern of action in the lyrical drama is a puzzling one. A rapid survey of character and plot is hardly possible, since the poem in a strict (and maddening) sense has neither, but a few points can be risked as introduction. Shelley's source is Aeschylus, insofar as he has a source, but his genuine analogues are in his older contemporary Blake, whom he had never read, and of whom indeed he never seems to have heard. Prometheus has a resemblance both to Blake's Orc and to his Los; Jupiter is almost a double for Urizen, Asia approximates Blake's Jerusalem, while Demogorgon has nothing in common with any of Blake's "Giant Forms." But, despite this last, the shape of Shelley's myth is very like Blake's. A unitary Man fell, and split into torturing and tortured components, and into separated male and female forms as well. The torturer is not in himself a representative of comprehensive evil, because he is quite limited; indeed, he has been invented by his victim, and falls soon after his victim ceases to hate his own invention. Shelley's Jupiter, like Urizen in one of his aspects, is pretty clearly the Jehovah of institutional and historical Christianity. George Bernard Shaw, one of the most enthusiastic of Shelleyans, had some illuminating remarks on *Prometheus Unbound* in *The Perfect Wagnerite*. Jupiter, he said, "is the almighty fiend into whom the Englishman's God had degenerated during two centuries of ignorant Bible worship and shameless commercialism." Shaw rather understated the matter, since it seems indubitable that the Jupiter of Shelley's lyrical drama is one with the cheerfully abominable Jehovah of *Queen Mab*, and so had been degenerating for rather more than two centuries.

Prometheus in Shelley is both the archetypal imagination (Blake's Los) and the primordial energies of man (Blake's Orc). Jupiter, like Urizen again, is a limiter of imagination and of energy. He may masquerade as reason, but he is nothing of the kind, being a mere circumscriber and binder, like the God of *Paradise Lost*, Book III (as opposed to the very different, creative God of Milton's Book VII). Asia is certainly not the Universal Love that Shaw and most subsequent Shelleyans have taken her to be. Though she partly transcends nature she is still subject to it, and she is essentially a passive being, even though the apparently central dramatic action of the poem is assigned to her. Like the emanations in

Blake, she may be taken as the total spiritual form or achieved aesthetic form quested after by her lover, Prometheus. She is less than the absolute vainly sought by the poet-hero of *Alastor*, though she is more presumably than the mortal Emilia of *Epipsychidion* can hope to represent. Her function is to hold the suffering natural world open to the transcendent love or Intellectual Beauty that hovers beyond it, but except in the brief and magnificent moment-of-moments of her transfiguration (end of Act II) she is certainly not one with the Intellectual Beauty.

That leaves us Demogorgon, the poem's finest and most frustrating invention, who has been disliked by the poem's greatest admirers, Shaw and Yeats. Had Shaw written the poem, Demogorgon would have been Creative Evolution, and had Yeats been the author, Demogorgon would have been the Thirteenth Cone of *A Vision*. But Shelley was a subtler dialectician than Shaw or Yeats; as a skeptic, he had to be. Shaw testily observed that "flatly, there is no such person as Demogorgon, and if Prometheus does not pull down Jupiter himself, no one else will." Demogorgon, Yeats insisted, was a ruinous invention for Shelley: "Demogorgon made his plot incoherent, its interpretation impossible; it was thrust there by that something which again and again forced him to balance the object of desire conceived as miraculous and superhuman, with nightmare."

Yet Demogorgon, in all his darkness, is a vital necessity in Shelley's mythopoeic quest for a humanized or displaced theodicy. The Demogorgon of Spenser and of Milton was the evil god of chaos, dread father of all the gentile divinities. Shelley's Demogorgon, like the unknown Power of *Mont Blanc*, is morally unallied; he is the god of skepticism, and thus the preceptor of our appalling freedom to imagine well or badly. His only clear attributes are dialectical; he is the god of all those at the turning, at the reversing of the cycles. Like the dialectic of the Marxists, Demogorgon is a necessitarian and materialistic entity, part of the nature of things as they are. But he resembles also the shadowy descent of the Holy Spirit in most Christian dialectics of history, though it would be more accurate to call him a demonic parody of the Spirit, just as the whole of *Prometheus Unbound* is a dark parody of Christian salvation myth. Back of Demogorgon is Shelley's difficult sense of divinity, an apocalyptic humanism like that of Blake's, and it is not possible therefore to characterize *Prometheus Unbound* as being either humanistic or theistic in its ultimate vision. Martin Price, writing of Blake's religion, observes that "Blake can hardly be identified as theist or humanist; the distinction becomes meaningless for him. God can only exist within man, but man must be raised to a perception of the infinite. Blake rejects both transcendental deity and natural man." The statement is equally true for the Shelley of *Prometheus Unbound*, if one modifies rejection of transcendental deity to a skeptical opening toward the possibility of such a Power. Though Demogorgon knows little more than does the Asia who questions him, that little concerns his relationship to a further Power, and the relationship is part of the imagelessness of ultimates, where poetry reaches its limit.

The events of *Prometheus Unbound* take place in the realm of mind, and despite his skepticism Shelley at this point in his career clung to a faith in the capacity of the human mind to renovate first itself, and then the outward world as well. The story of the lyrical drama is therefore an unfolding of renovation after renovation, until natural cycle itself is canceled in the rhapsodies of Act IV. Of actions in the traditional sense, I find only one, the act of pity that Prometheus extends toward Jupiter at line 53 of Act I. Frederick A. Pottle, in the most advanced essay yet written on the poem, insists that there is a second and as crucial action, the descent of Asia, with her subsequent struggle to attain to a theology of love: "Asia's action is to give up her demand for an ultimate Personal Evil, to combine an unshakable faith that the universe is sound at the core with a realization that, as regards man, Time is radically and incurably evil." Behind Pottle's reading is a drastic but powerful allegorizing of the poem, in which Prometheus and Asia occupy respectively the positions of head and heart: "The head must sincerely forgive, must willingly eschew hatred on purely experimental grounds . . ." while the heart "must exorcize the demons of infancy." One can benefit from this provisional allegorizing even if one finds *Prometheus Unbound* to be less theistic in its implications than Pottle appears to do.

Further commentary on the complexities of the poem can be sought in works listed in the bibliography of this volume, but the aesthetic achievement needs to be considered here. Dr. Samuel Johnson still knew that invention was the essence of poetry, but this truth is mostly neglected in our contemporary criticism. It may be justly observed that Shelley had conquered the myth of Prometheus even as he had transformed it, and the conquest is the greatest glory of Shelley's poem. One power alone, Blake asserted, made a poet: the divine vision or imagination, by which he meant primarily the inventive faculty, the gift of making a myth or of so re-making a myth as to return it to the fully human truths of our original existence as unfallen men. If Johnson and Blake were right, then *Prometheus Unbound* is one of the greatest poems in the language, a judgment that will seem eccentric only to a kind of critic whose standards are centered in areas not in themselves imaginative.

IV

Nature has appointed us men to be no base or ignoble animals, but when she ushers us into the vast universe . . . she implants in our souls the unconquerable love of whatever is elevated and more divine than we. Wherefore not even the entire universe suffices for the thought and contemplation within the reach of the human mind.

(Longinus, *On the Sublime*)

Published with *Prometheus Unbound* in 1820 were a group of Shelley's major odes, including "Ode to the West Wind," "To a Skylark," and "Ode to Liberty." These poems show Shelley as a lyricist deliberately seeking to extend the sublime mode, and are among his finest achievements.

Wallace Stevens, in one of the marvelous lyrics of his old age, hears the cry of the leaves and knows "it is the cry of leaves that do not transcend themselves," knows that the cry means no more than can be found "in the final finding of the ear, in the thing / Itself." From this it follows, with massive but terrible dignity, that "at last, the cry concerns no one at all." This is Stevens' modern reality of *decreation*, and this is the fate that Shelley's magnificent "Ode to the West Wind" seeks to avert. Shelley hears a cry of leaves that do transcend themselves, and he deliberately seeks a further transcendence that will metamorphosize "the thing itself" into human form, so that at last the cry will concern all men. But in Shelley's "Ode," as in Stevens, "there is a conflict, there is a resistance involved; / And being part is an exertion that declines." Shelley too feels the frightening strength of the *given*, "the life of that which gives life as it is," but here as elsewhere Shelley does not accept the merely "as it is." The function of his "Ode" is apocalyptic, and the controlled fury of his spirit is felt throughout this perfectly modulated "trumpet of a prophecy."

What is most crucial to an understanding of the "Ode" is the realization that its fourth and fifth stanzas bear a wholly antithetical relation to one another. The triple invocation to the elements of earth, air, and water occupies the first three stanzas of the poem, and the poet himself does not enter those stanzas; in them he is only a voice imploring the elements to hear. In the fourth stanza, the poet's ego enters the poem, but in the guise only of a battered Job, seeking to lose his own humanity. From this nadir, the extraordinary and poignantly "broken" music of the last stanza rises up, into the poet's own element of fire, to affirm again the human dignity of the prophet's vocation, and to suggest a mode of imaginative renovation that goes beyond the cyclic limitations of nature. Rarely in the history of poetry have seventy lines done so much so well.

Shelley's other major odes are out of critical favor in our time, but this is due as much to actual misinterpretations as to any qualities inherent in these poems. "To a Skylark" strikes readers as silly when they visualize the poet staring at the bird and hailing it as nonexistent, but these readers have begun with such gross inaccuracy that their experience of what they take to be the poem may simply be dismissed. The ode's whole point turns on the lark's being out of sight from the start; the poet *hears* an evanescent song, but can see nothing, even as Keats in the "Ode to a Nightingale" never actually sees the bird. Flying too high almost to be heard, the lark is crucially compared by Shelley to his central symbol, the morning star fading into the dawn of an unwelcome day. What can barely be heard, and not seen at all, is still discovered to be a basis upon which to rejoice, and indeed becomes an inescapable motive for metaphor, a dark justification for celebrating the light of uncommon day. In the great revolutionary "Ode to Liberty," Shelley successfully adapts the English Pindaric to an abstract political theme, mostly by means of making the poem radically its own subject, as he does on a larger scale in *The Witch of Atlas* and *Epipsychidion*.

In the last two years of his life, Shelley subtly modified his lyrical art, making the best of his shorter poems the means by which his experimental intellectual temper and his more traditional social urbanity could be reconciled. The best of these lyrics would include "Hymn of Apollo," "The Two Spirits: An Allegory," "To Night," "Lines . . . on . . . the Death of Napoleon," and the final group addressed to Jane Williams, or resulting from the poet's love for her, including "When the lamp is shattered," "To Jane: The Invitation," "The Recollection," "With a Guitar, to Jane," and the last completed lyric, the immensely moving "Lines written in the Bay of Lerici." Here are nine lyrics as varied and masterful as the language affords. Take these together with Shelley's achievements in the sublime ode, with the best of his earlier lyrics, and with the double handful of magnificent interspersed lyrics contained in *Prometheus Unbound* and *Hellas*, and it will not seem as if Swinburne was excessive in claiming for Shelley a rank as one of the two or three major lyrical poets in English tradition down to Swinburne's own time.

The best admonition to address to a reader of Shelley's lyrics, as of his longer poems, is to slow down and read very closely, so as to learn what Wordsworth could have meant when he reluctantly conceded that "Shelley is one of the best *artists* of us all: I mean in workmanship of style":

There is no dew on the dry grass tonight,
  Nor damp within the shadow of the trees;
The wind is intermitting, dry and light;
  And in the inconstant motion of the breeze
The dust and straws are driven up and down,
And whirled about the pavement of the town.
              ("Evening: Ponte Al Mare, Pisa")

This altogether characteristic example of Shelley's workmanship is taken from a minor and indeed unfinished lyric of 1821. I have undergone many unhappy conversations with university wits, poets, and critics, who have assured me that "Shelley had a tin ear," the assurance being given on one occasion by no less distinguished a prosodist than W. H. Auden, and I am always left wondering if my ears have heard correctly. The fashion of insisting that Shelley was a poor craftsman seems to have started with T. S. Eliot, spread from him to Dr. Leavis and the Fugitive group of Southern poets and critics, and then for a time became universal. It was a charming paradox that formalist and rhetorical critics should have become so affectively disposed against a poet as to be incapable of reading any of his verbal figures with even minimal accuracy, but the charm has worn off, and one hopes that the critical argument about Shelley can now move on into other (and more disputable) areas.

V

Cruelty has a Human Heart,
And Jealousy a Human Face;
Terror the Human Form Divine,
And Secrecy the Human Dress.
The Human Dress is forged Iron,
The Human Form a fiery Forge,
The Human Face a Furnace seal'd,
The Human Heart its hungry Gorge.
              (Blake, "A Divine Image")

The Cenci occupies a curious place in Shelley's canon, one that is overtly apart from the sequence of his major works that goes from *Prometheus Unbound* to *The Triumph of Life*. Unlike the psuedo-Elizabethan tragedies of Shelley's disciple Beddoes, *The Cenci* is in no obvious way a visionary poem. Yet it is a tragedy only in a very peculiar sense, and has little in common with the stage-plays it ostensibly seeks to emulate. Its true companions, and descendants, are Browning's giant progression of dramatic monologues, *The Ring and the Book*, and certain works of Hardy that

share its oddly effective quality of what might be termed dramatic solipsism, to have recourse to a desperate oxymoron. Giant incongruities clash
in *Prometheus Unbound* as they do in Blake's major poems, but the clashes
are resolved by both poets in the realms of a self-generated mythology.
When parallel incongruities meet violently in *The Cenci*, in a context that
excludes myth, the reader is asked to accept as human characters beings
whose states of mind are too radically and intensely pure to be altogether
human. Blake courts a similar problem whenever he is only at the
borderline of his own mythical world, as in *Visions of the Daughters of
Albion* and *The French Revolution*. Shelley's Beatrice and Blake's Oothoon
are either too human or not human enough; the reader is uncomfortable
in not knowing whether he encounters a Titaness or one of his own kind.

Yet this discomfort need not wreck the experience of reading *The
Cenci*, which is clearly a work that excels in character rather than in plot,
and more in the potential of character than in its realization. At the heart
of *The Cenci* is Shelley's very original conception of tragedy. Tragedy is
not a congenial form for apocalyptic writers, who tend to have a severe
grudge against it, as Blake and D. H. Lawrence did. Shelley's morality was
an apocalyptic one, and the implicit standard for *The Cenci* is set in *The
Mask of Anarchy*, which advocates a nonviolent resistance to evil. Beatrice is tragic because she does *not* meet this high standard, though she is
clearly superior to every other person in her world. Life triumphs over
Beatrice because she does take violent revenge upon an intolerable oppressor. The tragedy Shelley develops is one of a heroic character "violently
thwarted from her nature" by circumstances she ought to have defied.
This allies Beatrice with a large group of Romantic heroes, ranging from
the Cain of Byron's drama to the pathetic daemon of Mary Shelley's
Frankenstein and, on the cosmic level, embracing Shelley's own Prometheus
and the erring Zoas or demi-gods of Blake's myth.

To find tragedy in any of these, you must persuasively redefine
tragedy, as Shelley implicitly did. Tragedy becomes the fall of the imagination, or rather the falling away from imaginative conduct on the part of
a heroically imaginative individual.

Count Cenci is, as many critics have noted, a demonic parody of
Jehovah, and has a certain resemblance therefore to Shelley's Jupiter and
Blake's Tiriel and Urizen. The count is obsessively given to hatred, and is
vengeful, anal-erotic in his hoarding tendencies, incestuous, tyrannical,
and compelled throughout by a jealous possessiveness even toward those
he abhors. He is also given to bursts of Tiriel-like cursing, and like Tiriel
or Jupiter he has his dying-god aspect, for his death symbolizes the
necessity of revolution, the breaking up of an old and hopeless order. Like

all heavenly tyrants in his tradition, Cenci's quest for dominion is marked by a passion for uniformity, and it is inevitable that he seek to seduce the angelic Beatrice to his own perverse level. His success is an ironic one, since he does harden her into the only agent sufficiently strong and remorseless to cause his own destruction.

The aesthetic power of *The Cenci* lies in the perfection with which it both sets forth Beatrice's intolerable dilemma and presents the reader with a parallel dilemma. The natural man in the reader exults at Beatrice's metamorphosis into a relentless avenger, and approves even her untruthful denial of responsibility for her father's murder. The imaginative man in the reader is appalled at the degeneration of an all-but-angelic intelligence into a skilled intriguer and murderess. This fundamental dichotomy *in the reader* is the theater where the true anguish of *The Cenci* is enacted. The overt theme becomes the universal triumph of life over integrity, which is to say of death-in-life over life.

The Cenci is necessarily a work conceived in the Shakespearean shadow, and it is obvious that Shelley did not succeed in forming a dramatic language for himself in his play. Dr. Leavis has seized upon this failure with an inquisitor's joy, saying that "it takes no great discernment to see that *The Cenci* is very bad and that its badness is characteristic." It takes a very little discernment to see that *The Cenci* survives its palpable flaws and that it gives us what Wordsworth's *The Borderers,* Byron's *Cain,* and Coleridge's *Remorse* give us also in their very different ways, a distinguished example of Romantic, experimental tragedy, in which a crime against nature both emancipates consciousness and painfully turns consciousness in upon itself, with an attendant loss of a higher and more innocent state of being. The Beatrice of Shelley's last scene has learned her full autonomy, her absolute alienation from nature and society, but at a frightful, and to Shelley a tragic, cost.

VI

> But were it not, that *Time* their troubler is,
> All that in this delightful Gardin growes,
> Should happie be, and have immortall blis
> (Spenser)

In the spring of 1820, at Pisa, Shelley wrote *The Sensitive Plant,* a remarkably original poem, and a permanently valuable one, though it is little admired in recent years. As a parable of imaginative failure, the poem is another of the many Romantic versions of the Miltonic Eden's transformation into a wasteland, but the limitations it explores are not the Miltonic ones of human irresolution and disobedience. Like all of Shelley's major poems, *The Sensitive Plant* is a skeptical work, the skepticism here manifesting itself as a precariously poised suspension of judgment on the human capacity to perceive whether or not natural *or* imaginative values survive the cyclic necessities of change and decay.

The tone of *The Sensitive Plant* is a deliberate exquisitiveness, of a more-than-Spenserian kind. Close analogues to this tone can be found in major passages of Keats's *Endymion* and in Blake's *The Book of Thel*. The ancestor poet for all these visionary poems, including Shelley's *The Witch of Atlas* and the vision of Beulah in Blake's *Milton*, is of course Spenser, whose mythic version of the lower or earthly paradise is presented as the Garden of Adonis in *The Faerie Queene*, Book III, Canto VI, which is probably the most influential passage of poetry in English, if by "influential" we mean what influences other poets.

The dark melancholy of *The Sensitive Plant* is not Spenserian, but everything else in the poem to some extent is. Like many poems in this tradition, the lament is for mutability itself, for change seen as loss. What is lost is innocence, natural harmony, the mutual interpenetrations of a merely given condition that is nevertheless whole and beyond the need of justification. The new state, experiential life as seen in Part III of the poem, is the world without imagination, a tract of weeds. When Shelley, in the noblest quatrains he ever wrote, broods on this conclusion he offers no consolation beyond the most urbane of his skepticisms. The light that puts out our eyes is a darkness to us, yet remains light, and death may be a mockery of our inadequate imaginations. The myth of the poem—its garden, lady, and plant—may have prevailed, while we, the poem's readers, may be too decayed in our perceptions to know this. Implicit in Shelley's poem is a passionate refutation of time, but the passion is a desperation unless the mind's imaginings can cleanse perception of its obscurities. Nothing in the poem proper testifies to the mind's mastery of outward sense. The "Conclusion" hints at what Shelley beautifully calls "a modest creed," but the poet is too urbane and skeptical to urge it upon either us or himself. The creed appears again in *The Witch of Atlas*, but with a playful and amiable disinterestedness that removes it almost entirely from the anguish of human desire.

The Witch of Atlas is Shelley's most inventive poem, and is by any just standards a triumph. In kind, it goes back to the English Renaissance epyllion, the Ovidian erotic-mythological brief epic, but in tone and procedure it is a new departure, except that for Shelley it had been prophesied by his own rendition of the Homeric "Hymn to Mercury."

Both poems are in *ottava rima*, both have a Byronic touch, and both have been characterized accurately as possessing a tone of visionary cynicism. Hermes and the Witch of Atlas qualify the divine grandeurs among which they move, and remind us that the imagination unconfined respects no orders of being, however traditional or natural.

G. Wilson Knight first pointed to the clear resemblance between the tone of *The Witch of Atlas* and Yeats's later style, and there is considerable evidence of the permanent effect of the poem's fantastic plot and properties upon Yeats. Shelley's *Witch* is Yeats's "Byzantium" writ large; both poems deal with Phase 15 of Yeats's *A Vision*, with the phase of poetic incarnation, and so with the state of the soul in which art is created. In a comparison of the two poems, the immediate contrast will be found in the extraordinary relaxation that Shelley allows himself. The nervous intensity that the theme demands is present in the *Witch*, but has been transmuted into an almost casual acceptance of intolerable realities that art cannot mitigate.

The Witch of Atlas, as Shelley says in the poem's highly ironic dedicatory stanzas to his wife, tells no story, false or true, but is "a visionary rhyme." If the Witch is to be translated at all into terms not her own, then she can only be the mythopoeic impulse or inventive faculty itself, one of whose manifestations is the Hermaphrodite, which we can translate as a poem, or any work of art. The Witch's boat is the emblem of her creative desire, and like the Hermaphrodite it works against nature. The Hermaphrodite is both a convenience for the Witch, helping her to go beyond natural limitations, and a companion of sorts, but a highly inadequate one, being little more than a robot. The limitations of art are involved here, for the Witch has rejected the love of every mortal being, and has chosen instead an automaton of her own creation. In the poignant stanzas in which she rejects the suit of the nymphs, Shelley attains one of the immense triumphs of his art, but the implications of the triumph, and of the entire poem, are as deliberately chilling as the Byzantine vision of the aging Yeats.

Though the Witch turns her playful and antinomian spirit to the labor of upsetting church and state, in the poem's final stanzas, and subverts even the tired conventions of mortality as well as of morality, the ultimate impression she makes upon us is one of remoteness. The fierce aspirations of *Prometheus Unbound*, were highly qualified by a consciously manipulated prophetic irony, yet they retained their force, and aesthetic immediacy, as the substance of what Shelley passionately desired. The ruin that shadows love in *Prometheus Unbound*, the *amphisbaena* or two-headed serpent that could move downward and outward to destruction again, the warning made explicit in the closing stanzas spoken by Demogorgon; it is these antithetical hints that survived in Shelley longer than the vehement hope of his lyrical drama. *The Sensitive Plant* and *The Witch of Atlas* manifest a subtle movement away from that hope. *Epipsychidion*, the most exalted of Shelley's poems, seeks desperately to renovate that hope by placing it in the context of heterosexual love, and with the deliberate and thematic self-combustion of the close of *Epipsychidion* Shelley appears to have put all hope aside, and to have prepared himself for his magnificent but despairing last phase, of which the enduring monuments are *Adonais* and *The Triumph of Life*.

VII

What man most passionately wants is his living wholeness and his living unison, not his own isolate salvation of his "soul." Man wants his physical fulfillment first and foremost, since now, once and once only, he is in the flesh and potent. For man, as for flower and beast and bird, the supreme triumph is to be most vividly, most perfectly alive. Whatever the unborn and the dead may know, they cannot know the beauty, the marvel of being alive in the flesh. The dead may look after the afterwards. But the magnificent here and now of life in the flesh is ours, and ours alone, and ours only for a time.

(D. H. Lawrence, *Apocalypse*)

Except for Blake's *Visions of the Daughters of Albion*, which it in some respects resembles, *Epipsychidion* is the most outspoken and eloquent appeal for free love in the language. Though this appeal is at the heart of the poem, and dominates its most famous passage (lines 147–54), it is only one aspect of a bewilderingly problematical work. *Epipsychidion* was intended by Shelley to be his *Vita Nuova*, celebrating the discovery of his Beatrice in Emilia Viviani. It proved however to be a climactic and not an initiatory poem, for in it Shelley culminates the quest begun in *Alastor*, only to find after culmination that the quest remains unfulfilled and unfulfillable. The desire of Shelley remains infinite, and the only emblem adequate to that desire is the morning and evening star, Venus, at whose sphere the shadow cast by earth into the heavens reaches its limits. After *Epipsychidion*, in *Adonais* and *The Triumph of Life*, only the star of Venus abides as an image of the good. It is not Emilia Viviani but her image that proves inadequate in *Epipsychidion*, a poem whose most turbulent and valuable element is its struggle to record the process of image-making. Of all Shelley's major poems, *Epipsychidion* most directly concerns itself with the mind in creation. "Mont Blanc" has the same position among Shelley's shorter poems, and has the advantage of its relative discursiveness, as the poet meditates upon the awesome spectacle before him. *Epipsychidion* is continuous rhapsody, and sustains its lyrical intensity of a lovers' confrontation for six hundred lines. The mind in creation, here and in *A Defense of Poetry*, is as a fading coal, and much of Shelley's art in the poem is devoted to the fading phenomenon, as image after image recedes and the poet-lover feels more fearfully the double burden of his love's inexpressibility and its necessary refusal to accept even natural, let alone societal, limitations.

There is, in Shelley's development as a poet, a continuous effort to subvert the poetic image, so as to arrive at a more radical kind of verbal figure, which Shelley never altogether achieved. Tenor and vehicle are imported into one another, and the choice of natural images increasingly favors those already on the point of vanishing, just within the ken of eye and ear. The world is skeptically taken up into the mind, and there are suggestions and overtones that all of reality is a phantasmagoria. Shelley becomes an idealist totally skeptical of the metaphysical foundations of idealism, while he continues to entertain a skeptical materialism, or rather he becomes a fantasist pragmatically given to some materialist hypotheses that his imagination regards as absurd. This is not necessarily a self-contradiction, but it is a kind of psychic split, and it is exposed very powerfully in *Epipsychidion*. Who wins a triumph in the poem, the gambler with the limits of poetry and of human relationship, or the inexorable limits? Space, time, loneliness, mortality, wrong—all these are put aside by vision, yet vision darkens perpetually in the poem. "The world, unfortunately, is real; I, unfortunately, am Borges," is the ironic reflection of a great contemporary seer of phantasmagorias, as he brings his refutation of time to an unrefuting close. Shelley too is swept along by what destroys him and is inescapable, the reality that will not yield to the most relentless of imaginings. In that knowledge, he turns to elegy and away from celebration.

Adonais, Shelley's formal elegy for Keats, is a great monument in the history of the English elegy, and yet hardly an elegy at all. Nearly five hundred lines long, it exceeds in scope and imaginative ambition its major English ancestors, the *Astrophel* of Spenser and the *Lycidas* of Milton, as well as such major descendants as Arnold's *Thyrsis* and Swinburne's *Ave Atque Vale*. Only Tennyson's *In Memoriam* rivals it as an attempt to make the elegy a vehicle for not less than everything a particular poet has to say on the ultimates of human existence. Yet Tennyson, for all his ambition, stays within the bounds of elegy. *Adonais*, in the astonishing sequence of its last eighteen stanzas, is no more an elegy proper than Yeats's "Byzantium" poems are. Like the "Byzantium" poems (which bear a close relation to it), *Adonais* is a high song of poetic self-recognition in the presence of foreshadowing death, and also a description of poetic existence, even of a poem's state of being.

Whether Shelley holds together the elegiac and visionary aspects of his poem is disputable; it is difficult to see the full continuity that takes the poet from his hopeless opening to his more than triumphant close, from:

> I weep for Adonais—he is dead!
> O, weep for Adonais! though our tears
> Thaw not the frost which binds so dear a head!

to:

> I am borne darkly, fearfully, afar;
> Whilst, burning through the inmost veil of Heaven,
> The soul of Adonais, like a star,
> Beacons from the abode where the Eternal are.

From frost to fire as a mode of renewal for the self: that is an archetypal Romantic pattern, familiar to us from *The Ancient Mariner* and the *Intimations* Ode (see the contrast between the last line of stanza VIII and the first of stanza IX in that poem). But *Adonais* breaks this pattern, for the soul of Shelley's Keats burns through the final barrier to revelation only by means of an energy that is set against nature, and the frost that no poetic tears can thaw yields only to "the fire for which all thirst," but which no natural man can drink, for no living man can drink of the whole wine of the burning fountain. As much as Yeats's "All Souls' Night," *Adonais* reaches out to a reality of ghostly intensities, yet Shelley as well as Yeats is reluctant to leave behind the living man who blindly drinks his drop, and *Adonais* is finally a "Dialogue of Self and Soul," in which the Soul wins a costly victory, as costly as the Self's triumph in Yeats's "Dialogue." The Shelley who cries out, in rapture and dismay, "The massy earth and spherèd skies are riven!", is a poet who has given himself freely to the tempest of creative destruction, to a reality beyond the natural, yet who movingly looks back upon the shore and upon the throng he has forsaken. The close of *Adonais* is a triumph of character over personality, to use a Yeatsian dialectic, but the personality of the lyric poet is nevertheless the dominant aesthetic element in the poem's dark and fearful apotheosis.

"Apotheosis is not the origin of the major man," if we are to credit

Stevens, but the qualified assertions of Shelley do proclaim such an imaginative humanism in the central poems that preceded *Adonais*. In *Adonais* the imagination forsakes humanism, even as it does in the "Byzantium" poems.

Though *Adonais* has been extensively Platonized and Neoplatonized by a troop of interpreters, it is in a clear sense a materialist's poem, written out of a materialist's despair at his own deepest convictions, and finally a poem soaring above those convictions into a mystery that leaves a pragmatic materialism quite undisturbed. Whatever supernal apprehension it is that Shelley attains in the final third of *Adonais*, it is not in any ordinary sense a religious faith, for the only attitude toward natural existence it fosters in the poet is one of unqualified rejection, and indeed its pragmatic postulate is simply suicide. Nothing could be more different in spirit from Demogorgon's closing lines in *Prometheus Unbound* than the final stanzas of *Adonais*, and the ruthlessly skeptical Shelley must have known this.

He knew also though that we do not judge poems by pragmatic tests, and the splendor of the resolution to *Adonais* is not impaired by its implications of human defeat. Whether Keats lives again is unknown to Shelley; poets are among "the enduring dead," and Keats "wakes *or* sleeps" with them. The endurance is not then necessarily a mode of survival, and what flows back to the burning fountain is not necessarily the *human* soul, though it is "pure spirit." Or if it is the soul of Keats as well as "the soul of Adonais," then the accidents of individual personality have abandoned it, making this cold comfort indeed. Still, Shelley is not offering us (or himself) comfort; his elegy has no parallel to Milton's consolation in *Lycidas*:

> There entertain him all the Saints above,
> In solemn troops, and sweet Societies
> That sing, and singing in their glory move,
> And wipe the tears forever from his eyes.

To Milton, as a Christian poet, death is somehow unnatural. To Shelley, for all his religious temperament, death is wholly natural, and if death is dead, then nature must be dead also. The final third of *Adonais* is desperately apocalyptic in a way that *Prometheus Unbound*, Act IV, was not. For *Prometheus Unbound* ends in a Saturnalia, though there are darker implications also, but *Adonais* soars beyond the shadow that the earth casts into the heavens. Shelley was ready for a purgatorial vision of earth, and no longer could sustain even an ironic hope.

VIII

Mal dare, e mal tener lo mondo pulcro
ha tolto loro, e posti a questa zuffa;
qual ella sia, parole non ci appulcro.
(*Inferno* 7:58–60)

That ill they gave,
And ill they kept, hath of the beauteous world
Deprived, and set them at this strife, which needs
No labour'd phrase of mine to set it off.
(Cary, *The Vision of Dante*)

There are elements in *The Triumph of Life*, Shelley's last poem, that mark it as an advance over all the poetry he had written previously. The bitter eloquence and dramatic condensation of the style are new; so is a ruthless pruning of invention. The mythic figures are few, being confined to the "Shape all light," the charioteer, and Life itself, while the two principal figures, Shelley and Rousseau, appear in their proper persons, though in the perspective of eternity, as befits a vision of judgment. The tone of Shelley's last poem is derived from Dante's *Purgatorio*, even as much in *Epipsychidion* comes from Dante's *Vita Nuova*, but the events and atmosphere of *The Triumph of Life* have more in common with the *Inferno*. Still, the poem is a purgatorial work, for all the unrelieved horror of its vision, and perhaps Shelley might have found some gradations in his last vision, so as to climb out of the poem's impasse, if he had lived to finish it, though I incline to doubt this. As it stands, the poem is in hell, and Shelley is there, one of the apparently condemned, as all men are, he says, save for "the sacred few" of Athens and Jerusalem, martyrs to vision like Socrates, Jesus, and a chosen handful, with whom on the basis of *Adonais* we can place Keats, as he too had touched the world with his living flame, and then fled back up to his native noon.

The highest act of Shelley's imagination in the poem, perhaps in all of his poetry, is in the magnificent appropriateness of Rousseau's presence, from his first entrance to his last speech before the fragment breaks off. Rousseau is Virgil to Shelley's Dante, in the sense of being his imaginative ancestor, his guide in creation, and also in prophesying the dilemma the disciple would face at the point of crisis in his life. Shelley, sadly enough, was hardly in the middle of the journey, but at twenty-nine he had only days to live, and the imagination in him felt compelled to face the last things. Without Rousseau, Shelley would not have written the "Hymn to Intellectual Beauty," and perhaps not "Mont Blanc" either. Rousseau, more even than Wordsworth, was the prophet of natural man, and the celebrator of the state of nature. Even in 1816, writing his hymns and starting the process that would lead to the conception of *Prometheus Unbound*, Shelley fights against the natural man and natural religion, but he fights partly against his own desires, and the vision of Rousseau haunts him still in the "Ode to the West Wind" and in the greatest chant of the apocalyptic fourth act of the lyrical drama, the song of the Earth beginning "It interpenetrates my granite mass." Shelley knew that the spirit of Rousseau was what had moved him most in the spirit of the age, and temperamentally (which counts for most in a poet) it makes more sense to name Shelley the disciple and heir of Rousseau than of Godwin, or Wordsworth, or any of the later French theorists of Revolution. Rousseau and Hume make an odd formula of heart and head in Shelley, but they are the closest parallels to be found to him on the emotional and intellectual sides respectively.

Chastened and knowing, almost beyond knowledge, Rousseau enters the poem, speaking not to save his disciple, but to show him that he cannot be saved, and to teach him a style fit for his despair. The imaginative lesson of *The Triumph of Life* is wholly present in the poem's title: life always triumphs, for life, our life, is after all what the preface to *Alastor* called it, a "lasting misery and loneliness." One Power only, the Imagination, is capable of redeeming life, "but that Power which strikes the luminaries of the world with sudden darkness and extinction, by awakening them to too exquisite a perception of its influences, dooms to a slow and poisonous decay those meaner spirits that dare to abjure its dominion." In *The Triumph of Life*, the world's luminaries are still the poets, stars of evening and morning, "heaven's living eyes," but they fade into a double light, the light of nature or the sun, and the harsher and more blinding light of Life, the destructive chariot of the poem's vision. The chariot of Life, like the apocalyptic chariots of Act IV, *Prometheus Unbound*, goes back to the visions of Ezekiel and Revelation for its sources, as the chariots of Dante and Milton did, but now Shelley gives a demonic parody of his sources, possibly following the example of Spenser's chariot of Lucifera. Rousseau is betrayed to the light of life because he began by yielding his imagination's light to the lesser but seductive light of nature, represented in the poem by the "Shape all light" who offers him the waters of natural experience to drink. He drinks, he begins to forget everything in the mind's desire that had transcended nature, and so he falls victim to Life's destruction, and fails to become one of "the sacred few." There is small reason to doubt that Shelley, at the end, saw himself as having shared in Rousseau's fate. The poem, fragment as it is, survives its own despair, and stands with Keats's *The Fall of Hyperion* as a marvelously eloquent imaginative testament, fit relic of an achievement broken off too soon to rival Blake's or Wordsworth's, but superior to everything else in its own age.

IX

The great instrument of moral good is the imagination.
(*A Defence of Poetry*)

Anti-Shelleyans have come in all intellectual shapes and sizes, and have included distinguished men of letters from Charles Lamb and De Quincey down to T. S. Eliot, Allen Tate, and their school in our day. To distinguish between the kinds of anti-Shelleyans is instructive, though the following categories are by no means mutually exclusive. One can count six major varieties of anti-Shelleyans, whether one considers them histori-cally or in contemporary terms:

1. The school of "common sense"
2. The Christian orthodox
3. The school of "wit"
4. Moralists, of most varieties
5. The school of "classic" form
6. Precisionists, or concretists.

It is evident that examples of (1), (2), and (4) need not be confuted, as they are merely irrelevant. We may deal with (3), (5), and (6) in their own terms, rather than in Shelley's, and still find Shelley triumphant.

The "wit" of Shelley's poetry has little to do with that of seventeenth-century verse, but has much in common with the dialectical vivacity of Shaw, and something of the prophetic irony of Blake. If irony is an awareness of the terrible gap between aspiration and fulfillment, then the skeptical Shelley is among the most ironical of poets. If it is something else, as it frequently is in the school of Donne, one can observe that there are many wings in the house of wit, and one ought not to live in all of them simultaneously.

Form is another matter, and too complex to be argued fully here. The late C. S. Lewis justly maintained against the school of Eliot that Shelley was more classical in his sense of form, his balance of harmony and design, than Dryden. One can go further: Shelley is almost always a poet of the highest decorum, a stylist who adjusts his form and tone to his subject, whether it be the hammer-beat low style of *The Mask of Anarchy*, the urbane middle style of the *Letter to Maria Gisborne*, or the sublime inventiveness of the high style as it is renovated in *Prometheus Unbound.* Shelley was sometimes a hasty or careless artist, but he was always an artist, a poet who neither could nor would stop being a poet. Dr. Samuel Johnson would have disliked Shelley's poetry, indeed would have considered Shelley to be dangerously mad, but he would have granted that it was poetry of a high, if to him outmoded, order. Critics less classical than Johnson will not grant as much, because their notions of classical form are not as deeply founded.

The precisionist or concretist is probably Shelley's most effective enemy, since everything vital in Shelley's poetry deliberately strains away from the minute particulars of experience. But this is oddly true of Wordsworth as well, though Wordsworth usually insisted upon the opposite. The poetry of renovation in the United States, in our time, had its chief exemplars in William Carlos Williams and in Wallace Stevens, and it is Stevens who is in the line of both Wordsworth and of Shelley. Williams's famous adage, "no ideas but in things," is the self-justified motto of one valid kind of poetic procedure, but it will not allow for the always relevant grandeurs of the sublime tradition, with its "great moments" of ecstasy and recognition. Wordsworth on the mountainside looks out and finds only a sea of mist, an emblem of the highest imaginative vision, in which the edges of things have blurred and faded out. Stevens, opening the door of his house upon the flames of the Northern Lights, confronts an Arctic effulgence flaring upon the frame of everything he is, but does not describe the flashing auroras. Shelley, at his greatest, precisely chants an energetic becoming that cannot be described in the concrete because its entire purpose is to modify the concrete, to compel a greater reality to appear:

> . . . the one Spirit's plastic stress
> Sweeps through the dull dense world, compelling there,
> All new successions to the forms they wear;
> Torturing th' unwilling dross that checks its flight
> To its own likeness, as each mass may bear;
> And bursting in its beauty and its might
> From trees and beasts and men into the Heaven's light.

Had Shelley been able to accept any known faith, he would have given us the name and nature of that "one Spirit." Unlike Keats, he would not have agreed with Stevens that the great poems of heaven and hell had been written, and that only the great poem of earth remained to be composed. His own spirit was apocalyptic, and the still unwritten poems of heaven and hell waited mute upon the answering swiftness of his own imaginings, when he went on to his early finalities:

> As if that frail and wasted human form,
> Had been an elemental god.

C. E. PULOS

Scepticism and Platonism

Shelley "felt the radiance and breathed the air of Plato's genius," said Edward Dowden, "as though he were himself a scholar in the garden at Colonus." But another nineteenth-century critic, Walter Bagehot, felt that "there is in Shelley none of that unceasing reference to ethical consciousness and ethical religion which has for centuries placed Plato first among the preparatory preceptors of Christianity." Early twentieth-century critics likewise disagreed sharply regarding Shelley's Platonism. Treating the subject more fully and systematically than had any of her predecessors, Lillian Winstanley arrived at the following conclusion: "Shelley was one of those men who are, by temperament, born Platonists, and it may be surmised that, had he never read a line of Greek or even heard of Plato, except by indirect tradition only, his work would still show a certain number of affinities. Natural resemblance and close study, taken together, have resulted in saturating his whole work with Platonic thought. . . ." Combining a similar verdict with considerations minimized by Lillian Winstanley, C. H. Hereford declared three years later: "Under forms of thought derived from the atheist and materialist Godwin, Shelley has given in *Prometheus Unbound* magnificent expression to the faith of Plato and of Christ." Hereford's remark drew this comment from Paul Elmer More: "The faith of Plato and of Christ! Shall I confess that to meet with such words in such a place is to be overborne with the futility of writing at all."

Faced with the question whether Shelley was a Platonist or a

From *The Deep Truth: A Study of Shelley's Scepticism*. Copyright © 1954 by University of Nebraska Press.

pseudo-Platonist, recent critics have avoided taking extreme positions and have sought, in various ways, the reaching of a compromise. Carl Grabo, for instance, discovers two factors that tended to differentiate Shelley's Platonism from Plato: the influence of the Neoplatonists and the desire to reconcile idealism with the speculations of current science. Another recent critic, Ellsworth Barnard, fully concedes the existence of fundamental differences between Shelley's and Plato's concepts of Beauty; but he argues that Shelley's concept may be as adequate as Plato's "to the actual needs of men in their struggle toward a higher state of existence than they have yet attained." Finally, James A. Notopoulos suggests that Shelley was not an expounder of Plato's philosophy but a "natural" Platonist, and that "those who condemn Shelley as a pseudo-Platonist confuse natural Platonism with Plato's expression of it."

If Shelley did not expound the philosophy of Plato, perhaps the philosophy that he did expound helped to determine the special character of his Platonism. This idea is no doubt implied in Mr. Grabo's theory that the Neoplatonists influenced Shelley's Platonism. The philosophy, however, that Shelley expounded was not that of Plotinus and Porphyry, but, as I have tried to show, that of Hume and Drummond. What the present chapter will attempt to suggest is that scepticism prepared the way for Shelley's acceptance of Plato and at the same time rendered inevitable his basic divergence from Plato.

The sceptical tradition prepared the way for Shelley's acceptance of Plato by resolving the objection to Plato held by the *philosophes* and by depicting Plato as a kind of sceptic himself—or as, at least, a forerunner of scepticism.

The attitude of the eighteenth century toward Plato was largely one of disparagement, characteristic of which was Bolingbroke's remark that Plato was "the father of philosophical lying." Owing to the increasing activity of Platonic scholars, this unappreciative point of view was questioned in the last forty years of the century. Little influenced, however, by this revival of Platonic scholarship, the *philosophes* continued to regard Plato as a mere poetic "dreamer" (see Notopoulos, 137 ff.), not to be taken seriously by modern philosophers. Shelley's first reference to Plato (I, 33–37), written before he had come under the influence of the *philosophes* (January, 1810), is quite free of any adverse criticism:

> Your writings may then with old Socrates vie,
> May on the same shelf with Demosthenes lie,
> May as Junius be sharp, or as Plato be sage. . . .

In the Notes to *Queen Mab* (1813), however, the poet employed the phrase "the reveries of Plato" (VII, 135–136) in a context clearly suggesting that he no longer regarded Plato as "sage," but had come to see him after the fashion of the *philosophes* as a kind of poetic "dreamer." From this point of view regarding Plato, Shelley was liberated, and liberated completely, by the influence upon him of the sceptical tradition. Although even the mature poet's unquestionable admiration for Plato is qualified by the admission of certain defects, that admission neither includes nor suggests the main charge directed against Plato by the *philosophes*.

Illustrative of the mature Shelley's attitude toward Plato is the Preface to his translation of *The Symposium*. The poet praises Plato's "view into the nature of mind and existence" as "profound" and "remarkable intuitions." On the other hand, he implies that he is not in complete agreement with Plato's views on "the government of the world" and "the elementary laws of moral action"; and he concedes, furthermore, that the dialogues are "stained by puerile sophisms" (VII, 161). This last charge contains the main substance of the mature poet's adverse criticism of the Greek philosopher. That it expresses a settled opinion, and not an echo of an earlier attitude, is indicated by its recurrence, as we shall see, in diverse references to Plato in the mature Shelley.

A comparison of this charge against Plato with that which the young Shelley had derived from the *philosophes* reveals a categorical difference: the mature poet objects to Plato's "sophisms," whereas the young poet had objected to his "reveries." The term "reveries" refers mainly to the Platonic myths and parables. The term "sophisms," however, refers not to the Platonic myths, but to the results of a mode of reasoning. A mode of reasoning that sometimes led Plato to utter what might conceivably impress one as "puerile sophisms" was the "induction of dialectic," which Diogenes Laertius explains as follows: "For instance, the question put is whether the soul is immortal, and whether the living come back from the dead. And this is proved in the dialogue *On the Soul* by means of a general proposition, that opposites proceed from opposites. And the general proposition itself is established by means of certain propositions which are particular, as that sleep comes from waking and *vice versa*, the greater from the less and *vice versa*" (iii. 55).

A consideration of the specific "sophisms" to which Shelley refers clearly indicates that they were the results of Plato's "induction of dialectic." To Socrates' question in the *Ion* (535) whether an actor is not mad who, with no one despoiling him or wronging him, "appears weeping or panic-stricken in the presence of more than twenty thousand friendly faces," Shelley replies in a note: "A sophism here. Tears did not indicate grief or horror. . . ." The error in this instance lies in a "particular proposition" of the "induction of dialectic." In his *On a Passage in Crito*, on the other hand, Shelley apparently objects to a "general proposition," for, after rewriting Socrates' account of a good citizen's duty to obey the laws of his country, the poet remarks: "Such are the arguments, which overturn the sophism placed in the mouth of Socrates by Plato" (VII, 265). Elsewhere Shelley's reference to a specific Platonic sophism recalls one of the examples cited by Diogenes Laertius in his explanation of the "induction of dialectic"—that the greater comes from the less and vice versa: "Perhaps all discontent with the *less* (to use a Platonic sophism) supposes the sense of a just claim to the *greater*" (X, 371).

But while the mature Shelley not infrequently finds fault with the results of Plato's "induction of dialectic," he still exhibits an extraordinary admiration for the Greek philosopher. No contradiction is involved here, for Shelley did not regard Plato as primarily a "mere reasoner," to be judged only by the standards of logic. In *A Defence of Poetry*, for instance, he writes: "Plato was essentially a poet—the truth and splendour of his imagery, and the melody of his language, is the most intense that it is possible to conceive" (VII, 114). In other words, Shelley came to set the highest value upon those very elements in the Platonic philosophy which in his youth, under the influence of the *philosophes*, he had contemptuously referred to as "the reveries of Plato."

In regarding Plato as essentially a poet, the mature Shelley was not partially following the example of the *philosophes*, as might at first appear; he was following the example of the sceptics. "Plato," said Montaigne, "is but a loose poet." The *philosophes* may sometimes describe Plato in almost the same words. But between Montaigne's meaning and that of the *philosophes* there lies a basic and significant difference. Montaigne was defining philosophy, not ridiculing Plato, when he called the Greek philosopher a poet. As a sceptic, he esteemed the "poetry" in Plato as the reaction of human nature to the unknown and unknowable. The *philosophes*, on the other hand, meant that Plato lacked their solidity of thought and knowledge. As dogmatists, they had no intention whatever of identifying metaphysics with poetry. For a time the young Shelley followed the view of the *philosophes*; but as he enlarged his acquaintance with the sceptical tradition, he discarded their view for that of Montaigne, whom he read in the fall of 1816.

The mature Shelley's revaluation of Plato may have owed something to another aspect of the sceptical tradition, pertaining not to the positive but to the negative side of the Greek philosopher's thought: I allude to the tendency among sceptics to claim Plato as an intellectual ancestor. Plato, of course, is not a sceptic. Socrates' claim of ignorance was largely ironic; his inconclusiveness in some of the dialogues resulted from his maieutic method, not from doubt and uncertainty. Socrates' disavowal of scepticism is clearly expressed in the *Meno*, 86: "Some things I have said of which I am not altogether confident. But that we shall be better and braver and less helpless if we think that we ought to enquire, than we should have been if we indulged in the idle fancy that there was no knowing and no use in seeking to know what we do not know;—that is a theme upon which I am ready to fight, in word and deed, to the utmost of my power."

Nevertheless, there have been sceptics in both ancient and modern times who have interpreted Plato as a sceptic rather than a dogmatist. Cicero, for instance, agreed with Philo of Larissa that the school of Plato and the New Academy were not two schools of thought but one (*Academica* i. 13). Disagreeing with Cicero regarding the classification of Plato, Varro granted, however, that Socrates was a sceptic, whose method was "to affirm nothing himself but to refute others, to assert that he knows nothing but the fact of his own ignorance" (*Academica* i. 16). Diogenes Laertius suggested a compromise on the issue: "where he has a firm grasp Plato expounds his own view and refutes the false one, but, if the subject is obscure, he suspends judgment" (iii. 51–52). Montaigne, however, returned to the position of Cicero: "They [Socrates and Plato] will not make open profession of ignorance, and the imbecility of man's reason, because they will not make children afraid: But they manifestly declare the same unto us under the show of a troubled Science and unconstant learning" (II, 255–256).

Though in a degree erroneous, this interpretation of Plato as a sceptic has enjoyed a respectable history; and it quite possibly contributed to the re-awakening of Shelley's interest in Platonism by relating Plato to a philosophical point of view that the poet himself had embraced. It is generally agreed that the renascence of Shelley's Platonism began at Marlow in 1817. By that date Shelley had virtually completed his study of the sceptical tradition—a study that had begun in earnest in the fall of 1813. By 1817, therefore, Shelley was quite familiar with the interpretation of Plato as a sceptic. That the poet endorsed this interpretation is suggested by his remark to Trelawny in 1822: "With regard to the great question, the System of the Universe, I have no curiosity on the subject. I am content to see no farther into futurity than Plato and Bacon."

Scepticism, however, not only prepared the way for Shelley's acceptance of Plato but also inevitably determined his basic divergence from Plato. While both Shelley and Plato exhibit tendencies often vaguely referred to as "transcendental," the nature of these tendencies is quite different in the two men. A brief comparison of the epistemological views of each with those of the strict transcendentalists may help to clarify this underlying difference.

Strict transcendentalism had its origin in Kant's effort to refute Hume. Kant presented two ways by which to surmount the obstacles to knowledge set up by the British sceptic. First, he held that such categories as time, space, and causality are not empirical concepts as Hume maintained but *a priori* concepts. Secondly, he pointed out that just as the "understanding" makes use of such *a priori* concepts in science, so "pure reason" employs the ideas of soul, universe, and God in metaphysics. Kant did not, however, assign to knowledge based on "pure reason" the certitude that he assigned to knowledge based on the "understanding"; it was possible, according to his principles, to know phenomena but not things-in-themselves or reality. But Kant's successors—Fichte, Schelling, and Hegel—rejected this reservation; while English and American writers who came under the direct or indirect influence of the German idealists seized upon Kant's distinction to sanction free intuitive thinking, by exalting "pure reason" and abasing the "understanding."

Plato's epistemology is both like and unlike that of the strict transcendentalists. Like them, Plato is no empiricist, for his doctrine of reminiscence amply recognizes the possibility of *a priori* knowledge. Socrates illustrates his view "that all knowledge is but recollection" by eliciting from a Greek slave of Meno's, previously ignorant of geometry, the proof of one of Euclid's theorems (*Meno* 81–85). To the extent that it rests on legends, particularly on the legend of the soul's pre-existence, the doctrine of reminiscence has, perhaps, the quality of a myth—the kind of myth to which Plato resorted when his subject was obscure. Aside from its mythical quality, however, the doctrine suggests the theory of innate ideas. At all events Plato seriously adhered to the view that all knowledge is latent in the mind, and that such knowledge can be recovered after we become conscious of our ignorance.

Since Plato held that all knowledge is latent in the mind, he was free, like the strict transcendentalists, to pass from the world of becoming to the world of being; to seek not the knowledge of phenomena but "that other sort of knowledge which reason herself attains by the power of dialectic, using hypotheses not as first principles but only as hypotheses—that is to say, as steps and points of departure into a world which is above hypotheses, in order that she may soar beyond them to the first principle of the whole; and clinging to this and then to that which depends on this, by successive steps she descends again with the aid of any sensible object, from ideas through ideas, and in ideas she ends" (*Republic* 511). But as this passage suggests, his method was dialectical rather than intuitive.

Innocent of the Kantian distinction, he could not, like Emerson, for instance, ignore logic because he was employing "pure reason."

Reared in the empirical tradition of British philosophy, Shelley never seriously considered the possibility of *a priori* knowledge, which constitutes so essential a feature of strict transcendentalism and Platonism. While a student at Oxford in the winter of 1810–1811, he was converted by Locke to the doctrine that all knowledge is derived ultimately from experience—a doctrine he never abandoned, although he accepted the slight modification of it involved in Hume's theory of innate passions. Shelley also embraced Hume's empirical concept of cause—a concept that played a major role in the poet's rejection of materialism for scepticism. His subsequent admiration for Plato, being an effect, as we have seen, of this development, can hardly be used as evidence of a change in his epistemological views. Nor is there any reason for suspecting that the poet's empiricism was ever undermined by the influence of strict transcendentalism. His letter to Claire Clairmont, dated February 18, 1821, suggests modesty and tact rather than approval of his correspondent's interest in German philosophy. Shelley, like Sir William Drummond, was hostile rather than friendly toward Kant and his "disciples," as the following passage in *Peter Bell the Third* makes abundantly clear:

> The Devil then sent to Leipsic fair,
>   For Born's translation of Kant's Book;
> A world of words, tail foremost, where
> Right—wrong—false—true—and foul—and fair,
>   As in a lottery-wheel are shook.
>
> Five thousand crammed octavo pages
>   Of German psychologies,—he
> Who his *furor verborum* assuages
> Thereon, deserves just seven months' wages
>   More than will e'er be due to me.
>
> I looked on them nine several days,
>   And then I saw that they were bad;
> A friend, too, spoke in their dispraise,—
> He never read them;—with amaze
>   I found Sir William Drummond had.
>   (Part the Sixth, ll.61–75)

One might insist that despite this hostility in theory, Shelley in practice resembles the strict trancendentalists; for in dealing with the great and eternal questions, he turns from reason to the imagination, exactly as they turn from the "understanding" to "pure reason." But this affinity has perhaps been overemphasized, its limitations ignored. To strict transcendentalists like Coleridge and Emerson, "pure reason" is a superior form of thinking and not a non-rational source of provisional assent. Wordsworth illustrates this point in his well known definition of the imagination as "reason in her most exalted mood"—a view with which most strict transcendentalists would agree. Never accepting, however, the distinction between a lower and a higher rational faculty, Shelley avoids such confounding of imagination with reason. In conceiving of what lies beyond phenomena, he resorts to the sceptic's faith or the sceptic's doctrine of probability. He does not make dogmatical assertions about unknowable things but expresses tentative feelings about things recognized as unknowable.

How Shelley's Humean theory of knowledge influenced his apprehension of ultimate being is illustrated by his Platonism. It is generally agreed that the main feature of Shelley's Platonism is his pursuit of Beauty. The major differences between his pursuit of Beauty and Plato's are well known. While Plato ascends progressively from particular beauties to Beauty, Shelley tends to reverse this process and to seek Beauty in its earthly manifestations. Furthermore, while Plato seeks Beauty through dialectic, Shelley apprehends it only through imagination and feeling. What we are concerned with attempting to demonstrate is that these differences between the two men were the direct result of their dissimilar theories of knowledge. This hypothesis may be tested by examining the development of their concepts of Beauty.

It is quite possible, as William Temple maintained, that in both Plato's case and Shelley's the concept of Beauty had its genesis in a mystical experience. In the *Symposium*, this critic held, Plato "prepares us for a doctrine that is not only quite unsocratic, but has about it the dignity of a religious dogma. It is the prophetess who speaks, but the experience described is Plato's. . . . The language of initiation is freely used; the prophetess is afraid Socrates may not be able to follow *ta telea kai epoptika*, in whose interest all other love exists." To proceed aright, according to Diotima, a person should begin in his youth to visit beautiful forms; if properly guided by his instructor, the youth will love but one such form, out of which he will create fair thoughts, until he perceives "that the beauty of one form is akin to the beauty of another" and "that the beauty in every form is one and the same." In the next stage he will discover "that the beauty of mind is more honourable than the beauty of the outward form," a realization enabling him to see the beauty of institutions, laws, sciences; until at last the vision is revealed to him of "beauty absolute, separate, simple, and everlasting, which without diminution and without increase, or any change, is imparted to the evergrowing and perishing beauties of all other things" (*Symposium* 210–211).

That Shelley's concept of Beauty owed its genesis to a mystical experience is suggested by the following passage in the *Hymn to Intellectual Beauty*:

> While yet a boy I sought for ghosts, and sped
> 　　Thro' many a listening chamber, cave, and ruin,
> 　　And starlight wood, with fearful steps pursuing
> Hopes of high talk with the departed dead.
> I called on poisonous names with which our youth is fed:
> 　　I was not heard: I saw them not:
> 　　When musing deeply on the lot
> Of life, at that sweet time when woods are wooing
> 　　All vital things that wake to bring
> 　　News of birds and blossoming,
> 　　Sudden, thy shadow fell on me;
> I shrieked, and clasped my hands in extacy!
>
> 　　　　　　　　　　　　　　　　(ll. 49–60)

Shelley's account of his experience makes no mention of an "instructor"; nor does it employ the "language of initiation." Nevertheless, it is analogous to Plato's in suggesting the mystical origin of the same philosophical concept.

But while Plato and Shelley may have owed the genesis of their vision to similar mystical experiences, they had to relate their concepts of Beauty to quite dissimilar theories of knowledge; and this difference in the nature of their problems led to a considerable difference in their solutions. In his early dialogues, including the *Meno*, Plato had treated the Ideas as being immanent in particular things. His first clear assertion of the transcendence of Beauty occurs in the mystical passage ascribed to Diotima in the *Symposium*. It is in the next dialogue, the *Phaedo*, that Plato for the first time relates his concept of Beauty to his theory of knowledge—the theory that all knowledge is recollection: "Then may we not say, Simmias, that if, as we are always repeating, there is an absolute beauty, and goodness, and an absolute essence of all things; and if to this, which is now discovered to have existed in our former state, we refer all our sensations, and with this compare them, finding these ideas to be pre-existent and our inborn possession—then our souls must have had a prior existence, but if not, then there would be no force in the argument" (76).

By relating the Ideas to his doctrine of reminiscence, Plato was able to convert the concept of Beauty, previously but the expression of a mystical experience, into a metaphysical doctrine, a theory of reality.

Apart from the world of phenomena, which is subject to the Heracleitean flux, exist, Plato now came to hold on rational grounds, certain perfect and immutable forms. Though the soul cannot perfectly apprehend these essences so long as it is chained to the body, the philosopher in considerable measure escapes this limitation, since he spends his life in the pursuit of death, that is, in emancipating the soul from the body's domination and control (*Phaedo* 63–69). Accordingly, Plato was led to disparage poets and to glorify philosophers, on the ground that only the latter seek the true objects of knowledge, not the perishing forms and shadows of becoming, apprehended by the senses and the feelings, but the fixed and eternal patterns of being, discoverable only by the reason (*Republic* 597–608).

But while Plato's theory of knowledge enabled him to convert Beauty into a metaphysical concept based on reason, Shelley's theory of knowledge prevented him from following a similar course. Shelley's theory of knowledge confined the scope of reason to that prescribed by Hume's theory of causation. Within these limits only science and a negative metaphysics were possible. In the poet's own words, "metaphysical science" is to be treated "as a source of negative truth" (VII, 71). Philosophy, in other words, can destroy superstition, disprove the theory of innate ideas, invalidate the assumption of the efficacy of causes; but it can shed no light whatever on the nature of ultimate reality. Curiosity about ultimate being is therefore futile. In a letter to Thomas Medwin, dated August 22, 1821, Shelley wrote: "What were the speculations which you say disturbed you? My mind is at peace respecting nothing so much as the constitution and mysteries of the great system of things;—my curiosity on the point never amounts to solicitude." Shelley's problem, therefore, was to relate his mystical experience of Beauty, not to Plato's doctrine of reminiscence, but to Hume's theory of knowledge.

Shelley's first effort in poetry to adjust his concept of Beauty to a sceptical theory of knowledge appears in *Alastor* (1815). We are told in the Preface to this poem that the hero "images to himself the Being whom he loves" and then "seeks in vain for the prototype of his conception." The misinterpretation of these two points in the Preface has done much to make *Alastor* seem confused to its critics. As Evan K. Gibson has recently pointed out, the "Being" imaged by the hero is "a creation of his own mind and not, as some writers have stated, a vision sent to him by some outside agency"; and the "prototype" he seeks is not "a copy of the vision in the actual world" but "the pattern or original of the vision itself," that is, absolute Beauty. The hero's quest during his life proves futile; and whether he finds what he seeks after his death is a question to which Shelley gives no clear and definite answer. In other words, Shelley implies in *Alastor* that Beauty, so far as we know, has no objective existence. The tragedy of the hero of *Alastor* lies in his failure to realize this conviction of his creator. Instead of looking for the likeness of his vision in a human maiden, the hero of *Alastor* vainly seeks to apprehend its pattern in ultimate reality.

Likewise adapted to a sceptical theory of knowledge is the concept described in *Hymn to Intellectual Beauty* (1816). Man, according to the poet, is confronted by certain unanswerable questions:

> No voice from some sublimer world hath ever
>> To sage or poet these responses given:
>> Therefore the name of Demon, Ghost, and Heaven,
> Remain the records of their vain endeavour:
> Frail spells, whose uttered charm might not avail to sever,
>> From all we hear and all we see,
>> Doubt, chance, and mutability.
>
> (ll. 25–31)

In contrast to the "vain endeavour" of past sages and poets, which recalls the vain quest of the hero of *Alastor*, stands Shelley's concept of Beauty:

> Thy light alone, like mist o'er mountains driven,
>> Or music by the night wind sent
>> Thro' strings of some still instrument,
>> Or moonlight on a midnight stream,
> Gives grace and truth to life's unquiet dream.
>
> (ll. 32–36)

Shelley cannot possibly mean that his concept embodies a truer version of ultimate reality than that of former sages and poets: such an attitude would be so presumptuous and egotistical as to be ridiculous. He means only that his concept involves no "vain endeavour" because it postulates nothing regarding ultimate reality. In the next stanza he analyzes Beauty into "Love, Hope, and Self-esteem"—that is, into three precious feelings or states of mind—which "like clouds depart / And come, for some uncertain moments lent" (ll. 37–38). Regarding the ultimate cause or metaphysical basis of these feelings or states of mind, the poet remains essentially noncommittal, describing it as "unknown":

> Man were immortal and omnipotent,
> Didst thou, unknown and awful as thou art,
> Keep with thy glorious train firm state within his heart.
>
> (ll. 39–41)

In short, man knows nothing of Beauty as a metaphysical concept; he knows it only as a rare "state within his heart"; and only this "state within his heart" can give "grace and truth to life's unquiet dream."

The concept of Beauty implied in *Alastor* and described in the *Hymn to Intellectual Beauty*—a concept not of an objective entity but of a feeling arising from an unknown cause or power—appears in other of Shelley's works. It occurs, for instance, in *Speculations on Metaphysics* (1815?): "The caverns of the mind are obscure and shadowy; or pervaded with a lustre, beautifully bright indeed, but shining not beyond their portals" (VII, 64); and in *Julian and Maddalo* (1818):

> Where is the love, beauty and truth we seek,
> But in our mind?
>
> (ll. 174–175)

This is a doctrine not of a solipsist but of a sceptic—a sceptic who knows only his own impressions but is far from identifying those impressions with ultimate reality.

While Shelley, however, generally conceives of beauty as a feeling arising from an unknown cause or power, he sometimes—particularly after 1818—expresses some sceptical form of faith in its objective and independent existence. Clearly referring to an aspect of ultimate reality rather than to a state of mind, the concept embodied in these lines of *Prometheus Unbound* (1819), for instance, owes its sceptical quality primarily to its conditional form of expression:

> How glorious art thou, Earth! And if thou be
> The shadow of some spirit lovelier still,
> Though evil stain its work, and it should be
> Like its creation, weak yet beautiful,
> I could fall down and worship that and thee.
>
> (II. iii. 12–16)

On the other hand the concept of an absolute Beauty in the conclusion of *The Sensitive Plant* (1820) possesses a sceptical quality, not because of any conditional form of expression, but because of its admitted elusiveness: the failure of our "organs," whose vision is "obscure," to apprehend an absolute Beauty, the poet implies, constitutes no demonstration of its non-existence:

> For love, and beauty, and delight,
> There is no death nor change; their might
> Exceeds our organs, which endure
> No light, being themselves obscure.

Shelley's belief in the existence of an absolute Beauty, although it cannot be apprehended in our mortal state, reaches a climax in *Adonais* (1812):

> The One remains, the many change and pass;
> Heaven's light forever shines, Earth's shadows fly;
> Life, like a dome of many-coloured glass,
> Stains the white radiance of eternity,
> Until Death tramples it to fragments.—Die,
> If thou wouldst be with that which thou dost seek!
> (ll. 460–465; cf. *Hellas*, ll. 766–769)

In each case it may be said that Shelley's concept of an absolute Beauty rests on faith, not on reason.

The differences in their theories of knowledge, therefore, inevitably conducted Plato and Shelley to fundamental differences in their concepts of Beauty. Plato's concept, adapted to the doctrine of reminiscence, involves a dialectical ascent into ultimate being; whereas Shelley's, adapted to scepticism, refers only to a rare experience or to a faith in the existence of a metaphysical basis for that experience which we cannot apprehend in our mortal state. Their attitudes toward their respective concepts, as we shall now see, likewise reveal differences traceable to differences in their theories of knowledge: both men reflect something less than entire satisfaction with their doctrines of Beauty, but they do so for different reasons.

After converting the Ideas into ultimate entities discoverable by reason, Plato was soon faced by some dialectical difficulties from which he was unable to escape. Parmenides, for instance, puts the following question to Plato's Socrates, as the latter admits having expressed some things of which he is not altogether confident: "And would you feel equally undecided, Socrates, about things of which the mention may provoke a smile?—I mean such things as hair, mud, dirt, or anything else which is vile and paltry; would you suppose that each of these has an idea distinct from the actual objects with which we come into contact, or not?" Socrates grants both the pertinence of this question and the absurdity of supposing the existence of any form of Ideal Ugliness; and these admissions lead him to wonder whether the Ideas may not "be thoughts only," having "no proper existence except in our minds," in which case the Ideas "would no longer be absolute" (*Parmenides* 130–133).

Shelley likewise was not entirely satisfied with his doctrine of absolute Beauty, although the difficulties confronting him were not dialectical. They arose, instead, from deferring the possibility of apprehending absolute Beauty until after death. By the pursuit of death, as we have already noted, Plato referred to the cultivation of an austere and disinterested dialectical pursuit of ultimate truth. But in adapting Plato's meaning to his own scepticism, Shelley substituted an attitude of otherworldliness for Plato's dialectics. Such an alternative, however, required a firm belief in the soul's immortality, whereas the poet's was most tenuous. In his notes to *Hellas*, for instance, he asserts that man's only valid basis for believing in immortality is his "inextinguishable thirst" for it: "Until better arguments can be produced than sophisms which disgrace the cause, this desire itself must remain the strongest and only presumption that eternity is the inheritance of every thinking being." That this "only presumption" was quite inadequate to banishing doubt finds expression in a sonnet of 1820 (IV, 64):

> Ye hasten to the dead! What seek ye there,
> Ye restless thoughts and busy purposes
> Of the idle brain, which the world's livery wear?
> O thou quick Heart, which pantest to possess
> All that pale Expectation feigneth fair!
> Thou vainly curious Mind which wouldest guess
> Whence thou didst come, and whither thou must go,
> And that which never yet was known wouldst know—
> Oh, whither hasten ye, that thus ye press
> With such swift feet life's green and pleasant path,
> Seeking alike from happiness and woe
> A refuge in the cavern of grey death?
> O heart, and mind, and thoughts! what thing do you
> Hope to inherit in the grave below?

It is no cause for wonder, therefore, to find Shelley sometimes exhibiting a tendency diametrically opposed to the otherworldliness of *Adonais*, that is, a tendency to identify his subjective vision of Beauty with a mortal creature. The glorification of Emilia Viviani in *Epipsychidion*, written a few months before *Adonais*, illustrates this tendency:

> I knew it was the Vision veiled from me
> So many years—that it was Emily.
> (ll. 343–344)

Critics have often compared Shelley's *Epipsychidion* with Dante's *Vita Nuova*, but perhaps Keats' *Endymion* represents a truer parallel:

> My sweetest Indian, here
> Here will I kneel, for thou redeemed hast
> My life from too thin breathing: Gone and past
> Are cloudy phantoms. Caverns lone, farewell!
> And air of visions, and the monstrous swell
> Of visionary seas! No, never more
> Shall airy voices cheat me to the shore
> Of tangled wonder, breathless and aghast.

Shelley, of course, was more at home in a rarefied atmosphere than was Keats; what he was seeking escape from in *Epipsychidion*—perhaps without being fully aware of it—was the concentration of hope upon an afterlife about which he knew that he knew nothing.

In *The Triumph of Life*, left unfinished when he died in 1822, Shelley approached his problem—that of arriving at a satisfactory reconciliation of his empiricism and his idealism—from a new angle. Avoiding personal involvement by the device of assuming a spectator's point of view, he solved his problem dramatically. This fact, I think, accounts for the unusually subdued tone of the poem. Shelley transfers his faith in an absolute Beauty to the "sacred few"—

> who could not tame
> Their spirits to the conquerors—but as soon
> As they had touched the world with living flame,
> Fled back like eagles to their native noon . . .
> (ll. 128–131)

But the poet is to be identified with the "sacred few" no more than with Rousseau, whose courage failed before their vision, so that he followed the "cold bright car" of worldly life. How Shelley might have ended his last great poem can only be conjectured, but it is difficult to see how he could have abandoned the dramatic point of view that governs much of the work as it stands.

Shelley, then, is not a pseudo-Platonist but a Platonist in the sceptical tradition. The renascence of Platonism in his mature writings—a development that previous critics have never satisfactorily explained— owed much to the poet's investigation of the sceptical tradition during the years 1813–1816. Scepticism liberated Shelley from the prejudice against Platonism which he had inherited from the French materialists and rationalists of the eighteenth century: it accomplished this result by depicting Plato as a poet of the unknown and unknowable and as a forerunner of the sceptical point of view in philosophy. But scepticism not only formed a transition between Shelley's early materialism and his later Platonism but also determined the specific character of that later Platonism. When they came to adapt the concept of Beauty to their respective theories of knowledge, Plato and Shelley faced different tasks, which led to different results. His theory of reminiscence enabled Plato to seek Beauty dialectically as an aspect of ultimate reality. On the other hand, Shelley's sceptical theory of knowledge led him to conceive of Beauty as the unknown cause of a fleeting sense of ecstasy, or as an aspect of reality supported only by faith.

FREDERICK A. POTTLE

The Role of Asia in the Dramatic Action of Shelley's "Prometheus Unbound"

Since it is a myth, *Prometheus Un-*
bound is capable of endless allegorization. Some readers like to work out a
detailed and particular allegory for it, others prefer to keep the allegory
vague and general. Some even deprecate any attempt to formulate a "second
meaning." All readers ought to agree that one should understand the myth
as dramatic action on its own terms before one starts allegorizing. It may be
legitimate to conclude that Demogorgon is Necessity because he says so-
and-so, but until we despair of making dramatic sense out of him, we should
not conclude that he says so-and-so because he is Necessity. What *happens*
in *Prometheus Unbound?*

Though the opposition counts distinguished names, majority opinion seems agreed that there is only one action in the whole so-called drama,
and that that action is completed before the First Act has hardly got under
way. Prometheus announces at line 53 that he pities Jupiter; the remaining
2557 lines, it is maintained, consist merely of the unrolling necessary consequences of that action, and of jubilation over those consequences. This
does not at all accord with what I find the text saying.

What has happened by the end of Act I? Prometheus, who cursed
Jupiter three thousand years ago and has remained till at least very

---

From *Shelley: A Collection of Critical Essays*, edited by George M. Ridenour. Copyright ©
1965 by Frederick A. Pottle. Prentice-Hall, Inc., Englewood Cliffs, New Jersey, 1965.

recently in a state of passionate enmity toward him, discovers that he no longer hates his persecutor and repents of his curse. This discovery by no means ends his sufferings or brings any alleviation of them; on the contrary, it precipitates a visitation of the Furies and a particularly horrible train of tortures. His state is then cheered by a chorus of prophetic spirits who announce that the hope, the prophecy they bear begins and ends in him (I, 690–91, 706–7). Two things are to be noted about these spirits and their songs. First, it is not intimated that they are now putting in an appearance for the first time as a result of Prometheus's change of heart. On the contrary, one would infer that they have been consoling him all along, just as the Furies have been tormenting him. Secondly, their songs are by no means expressions of unmixed joy and hope: they are as sad as they are sweet. No portion of *Prometheus Unbound* has been so generally ignored as the songs of the Fifth and Sixth Spirits (I, 763–79). Ione (I, 756–57) characterizes their voices as despair mingled with love, and surely despair is not too strong a word for the sentiments these beautiful beings utter. "Yes," says the Fifth Spirit, "Love exists, I have seen him. But he was closely followed by Ruin." "Ah," rejoins the Sixth Spirit, "it is worse than that. Ruin—or Pain—masquerades as Love to betray the best and gentlest." The Chorus, speaking after Prometheus's recantation, does not deny that this is a true description of things as they still stand, but announced confidently that Prometheus will overcome Ruin: they know it as herdsmen know that the hawthorn will blow when they feel the winds of spring. The winds they have felt breathe from Prometheus:

> Wisdom, Justice, Love, and Peace,
> When they struggle to increase,
> Are to us as soft winds be.
> (I, 796–98)

Undoubtedly Prometheus begins the action and will end it; we are told so explicitly. But one can begin and end an action without being able to perform all the middle parts of it. At the end of the First Act Prometheus has realized that only through Love can he be freed. All he can do now is to endure and willingly accept his destiny as "the saviour and the strength of suffering man" (I, 816–17). He has passed beyond agony and solace (I, 819), and is just as firmly pinned to the crag as he was when he cursed Jupiter. Only love can help, and his beloved is far from him (I, 808). And the prophecy of his triumph, though the seasonal metaphor makes it seem more immediate than his own bleak vision of victory after an agony of literally innumerable years (I, 424), is actually conditional and ambiguous. Wisdom, Justice, Love, and Peace must go on struggling to increase; even if spring comes, there may be delays and setbacks. Frost may blast the young blossoms.

The First Act is the action of Prometheus, the Second is devoted entirely to the action of Asia. She goes to her spouse in response to a summons—not *his* summons, for he has not consciously issued one, but a summons conveyed in two dreams which Panthea has dreamed at his feet. The first presents Prometheus freed, unscarred and rejuvenated, an ardent bridegroom awaiting his bride. But Asia is not summoned to go to her husband by the direct route that Panthea travels. Panthea's second dream was ostensibly another vision of things as they are, a vision of Ruin dogging the steps of Love. She saw a blasted almond-tree bloom, and the miraculous flowers were immediately thrown down by frost. But the fallen petals in this case bore no message of despair; they were stamped with the hopeful directive FOLLOW. And Asia then remembers that she too had had a dream in which FOLLOW was written across the mountain shadows and the leaves of the plants, and the wind in the pines had taken up the message. Echo-songs in the air now repeat the summons and indicate what is to be followed, whither, and why. Asia is to follow the aerial voices through caverns and forest, by lakes and fountains, through mountains growing ever more rugged, to rents, gulfs, and chasms in the earth (II, i, 175–202). She is to do it because

> In the world unknown
> Sleeps a voice unspoken;
> By thy step alone
> Can its rest be broken;
> Child of Ocean!
> (II, i, 190–94)

She accordingly sets out, hand in hand with Panthea. The eddies of echoes, we are informed, are actually much more than the mere guide they appear to her to be. They are a positive force attracting and impelling her, and they grow steadily stronger as she yields to their impetus; she half walks, half floats on her way, thinking her motion due to her own limbs (II, ii, 41–63). She and Panthea pass through a shady damp forest thronged with nightingales, and are finally borne to the top of a pinnacle of rock among the mountains which they recognize as marking the portal to the abode of Demogorgon, a mysterious power already identified as directing the stream of sound (II, ii, 43). As they stand admiring the Alpine landscape, which moves Asia to overt theologizing, the spirits, now for the first time become visible, urge her to put herself utterly into their hands and allow herself to be borne unresisting down to the throne of Demogorgon in an abyss below all natural caverns. A spell is treasured there for her alone (II, iii, 88), but she can exert it only by utter surrender:

> We have bound thee, we guide thee;
> Down, down!
> With the bright form beside thee;
> Resist not the weakness,
> Such strength is in meekness
> That the Eternal, the Immortal,
> Must unloose through life's portal
> The snake-like Doom coiled underneath his throne
> By that alone.
> (II, iii, 90–98)

The lyric (there are five stanzas in all) is apparently not merely an invitation to the descent but accompanies it. At any rate, when the next scene opens, Asia and Panthea are in the Cave of Demogorgon, and there is no reason to doubt that they got there on the Spirits' terms.

The statements that only Asia can rouse Demogorgon to action, that in Demogorgon's cave is treasured a spell for Asia alone, are as express as the earlier statement that the prophecy of regeneration begins and ends in Prometheus. Why then the critics' reluctance to grant that Asia performs an independent and essential part of the action? Undoubtedly because of her seeming passivity in the first three scenes of the Second Act. She follows, she is borne, she does not resist an invading weakness. Significant action, the critics seem to feel, needs to be embodied in language like that of the First Act, language that testifies to a struggle against resistance, language that asserts difficulty. Now, one very important critic, C. S. Lewis, of course does maintain that difficulty is precisely the subject of these scenes, but I do not see any evidence for thinking that the journey was meant to seem physically arduous. We might take as the norm of a really arduous journey that portion of the Second Book of *Paradise Lost* which deals with Satan's ascent from the gates of Hell up through Chaos. If the Second Act of *Prometheus Unbound* were presenting external or physical difficulty, as the Second Book of *Paradise Lost* is, we should hear of lacerating, almost impenetrable, undergrowth in the forest, of rough stones that draw blood from clinging hands and clambering knees, of abysses that the giddy traveler must hang over with inadequate support, of tunnels and chimneys that narrow and threaten to hold him fast. The forest in *Prometheus Unbound* is damp and very shady, but it has the open pathways between the tree trunks that one would expect in a stand of large evergreens (II, ii, 1–2). If the poet had wished us to feel that passage through it was physically difficult, he would not have called its gloom "divine" (II, ii, 22), and he would not have devoted seventeen lines to a description of the songs of the nightingales. If Asia and Panthea encounter any physical difficulties in the ascent to the pinnacle, they are not reported or alluded to, while the help they are getting from the stream of sound is insisted on.

Yet no careful reader can feel that Asia is an automaton or even that she is naturally impassive. When we first meet her, she is displaying extreme impatience for Panthea's return. She does not instantly follow the echo guide, but ponders her action and takes time to make up her mind (II, i, 188–89, 207–8). She says nothing further to indicate that she is on the alert, but the spirits, in everything *they* say, assume that her assent is not irrevocable, that she might balk at any moment. In short, she wills to follow, she wills to continue to follow, and that constitutes her action in these scenes. *Pace* Professor Lewis, her progress is not physically difficult but rather the opposite: it is so easy and pleasant as to raise doubts whether it can possibly conduct to an heroic goal. Asia's difficulty in these scenes is to overcome the scruples that would keep her from surrendering herself to a duty which is disquietingly pleasant. And this difficulty, which I feel to be real, is expressed only indirectly.

This may be considered too subtle for drama. Drama is the most primitive of all literary forms, and our own dramatic tradition is especially committed to physical violence. It has, indeed, often been stated as a truism that physical non-resistance is essentially undramatic. That seems to me simply not true. Willing, not muscular action, is the essential of drama. A physical non-resistance which we see to be gravely and consciously willed, though not the usual stuff of drama in our tradition, will function dramatically in our experience if we will allow it to.

Difficulty in the Fourth Scene is of a more obvious sort, and is expressed directly in Asia's speeches. In the Cave of Demogorgon she performs an action parallel to and of equal importance with that of Prometheus in the First Act. He forgave Jupiter; she works her way to the word that will topple Jupiter from Olympus. In a way, the action is more difficult than his. He had to struggle with excruciating pain, both physical and mental, but it does not appear that he had to struggle with his hatred in order to overcome it. Reaching for it one day, he found it evaporated (I, 53). On the other hand, we see her in the agony of struggling through and out of some of her most passionately held attitudes.

One should not speak too confidently of "understanding" this pregnant and subtle colloquy, but two remarks concerning it seem warranted.

Demogorgon, though definitely a mighty power who can tell Asia all she dares ask (II, iv, 7), always in fact answers her in her own terminology and at the level of her own understanding. We are not to assume that she is merely talking to herself, but she certainly gets no answers she has not herself thought her way to. Secondly, because Demogorgon adapts his answers to her understanding, his oracular utterances must be taken as provisional and progressive. They are not coordinate articles of a creed, but a progress through dogma to the utterly undogmatic faith which will unloose the Doom sleeping under Demogorgon's throne:

> So much I asked before, and my heart gave
> The response thou hast given; and of such truths
> Each to itself must be the oracle.
>   (II, iv, 121–23)

Prometheus, the god-defier, engages in no theological speculation whatever. To him Jupiter is god and all but omnipotent; Jupiter is wicked, cruel, ungrateful, and unjust; Jupiter will ultimately fall. Until he falls, Prometheus expects to be tortured. To Prometheus evil is a fact of experience. He never asks why evil should exist, or if Jupiter comprehends all the evil there is in the cosmos.

Asia, on the other hand, is a passionate theologian or, to be precise, is passionately interested in the problem of evil. On the pinnacle, before descending to the Cave of Demogorgon, she had tentatively suggested that the glories and shortcomings of the physical universe might be explained by assuming that it was the work of some beautiful spirit too weak to prevent evil from invading and staining its work. She says she could worship that kind of Creator (II, iii, 11–16). Her cast of mind, we see, leads her to posit creation and a Creator with human attributes, and to repel any suggestion that the Creator of the physical universe may be responsible for evil.

But she is not so sure as to other possible creators, and in the Cave of Demogorgon she at once begins putting the questions that trouble her profoundly. Who made the *living* world, the world of Mind? Who made thought, passion, reason, will, imagination? Who made the sense of love? Demogorgon, in the tersest possible fashion, replies God, Almighty God, Merciful God. He will later suggest that she relinquish this terminology and some of the concepts associated with it, but the important thing at this stage is to give emphatic confirmation, in such terms as possess reality for her, to her intuition that the world of mind is fundamentally divine, or is like divinity, beneficent divinity. Who then, she continues, made terror, madness, crime, remorse, hate, self-contempt, all the varieties of pain? Demogorgon again uses her implied references, but to cover the facts this time he has to resort to ambiguity. "He reigns" may be taken as a virtual repetition of his previous answer, "Almighty God," or it may mean that the Maker of Evil is a usurper. Actually, it means both things at the same time. "Almighty God," the Primal Power, did not make Evil, but if one is to use this kind of language, he "made" the "evil things" which the malignancy of Jupiter converted into positive evil. Demogorgon at this stage wishes to give emphatic confirmation to Asia's intuition that the world of mind is dominated by an Evil Power which it is possible and proper to dethrone, but also to prepare the ground for his next and final position, which will be that when the usurper goes and the Primal Power alone "reigns," the means or occasion of evil, relative to man, will still inhere in the universe.

Asia not unnaturally takes him to be referring solely to a Usurper, and passionately demands the Usurper's name. The world asks but his name, she says; curses shall drag him down. She of course knows Jupiter's name, though she has not yet spoken it, but she confidently expects a curse already uttered to drag *him* down. Before ever she entered the Cave of Demogorgon she had come to the conclusion that the evil of Jupiter, real and horrible as it is, cannot cover all the evil in the universe. There is, she feels sure, an Evil more radical; Jupiter is only a front man. And Demogorgon, by saying "He reigns" rather than "Jupiter," has told that she is so far on the right track.

Well, who *does* reign? Demogorgon's first three utterances might make us think that we had left Greek theology for the Judaeo-Christian, but that would be too hasty. We are still within the Greek system, and in that system the question is highly pertinent. Greek myth records a succession of reigning deities, none of them omnipotent. Jupiter (Zeus) had dethroned Saturn (Kronos), just as Saturn had dethroned Uranus, but Jupiter himself was held to be subject to Fate or Necessity. He took over a created universe, and (in Shelley's version) had made nothing but evil. But he was not the originator of evil. So far as Asia could make out, evil entered the world in the reign of Saturn, when Time first appeared. Evil under Saturn had been negative or privative: men lived in joy but in a calm vegetable joy, denied the knowledge that was their birthright. Positive evil—famine, heat, cold, toil, disease, war, violent death, raging and lacerating passions—arrived with Jupiter, and increased in direct proportion as men received knowledge and skill from Prometheus. Prometheus's gifts were obviously not in themselves evil but glorious. Who then rains down evil? Surely not Jupiter. Prometheus pretty much set him up in business, and he is obviously afraid of Prometheus. He does not act like the Creator of Evil, he acts like someone who takes orders. Who is his hidden master? Is his master perhaps a slave too? Where does it all end?

My paraphrase, though highly speculative in its inferences, has so far been content to base itself on what is explicitly provided by Shelley's text. I want now, however, not merely to read *into* the dialogue, but to read *in* some dialogue, and I shall not be deterred if the result sounds more like Shaw than like Shelley.

ASIA: Who is his master? Is he too a slave?
DEMOGORGON: All spirits who serve evil things are enslaved. You are right in thinking Jupiter enslaved.
ASIA: But how about the Being you called God some lines back? If he made the living world, if he is almighty, must *he* not be the hidden master of Jupiter? If he is using evil, is he not enslaved by it?
DEMOGORGON: I employed the terminology and the concepts you gave me, and am glad to note that you now see some difficulties in them. If you load your questions concerning the Primal Power with demands that that Power be a personal, omnipotent Creator, you are going to run into irresolvable contradictions. And "God" is not a very good term either. I suggest that it had better be left to Jupiter.
ASIA: Very well, I give up those demands, holding on only to your assurance that the universe of mind is god-like and beneficent. But is it not possible to carry Jupiter any farther back? If he is a slave, who is his master?
DEMOGORGON: I said that spirits who serve evil *things* are enslaved; I did not say that Jupiter serves the Evil One. I grant that "slave" implies "master"; all figures from the world of human experience are misleading when applied to ultimates. *The deep truth is imageless.* Would it be at all helpful if I told you that the evil Jupiter serves is not personal, that it is, as you yourself hinted, Time? Time, relative to man, is evil, and Time is a mystery. Everything on earth is subject to Time, but not because of malignancy in the will of some Power superior to Jupiter. The Ultimate Power wishes man well and can and does get through to him. Love is not subject to Time.
ASIA: I have asked these questions before, and you have now confirmed the answers that my heart gave me. These truths must not be elaborated, systematized, institutionalized. In such matters each heart must be its own oracle. One question more, a question I would not ask if I had the answer anywhere within my own being. Prometheus will be freed, but when?
DEMOGORGON: Now.

Prometheus's action was to repent of his curse, to stop hating the manifested evil he continued unyieldingly to resist. Asia's action is to give up her demand for an ultimate Personal Evil, to combine an unshakable faith that the universe is sound at the core with a realization that, as regards man, Time is radically and incurably evil. That action is now finished. Demogorgon ascends the car to dethrone Jupiter, Asia rises from the abyss transfigured by the pouring in of that Eternal Love which is not subject to Time and Change.

Allegorization of myth has exactly the same values and is subject to the same dangers as any other kind of paraphrase of poetry. A paraphrase that is substituted for or imported into a poem is reductive, but a paraphrase that is annotative or exploratory may lead us deeper into the poem's concreteness. My allegorization of *Prometheus Unbound* will be justified if it backs up my reading of the action.

Shelley's Prometheus has too often been taken to represent the human mind, Asia to represent Eternal Love or Intellectual Beauty, and Jupiter to be the embodiment of merely external evil. Though in one aspect (an important one) Prometheus does seem to symbolize human mind and Asia Nature, a more profound and consistent reading would regard human mind as divided between Prometheus, Asia, and Jupiter. Prometheus (whose name in Greek means "forethought") symbolizes intellect, understanding, the inventive, rational faculties of mankind. Asia is the affective side of mind: emotion, passion, imagination. The separation of Asia from Prometheus is a "fall" of the Blakean sort which produced Urizen and Ahania, Los and Enitharmon. Asia is not Intellectual Beauty or Eternal Love, for she dwells in, and is wholly subject to, the world of Time and Change, but she is the chief conduit of Eternal Love into that world. Jupiter does not represent all the evil of human experience. He is subjective or man-made evil: custom, reaction, tyranny, superstition, outworn creeds. Man's intellect gave this kind of evil all its strength and has then been confined and tortured by it. Intellect of itself is capable of realizing that we make our own mental tortures by hating what we should merely resist, but knowledge alone will not bring reform or regeneration. Prometheus will never get free without help from Asia. "Until," Shelley says in his Preface to *Prometheus Unbound*, "the mind can love, and admire, and trust, and hope, . . . reasoned principles of moral conduct are seeds cast upon the high-way of life." Or again, in A *Defence of Poetry*, "The great instrument of moral good is the imagination" (paragraph 13).

But not the unregenerate Imagination. Asia must go down to the Cave of Demogorgon, the affections must sink back on themselves down into the unconscious depths of being and be made over. Specifically, the affections must exorcize the demons of infancy, whether personal or of the race, and must rebuild themselves in accord with a mature theology. But is not this to turn matters precisely upside down? Surely it is the function of the heart to forgive and of the head to construct theologies? No, would certainly be Shelley's firm rejoinder. The head must sincerely forgive, must willingly eschew hatred on purely experimental grounds. "Revenge, retaliation, atonement, are pernicious *mistakes*"; intellect must "discover the *wisdom* of universal love" (emphasis mine). And since the evidence on which all religions are founded is revealed to the heart and does not have the character of experimental verifiability which the intellect demands for its operations, intellect, to be true to itself, must remain scrupulously agnostic. If it does apply the operations of logic to the content of revelation, it produces precisely Jupiter. Theology, in the form of concrete poetic speculation, is the domain and the duty of the imagination.

The Imagination will not get a mature theology and a right religion until, as I have said, it is able to reconcile an unshakable but unelaborated faith that the universe is good and radically beneficent with a calm acceptance of the fact that when all man-made evil is cast off, men will still be confronted by chance and death and mutability.

And a right religion is essential for the overthrow of man-made evil. *Prometheus Unbound* is not humanist in its implications. The power we need to help ourselves is not our own but comes from on high, and will be granted if we make ourselves receptive of it. Eternal Love will stream with increasing power through us to reform the world, not merely the world of mind but also the world of matter. Human intellect thus empowered will build a new heaven and a new earth. The action which began in Prometheus will end in him.

JAMES RIEGER

Orpheus and the West Wind

" 'This is a fine, clever fellow!' "
Hogg said to himself after his first conversation with Shelley, " 'but I can
never bear his society; I shall never be able to endure his voice; it would
kill me. What a pity it is'! I am very sensible of imperfections, and especially
of painful sounds,—and the voice of the stranger was excruciating: it
was intolerably shrill, harsh, and discordant; of the most cruel intension,—
it was perpetual, and without any remission,—it excoriated the ears."

When modern readers complain of Shelleyan "shrillness," they do
not mean that they have heard cacophonies in the verse itself. They refer
to "tone," which may be defined as the emotional quality of a speaker's
relationship to his primary auditor. This listener is almost never the
reader. To borrow Mill's aphorism, the reader, by "overhearing" the
auditor, catches ironies that qualify or even subvert the tone. Only lyric
and dramatic utterances properly have tone, and lyrics have it only insofar
as they *become* dramatic by including two persons: "I" and the object
addressed, Peele Castle, Euphrosyne, Stella, a cuckoo, or God. No reader
confuses himself with these objects, but unless he is careful, he will on the
other hand mistake the poet's persona for the poet himself. The writer
may encourage the neglect of this distinction by painting the mask to
resemble his own face, but always, as Rimbaud remarked, *je suis un autre.*
Childe Harold is no more Lord Byron than Porphyria's strangler is Robert
Browning. Thus we hardly need to be told that the young man who sings,

> Oh lift me from the grass!
> I die! I faint! I fail!

is a Champak-drunk East Indian; he could not in any case be P.B. Shelley.

To take a less obvious example, the moth who recites quatrains to the star is not Shelley writing mash-notes to a woman of flesh and blood. One might, he said, as well look for a leg of mutton in a gin-shop as come to him for "human or earthly" articles. The inferior, passive, and weakly yearner who speaks most of these lyrics is Eros himself, the homeless and ugly offspring of Poverty and Plenty, who desires what he does not have, the Beautiful. Heavenly Love and Beauty reside in the third Neoplatonic Heaven, the sphere of Hesperus or the Venus Coelestis. Whoever condemns this metaphor as sentimental should know that he rejects Plotinus and Ficino with it, and through them, at either end, Sidney's Astrophel and the *Symposium*.

A poem's existence, then, depends upon four persons: the author, the speaker, the object addressed, and the reader. The posture called "tone" is a form of narrative irony. If, reading Shelley, we forget these axioms, the Amelia Curran portrait and Arnold's even more disastrous caricature will flash before our sight, and we shall find little in the tone of these lyrics but shrillness. By this we shall mean effeminacy, self-pity, and Ozymandiac arrogance. Interpreting the mask according to our notion of the man, we shall lose Shelley's voice in a whine of our own fancying.

[I have previously explored] the theological dimensions of Shelley's doctrine that Love is to the Imagination as the "great secret" is to the "instrument" of moral good. This formula also contains a pragmatic truth of literary criticism: if we dislike a poem, we shall probably misread it. Dr. Leavis' failure to make out the grammatical sense of "Lines: 'When the lamp is shattered'" exactly illustrates this fruitless clash of sensibilities. Suppose further that a reader sophisticated enough to register disgust at André Maurois' epicene cartoon in *Ariel* is just naïve enough to confuse the speaker of the "Hymn to Intellectual Beauty" with its author. What will he make of the poem's epiphanic climax?

> Sudden, thy shadow fell on me;
> I shrieked, and clasped my hands in ecstasy!

If Saint Teresa or Saint John of the Cross were credited with those lines, we would know at once what was meant. "Ecstasy," from the Greek word for "derangement," is the mystic's precise term for his loss of outward sense and voluntary motor control in the presence of his God. When wings come between Shelley and the sun, his reaction is traditional: he shrieks and clasps his hands in what looks like prayer. He does not squeal, or giggle, or skip about the room. And yet we smile, for we had heard of the plaster Cupid, "beautiful but ineffectual," before we read the poem.

Douglas Bush's stigmatization of Shelley's heroes and martyrs as "variations on the portrait of himself as an effeminate romantic idealist" is a *locus classicus* of the biographical fallacy. "It is painful," Professor Bush writes, "doubly painful when we remember that Christ is in the background, to think of the Aeschylean god in terms of 'pale feet,' 'pale wound-worn limbs,' 'soft and flowing limbs And passion-parted lips.' " A note follows to Shelley's description of Correggio's Christ, whose lips are parted (like those of many a Mannerist John the Baptist) in ambiguous if not indecent warmth. But we can spare ourselves all that pain if we will look only at the words themselves. Shelley did not decorate his text with a facing reproduction of Correggio's model; he used the word "passion" in a general Christic context, where it can only mean "suffering," the Passion of Our Lord. As for the pallor of the Prometheus-Christ's feet and lacerated limbs, the continued gnawing of a man's heart by a vulture will, like crucifixion, cause him to lose great quantities of blood.

Shelley's three major self-portraits appear in "Ode to the West Wind," *Epipsychidion*, and *Adonais*. A close reading of these passages will not only distinguish the persona from the man, but will also show that the persona's character and the tone of his grief are dictated in each case by the myth common to all three poems. The myth is again occult, though nominally classical. It tells of the first lyrist, whose mangled body was a blood sacrifice to his songs. The myth is that of Orpheus, poet and priest, and of the vegetative deities whose worship he reformed and whose annual slaughter and resurrection his words, by imitation, celebrate.

In the last three years of Shelley's life, the idiosyncrasy that had determined his choice of the most recondite symbologies research could yield invaded his prosody as well. Dante's chain-rhyme is the classic vernacular scheme for a purgatorial dream-vision; *The Triumph of Life* was therefore composed in tercets. Spenser's stanza, whose languid conclusion perfectly suits an elegiac mood (Latin elegy alternates pentameters with hexameters), was selected for *Adonais* at least partly because the poem is a parabolic variation on the "Garden of Adonis" episode in the Third Book of *The Faerie Queene*. Shelley had always insisted that his non-political verse was directed to a small and highly-educated audience. Today that audience necessarily consists of students of literary history. An awareness of the technical antecedents of Shelley's poems alone can trigger a full response to the thematic ironies implicit in them and suggest the mythological ancestors of their personages. In this sense Shelley may be called an academic poet.

The rhyme-scheme of "Ode to the West Wind" conforms to the larger numerological pattern within which Shelley develops his chief images. The historical connotations of *terza rima* take second place to certain overall ritualistic correspondences, which we shall now examine at some length.

The "Ode" is divided into five sections, each of which contains fourteen lines and ends with a couplet: the rhyme scheme is *ababcbcdcdedee*. If the tercets were not visibly separated on the page, the reader would not know until the end of the sixth line, when the *b*-rhyme repeats once too often, that the poem was to be something other than a sequence of Shakespearean sonnets. The obvious question—why, having fourteen lines to work with, a poet should confine himself to five rather than seven rhymes—leads nowhere. Shelley shared with Keats, Byron, and Words-worth a distaste for the English sonnet, but not, significantly, their devotion to the tighter, four- or five-rhyme Italian form. He wrote com-paratively few sonnets, almost none of which adheres to a strict pattern. Even the pallid, ostensibly Petrarchan "To the Nile" (1818) is spoiled by two feminine endings and two forced rhymes. "Ozymandias" (1817) fol-lows the scheme *ababacdcedefef,* and the *e*-rhyme of the "Sonnet to Byron" (1821) dangles in isolation. "Lift not the painted veil" (1818) and "England in 1819" both reverse the normal order of octave and sestet; the first six lines (*ababab*) are succeeded by the equally mechanical alternation of *c*- and *d*-rhymes in the final eight. Such sloppiness is freakish in Shelley and indicates nothing less than boredom with the form. It forces the reader to presume that the contrasting intricacy, strength, and consistency, from section to section, of the "Ode" stanza conceal a more typical symbolic intent.

That symbolism has venerable antecedents. The Romantic renas-cence of Petrarch's sonnet coincided with the importation from Germany of a transcendentalism that revived, by restating, older "platonizing" habits of mind. When, for example, a Tudor Laura was something less than chaste, the opposition of octave to sestet adumbrated, no less than did the words themselves, the half-remembered but inescapably formative tension between Urania and Pandemos. So Keats measured his reactions to the brevity of sexual climax and to the *tristitia* that follows it against the "steadfastness" of the Pole Star. Mutability, armed with a bending sickle and envious of smooth complexions—"indifferent in a week," says Auden, "to a beautiful physique"—also reappeared with the genre, but mainly as the ravisher of statuary and architecture. These are "too weak," Shelley says of Rome's ruins, "The glory they transfuse with fitting truth to speak." Wordsworth in "Mutability" subjects a weed-crowned tower to that abstraction's "unimaginable touch," and Keats in another sonnet mingles "Grecian grandeur with the rude / Wasting of Old Time."

The Italian form imposes Ciceronian syntax on the poet: octave and sestet reinforce, for example, the "when . . . then" construction which, surviving in Shakespeare, strengthens his looser framework. If the sonnet is broken down further into two quatrains and a sestet, the sentiment fits naturally into a pattern determined by, say, an "if . . . then . . . but" sequence of clauses. Syntax is logic, and the logic of romantic irony perfectly suits the sonnet's periodic structure.

Shelley and Byron, of course, preferred other Italian stanza forms as vehicles for their wry sense of the light years separating Heavenly Love from the Yeatsian complexities of mire or blood. A canceled passage of *Epipsychidion* pays tribute to Shakespeare's sonnets, but the poem itself imitates the first canzone of the *Convivio* in memorializing the poet's "rash" search for a mortal form of his "idol"—the One Venus, emblematically rendered by a fusion of the Pole and Evening Stars. Byron's *ottava rima* builds loosely to a terse and epigrammatic final turn whose inevitability invites flippancy. For six lines the intertwined arms and legs of Juan and Haidée writhe and glisten on the twilit beach; the dry, weary, and faintly pitying accents of the aging voyeur break in with the couplet. Connoisseurship ("a *group* that's quite *antique*, / Half naked, loving, natural, and *Greek*") establishes distance and a worldly-wisdom against which there is no argument, for it hints the truth: that these lovers will degenerate into voluptuaries as soon as they move indoors.

If Shelley's tercets were not run-on, his "Ode" stanza and the Shakespearean sonnet, with its three discrete quatrains, would be roughly similar in effect. The English has one emblematic advantage over the Italian form. Because the quatrains are independent degrees by which the speaker climbs to an emotional *aperçu*, they can be taken to represent the rungs of Eros' ascent towards a glimpse of the beautiful Idea. Sir Philip Sidney, for example, rejects in an opening line the love that reaches "but to dust"; his mind, aspiring to "higher things" and the "light" of a vaguely Christian "heaven," rises to the perception and direct address of "Eternal Love" in the couplet. In his great cycle he writes, like Shelley, as star-lover to star. The same accommodation of sense to structure has, of course, been attempted within the Petrarchan pattern. Thomas Wyatt, called by "Senec and Plato" from the "baited hooks" of profane love, proclaims in a final line that he will no longer climb the "rotten boughs" of any worldly copy of the *Symposium*'s ladder. But the formal correlative of his steps to this renunciation is more shadowy, though visible, than it would be if the octave were clearly broken in the middle.

Shelley rejects this entire tradition. The gnostic and Platonic tendencies found elsewhere in his work have been excluded from the "Ode," whose stanza mimics only the Wind. The enjambment of most tercets combines a double effect of momentum and suspension, of un-checked onrush and escape, with a piling up of pressure, a gathering of breath, for each final explosion: "oh, hear!" Although the Wind literally informs all the elements of the poem, it is not, as we shall see, one of them. For these we must look once more at the rhyme-scheme.

The special virtue of *terza rima* or of any chain-rhyme is its perpet-ual instability. Typography imposes an apparent unit of three lines, but "terza" more properly should denote the triple occurrence of each rhyme than the spurious tercet—spurious because it does not exist in the ear. Each sequence, beginning with the *b*-rhyme, perfects itself in five lines, the fourth of which disrupts the pattern otherwise nearing completion by introducing the next sequence. This discordant-concordant opposition of *visible* three to *audible* five not only underpins the tension between impetus and stasis enforced in this case by enjambment, but also establishes a numerological configuration that determines the poem's overall structure and its symbology. Before examining the total geometry, we should note a further tension between the 3:5 pattern and that of *four* tercets against *one* couplet (yielding both 4:1 and 4:5—which in the end will prove identical) in each stanza.

The first three of the "Ode's" five stanzas describe the action of the Wind upon three of the essences of ancient natural philosophy: earth, air and water. The fourth essence—destroyer, cleanser, regenerator, and therefore the element proper to the poet as a political reformer—is held in reserve until the end:

> Scatter, as from an unextinguished hearth
> Ashes and sparks, my words among mankind!

Insofar as these purely descriptive stanzas can be detached from the last two, which convert uneditorialized observation into personal metaphor, the "Ode's" structure magnifies the eye-ear ratio of three against five. It should be noted in passing that three and five are among the possible dimensions of the Golden Rectangle. Also, as neighbors in the Fibonacci series (1:2:3:5:8:13:21:34, and so forth), they recur as a clockwise-counterclockwise proportion throughout nature, from the seeds of conifers to the chambers of the nautilus.

The opening of the fourth stanza recapitulates the established imagery in epitome:

> If I were a dead leaf thou mightest bear;
> If I were a swift cloud to fly with thee;
> A wave to pant beneath thy power . . .

Shelley's speaker then prays the Wind to deal with him as with the grosser elements ("Oh, lift me as a wave, a leaf, a cloud!"); he also implies that he craves liberation from them. They smell of mortality and change and are subject to the "heavy weight of hours" which has "chained and bowed" him too; they suggest the "thorns" on which he falls.

The amalgamation of all subigneous essences into the clay that composes breathing but unenlightened flesh (including the dormant poet's) has been long in preparation. The Wind's "stream" in the second stanza has recalled the forest and anticipated the sea:

> Loose clouds like earth's decaying leaves are shed,
> Shook from the tangled boughs of Heaven and Ocean.

So too the Mediterranean has drowned "old palaces and towers," now "overgrown with azure moss"; even farther below the surface the speaker imagines

> The sea-blooms and the oozy woods which wear
> The sapless foliage of the ocean.

The poem's conclusion reveals the Wind to be something other than the lightest of the three lower elements: not air in motion but the force that drives the air. It can be addressed in the second person without license because like the skylark it is alive. This fact explains the pictorial vagueness so often objected to in the second stanza. How could the poet represent the Wind behind the wind, the agency of Spirit upon corporeal air, without confusion? He chose instead to let clouds stand for the atmosphere which supports them, although he knew remarkably well (see, of course, "The Cloud") that they consist of tiny drops of water. He also rendered their interaction with the sea from which they rose in terms of the forest. And he had no choice. When Shelley tangled the "boughs of Heaven and Ocean," he tangled the imagery too, but he saved the larger metaphor. The fifth stanza confirms that the Wind is literally a fifth element interpenetrating the others. It is the Pythagorean ether, the *Quinta Essentia*. This information justifies the secondary structural ratio of four tercets against a total of five stanzaic elements (the fifth, again, being the couplet) and proves it the same as 4:1. For the Wind is consubstantial with all.

As fire quickens with intelligence the tenement of clay, so the Quintessence informs mineral and vegetable nature. It evaporates water and condenses vapor; every spring it arouses "the wingèd seeds," each "like a corpse within its grave," from "their dark wintry bed." Equivalent like Brahma to the universe it perpetually creates, this "Wild Spirit" is

Siva and Vishnu as well—"Destroyer and preserver"—and thus a trinity. It had killed William Shelley in June, and now in late October Mary was in her ninth month of pregnancy with the only son who would survive the poet. That ecology is the theme of this completely syncretistic and—one might as well say it—completely Christian poem:

> Thou fool, that which thou sowest is not quickened, except it die. . . .
> So also is the resurrection of the dead. It is sown in corruption, it is raised in incorruption:
> It is sown in dishonor, it is raised in glory: it is sown in weakness, it is raised in power.
>
> (I Corinthians XV. 36, 42–43)

A taste for numerology and medieval chemistry seems queer in a poet with an advanced aesthetic and years of laboratory experience; the connection between such lore and Orphic ritual will seem even more capricious until we recall a tradition usually neglected in the study of post-Renaissance English literary culture. Francesco Giorgio's *De Harmonia Mundi* (1525) measured the universe according to the fifth (*diapente*) and octave (*diapason*) of music. Through such transmitters as Robert Fludd (1574–1637), his work eventually influenced the cosmology of Milton. Giorgio was a Neoplatonic friar and a dabbler in the Kabalah, but his "Musical Philosophy" derives ultimately from Pythagoras. It appealed to a fascination with the mystical significances of numbers, which was as widespread in the sixteenth century as it had been in Dante's and remains prominent in *The Faerie Queene*. All such systems of cosmic harmony—popularly known as the "music of the spheres"—were wedded to occult learning generally, and expecially to a concern with the writings then ascribed to Orpheus and Hermes Trismegistus.

Ficino claimed in his translation of the *Corpus Hermeticum* (1463) that these pseudonymous teachers were the doctrinal ancestors of Pythagoras, who thus emerges as a mathematician grafted onto an adept. If Désirée Hirst is right, Agrippa, Paracelsus, and the Florentine and French academicians handed down their syncretistic occultism through Boehme and the Philadelphians, Henry More and the Cambridge Platonists, William Law, Swedenborg and later eighteenth-century "enthusiasts" to William Blake, who purged it of the vulgarities it had picked up along the way, and whose mythological symbolism is in many respects startlingly like Shelley's. In 1813, Fabre d'Olivet's translation, *Les Vers dorés de Pythagore*, gave new life to a pre-Revolutionary fad for numerology. Shelley's own interest in such systems grew out of his long-standing practice of "the Orphic and Pythagoric system of diet." Let us look first at the Musical Philosophy in "Ode to the West Wind" and pass through it to Orpheus.

Pythagoras' great contribution to physics was his discovery that, in Arthur Koestler's words, "the pitch of a note depends upon the length of the string which produces it, and that concordant intervals in the scale are produced by simple numerical ratios (2:1 octave, 3:2 fifth, 4:3 fourth, etc.)." His disciples adopted the Orphic belief in metempsychosis, which they feared, and worshiped number as the secret strength of all things, but the Renaissance received as doctrine only the sect's extension of their master's acoustics to cosmic sound. As the planets revolve through the upper air, fixed to concentric spheres, they produce tones which differ according to the length of the orbit of each and yield a chord of eight notes, a celestial concert which, if heard, would paradoxically be judged a dissonance. In his *Utriusque Cosmi . . . Historia* (1617) Fludd illustrates this "harmony" by the *monochordus mundanus*, a guitar-like instrument whose frets are formed by the intersection of planetary orbits (and the regions of the sublunary elements) with a single string, tuned in the drawing by an angelic hand. But the more common analogy is to Orpheus' own instrument: a gigantic lyre whose strings have been bent into circles.

Shelley urges the West Wind to make him

> thy lyre, even as the forest is:
> What if my leaves are falling like its own!

The germ of this metaphor had been present five years earlier. "Hark! whence that rushing sound?" Shelley had asked as the chariot of the Daemon of the World began its descent:

> 'Tis like a wondrous strain that sweeps
>   Around a lonely ruin
> When *west winds* sigh and evening waves respond
>   In whispers from the shore:
> 'Tis wilder than the unmeasured notes
> Which from the unseen *lyres of dells and groves*
>   The genii of the breezes sweep.
>
> (I, 48–55)

Although daemonic influence is rather a property of Neoplatonic panpsychism than of the Pythagorean Quintessence, the action of "genius" here is startlingly like the Wind's.

The mythological connotations of the metaphor become even more explicit in the dramatic lyric "Orpheus" (1820). The chorus leader describes a stand of cypresses and a cave,

> from which there eddies up
> A pale mist, like aëreal gossamer,
> Whose breath destroys all life . . .
>
> (19–21)

until the breeze scatters it. Meanwhile the "weak boughs" of the cypresses "Sigh as the wind buffets them, and they shake / Beneath its blasts" (32–34). Because Eurydice is dead, the air carries pestilence, and the wind-harp of the grove cries out in pain. All this changes the moment Orpheus begins to play:

CHORUS: What wondrous sound is that, mournful and faint,
    But more melodious than the murmuring wind
    Which through the columns of a temple glides?
A: It is the wandering voice of Orpheus' lyre,
    Borne by the winds, who sigh that their rude king
    Hurries them fast from these air-feeding notes;
    But in their speed they bear along with them
    The waning sound, scattering it like dew
    Upon the startled sense.

                                              (35–43)

The winds clearly stand for poetry itself, that is, for "making" and unmaking. What one breeze kills, the other mourns. But Orpheus' song, by purging his grief, renews the natural world, which falls silent with love. The trees and animals crowd in to hear him, and the wind resumes its normal neutrality (as regards the immediate felicity of man) in its third appearance, a dialectically necessary epic simile from "mighty poesy" to "a fierce south blast" which tears

        through the darkened sky,
    Driving along a rack of wingèd clouds,
    Which may not pause, but ever hurry on,
    As their wild shepherd wills them.
                        (86, 88–91)

"Ode to the West Wind" exists on three levels of myth. Orpheus' music once tamed wild beasts, caused trees and stones to start from their places, and arrested the flow of rivers. Even so the Quintessence forces the grosser elements it interpenetrates to dance to the numbers of a celestial harmony, from birth through corruption to regeneration. The "plastic stress" of this divine Afflatus sweeps through the "dull dense world" of *Adonais* and compels form to follow form there in "new successions." Finally, the poet is himself a variant of that Romantic commonplace, the Aeolian lyre. The world's soul, as it breathes through the Orphic mouth, performs a Promethean work of ordering and illumination:

    Language is a perpetual Orphic song,
    Which rules with Daedal harmony a throng
Of thoughts and forms, which else senseless and shapeless were.
            (*Prometheus Unbound*, IV, 415–417)

Shelley wrote in *A Defence of Poetry* that "the mind in creation is as a fading coal, which some invisible influence, like an inconstant wind, awakens to transitory brightness." The West Wind scatters "ashes and sparks" from this ember. Insofar as they are revolutionary, the poet's enlightening "words among mankind" are incendiary too. The fire can only catch outside the poem, for the voice that fans the blaze must expire in doing so. The "unextinguished hearth" must be blown out. The mind itself must be offered in sacrifice.

The "Ode" contains only one classical allusion. The cirrus clouds, portending storm, are metamorphosed into a rout of ecstatic Thracian women:

> there are spread
> On the blue surface of thine aëry surge,
> Like the bright hair uplifted from the head
>
> Of some fierce *Maenad*, even from the dim verge
> Of the horizon to the zenith's height,
> The locks of the approaching storm.

Shelley visited the Florentine galleries, notebook in hand, at least twice in the week before he began the "Ode." He was not impressed by the statue of "A Bacchante with a Lynx," but jotted down a description of it anyway: "*The effect of the wind* partially developing her young and delicate form upon the light and floating drapery, and the aerial motion of the lower part of her limbs are finely imagined." Then he saw "A Statue of Minerva," which shocked him because it stood on an altar to Bacchus, decorated with the skulls of goats and, in moderate relief, the figures of four Maenads. His note on this group is as impressionistic as the earlier one, recording a concrete, windblown effect, had been photographic; it establishes that analogy from storm to the hair and clothing of the Dionysiac celebrant which within a few days would become the dominating metaphor of the second stanza of "Ode to the West Wind":

> The tremendous spirit of superstition aided by drunkenness and pro-ducing something beyond insanity, seems to have caught them in its *whirlwinds*, and to bear them over the earth *as the rapid volutions of a tempest bear the ever-changing trunk of a waterspout*, as the torrent of a mountain river *whirls the leaves* in its full eddies. *Their hair loose and floating seems caught in the tempest* of their own tumultuous motion, their heads are thrown back leaning with a strange inanity upon their necks, and looking up to heaven, while they totter and stumble even in the energy of their *tempestuous dance*.

Shelley goes on to condemn this "monstrous superstition," which inflicted on Roman art and morals "a deep injury little analogous to its effects upon the Greeks who turned all things, superstition, prejudice, murder, madness—to Beauty." And yet the Bacchantes call up favorable suggestions wherever they appear in the poems of 1819 and 1820. According to the "Ode to Liberty" (1820), Rome sucked "the milk of greatness" from Athens' bosom, "Like a wolf-cub from a Cadmaean Maenad" (92–93). And Panthea compares the mists rising from the portal of Demogorgon's cave to the "oracular vapour"

> Which lonely men drink wandering in their youth,
> And call truth, virtue, love, genius, or joy,
> That maddening wine of life, whose dregs they drain
> To deep intoxication; and uplift,
> Like Maenads who cry loud, Evoe! Evoe!
> The voice which is contagion to the world.
>   (P.U, II, iii, 4–10)

Asia replies that the "contagion" is liberty and a refreshed awareness of the splendors of nature. Finally, the Moon sings as she traces the circle of her mating dance with Earth:

> I, a most enamoured maiden
> Whose weak brain is overladen
> With the pleasure of her love,
> Maniac-like around thee move
> Gazing, an insatiate bride,
> On thy form from every side
> Like a Maenad, round the cup
> Which Agave lifted up
> In the weird Cadmaean forest.
>   (IV, 467–475)

How does Shelley justify the use of symbols condemned in his notebook? The apparent conflict between the poet and the moralizing connoisseur can be resolved by an examination of two of the many competing versions of the death of Orpheus.

The first and less popular version came down to Shelley through the *Periegesis* of Pausanias. In the course of his wanderings over Greece, Orpheus established the Mysteries of Hecate, of the Subterrene Demeter, and especially of Apollo, who had given him his lyre in the first place. Too enthusiastic a proselytizer, Orpheus gave away so many holy secrets that Zeus, as a security measure, blasted him with a thunderbolt. The first of the Bixby-Huntington Notebooks contains a fragment of *terza rima* (generally agreed to be connected with the "Ode"), whose canceled opening reads as follows:

> And what art thou presumptuous boy who wearest
>> The bays to mighty Poets only due?
> The ivy tresses of Apollo's fairest
>> Prophaning . . .

Shelley admits that he wears the poisonous, "false laurel," not "that which bound Milton's immortal hair." He is none the less exultant:

> And that I walk thus proudly crowned withal
>> Is that I know *it may be thunderstricken*
> And this is my distinction, if I fall
> I shall not creep out of the vital day
>> To common dust nor wear a common pall
> But as my hopes were fire, so my decay
>> Shall be as ashes covering them. Oh, Earth
> Oh friends, if when my   has ebbed away
>> One spark be unextinguished of that hearth
> Kindled in. . . .

These lines may or may not echo Pausanias. In either case they were soon abandoned.

The second account is Ovid's, who reports that after Orpheus had lost Eurydice the second time, he forswore heterosexual love, sang such tragic amours as that of his father Apollo for Hyacinth, and converted the men of Thrace to pederasty:

> ille etiam Thracum populis fuit auctor amorem
> in teneros transferre mares citraque iuventam
> aetatis breve ver et primos carpere flores.
>> (*Metamorphoses*, X, 83–85)

The Maenads, understandably vexed by this development, spotted Orpheus one day from a hilltop. The first of the women to recognize their disparager shrieked out against him and, *her hair streaming in the wind*, hurled a spear straight at his mouth:

> e quibus una leves iactato crine per auras,
> "en," ait "en, hic est nostri contemptor!" et hastam
> vatis Apollinei vocalia misit in ora.
>> (*Metam.*, XI, 6–8)

After bloodying him with stones, the Maenads ripped Orpheus to pieces with hoes and mattocks. The birds and beasts mourned the dismembered poet, the rivers swelled with their own tears, and the trees *shed their leaves as if tearing their hair* in grief:

te carmina saepe secutae
fleverunt silvae, positis te frondibus arbor
tonsa comas luxit.
(Meta., XI, 45–47)

Orpheus had taught the Dionysiac Mysteries to the Athenian
Eumolpus and to Midas, the king of Phrygia. Bacchus therefore did not
suffer his priest's murder to go unavenged:

Non impune tamen scelus hoc sinit esse Lyaeus
amissoque dolens sacrorum vate suorum . . .
(Meta., XI, 67–68)

Before leaving Thrace forever, he turned the Maenads into oak trees.
Their offending arms changed to branches, and their wind-tossed hair
became leaves.

Shelley's debt to Ovid is clear. Both poets manipulate their imagery in such a way that mourning and murder, the depilated leaves of the
trees and the transformed hair of the Maenads, blend into one symbol.
Comparison of the "Ode" with its source adds still greater value to the
"tangled boughs" of the second stanza, explains away what had seemed
Shelley's ethical confusion with regard to the Maenads, and, most important of all, underscores the paradox which in the end defines the tone.
The Maenads are votaries of Dionysus, and Orpheus is his hierophant. If
mourner and murderess are identical, so are priest and victim.

Proclus, commenting on Plato, reports that "Orpheus, because he
was the principal in the Dionysian [sic] rites, is said to have suffered the
same fate as the god." In some versions of the story—including, as we shall
see, Adonais—Orpheus is an incarnation of Dionysus, and his death
recapitulates the Titans' dismemberment of the newly born, horned god.
Each year at the summer solstice the priests of the Dionysiac rites re-
enacted this murder in the omophagia, their highest mystery, by tearing a
bull apart and eating its flesh raw. Various horned animals, representing
the god's metamorphoses in this struggle to escape the Titans, sometimes
replaced the Thracian bull in other Greek lands. The Cretans substituted a
wild goat and merged the ceremony with the cult of Zagreus. Wherever a
stag was used, Dionysus became confused with Actaeon, as he does in
Adonais and as Orpheus does in the poem that bears his name:

Awhile he paused. As a poor hunted stag
A moment shudders on the fearful brink
Of a swift stream—the cruel hounds press on
With deafening yell, the arrows glance and wound,—
He plunges in: so Orpheus, seized and torn

> By the sharp fangs of an insatiate grief,
> Maenad-like waved his lyre in the bright air,
> And wildly shrieked "Where she is, it is dark!"
>
> (46–53)

The identification of Orpheus with the Bacchantes is subliminally present in the "Ode" as well. When the speaker begs to be dealt with as the forest—"What if my leaves are falling like its own!"—he is not straining a metaphor. He refers neither to incipient baldness nor to the pages of his book—even though "the leaves of the tree" are, in the words of Saint John of the Apocalypse, "for the healing of the nations." He wears the bays of Apollo's bard, the vine leaves of Bacchus, and the Maenads' crown of oak and ivy. He celebrates a feast in which he is at once the minister, the eaten god, and the human devourer, fulfilling thereby the triple function formulated by the terrible figure at the center of every Eucharist: *hoc est enim meum corpus*. In the passage last quoted, Orpheus cannot decide whether to take up his lyre or to drown himself. The singer of "Ode to the West Wind" need not so choose, or rather has no choice to make. The trumpet of his prophecy will awaken earth *by virtue of* the death he embraces. In the hair of the Maenads—"the locks of the approaching storm"—we recognize that obsessive image of the sailor's suicide which will recur to the Orphic-Actaeontic speaker of *Epipsychidion* and *Adonais*.

Priest, divine victim, and ravenous communicant, Orpheus is first and last a singer of songs. The leaves run before the Wind "like ghosts from an *enchanter* fleeing," and, "by the *incantation* of this verse," the Wind also scatters the evangel of a human spring. Shelley borrowed the pun from Milton:

> What could the Muse her self that Orpheus bore,
> The Muse her self for her *inchanting* son
> Whom universal nature did lament . . .

The diction of "Lycidas" and "Ode to the West Wind" reaches back beyond *canere* ("to sing or prophesy") and *cantare* ("to sing or bewitch") to the Indo-Germanic KAN or HAN ("to sound"). It evokes memories of the birth of language itself, the "perpetual Orphic song," and of villages where music had the potency of magic and the lyrist and the shaman were a single person. Shelley's poem concerns the human voice, which sets stones dancing and echoes the spheres; it concerns the *vates* who immolates himself for the regeneration of his fellows and of the god who possesses him. "That which thou sowest is not quickened, except it die." That is why the poet must fall and bleed, and why the poem takes the "tone" it does.

STUART CURRAN

"The Cenci":
The Tragic Resolution

With the exception of Beatrice the characters of *The Cenci* are fixed, changing only in intensity. Whether this indicates Shelley's immaturity as a playwright is, like other such questions, debatable, and the dramatic effect is at any rate far more important than its possible causes. The villainy and the weakness that circumscribe the experience of Beatrice Cenci do not alter during the course of the tragedy, but they do intensify, making her own insecure position more and more acute. She is driven to suffer between fixed poles, which reverse the ordinary values of her world to the extent that the only positive force is evil; the good of Lucretia or Camillo is negative. Beatrice's slow recognition, first, of these reversed values and, second, of her inability to withstand the magnetic power of the evil confronting her, determines the underlying structure of Shelley's tragedy. His play is a psychological study whose focus is Beatrice, the Romantic Everyman with whom we identify and in whose defeat we are forced to see our own. The development of her awareness can be precipitated by the action, but can only partially be explained by it. Thus, the very structure of the play necessitates Shelley's heavy reliance on patterns of imagery: in their combination he can set for any given moment the precarious balance between Beatrice and the evil forces threatening her, as well as illuminate the basic characteristics of the world in which she is forced to act. That world is remarkably similar to the pessimistic conceptions of our own time.

From *Shelley's Cenci: Scorpions Ringed with Fire.* Copyright © 1970 by Princeton University Press.

In the commonplaces of twentieth-century philosophy Beatrice Cenci would be considered an existential heroine. She endures both a crisis of faith and a crisis of identity. If we examine in the abstract her progress through the play, we find a familiar path at least to a point: that of Kierkegaard, who, confronting a Nothingness where values were without meaning, posited with ruthless persistence a God who would give them meaning. But *The Cenci* is the tragic history of a human being, not the record of a victorious logician. Though the play often moves in the realms of philosophical argument, the final questions that it asks are subordinate to a dramatic purpose resolved only in the concluding lines. Beatrice is another Shelleyan "Spirit that strove / For truth, and like the Preacher found it not." Beginning as a sensitive and basically good human being whose values are civilized, she finds herself inhabiting a bestial world whose denizens satisfy only a selfish appetite for power and personal gain. Always these men are alone, alienated from the world on which they prey, isolating their victims in turn. Both Cenci and Orsino bar her exit from the prison of their separate designs. And then that external savage chaos is perpetrated upon her person—not simply upon, but within as well. To keep from being swirled into that vortex of evil, Beatrice must use evil means to support good, to destroy the bestiality that would destroy her. But the external forms of the world unite to prevent her return to normal human society. God has allowed evil to disfigure her; man has acquiesced; and now neither God nor man will act to save her. Beatrice is forced into her own alienation from the world, in which she questions the very roots of human society, the values that she has been taught to accept. To her condition they have nothing to say; they contradict the history of her life. The elemental paradoxes she confronts on every hand resolve only in meaninglessness, whose acceptance leads to despair. Through the development of the play Beatrice has increasingly been forced to uphold her universal values simply through the force of her belief. Her final act—and a singular triumph in the face of despair—is to accept the meaninglessness of the external world without relinquishing the meaningfulness of her internal values, to posit order in the face of chaos even as she must succumb to it. Having passed through the dark night of the soul and having resolved the deepest crises of her existence, Beatrice can die in peace with herself, "fear and pain / Being subdued" (V,iv,155–156).

The values preserved through her mere act of faith allow Beatrice to face death with measured equanimity, but such an internal commitment would appear inadequate to sustain her life in a world where these values can have no reality beyond the confines of the mind. Beatrice's experience has proved the world insidious and treacherous. Here, nothing is as it seems: beneath the deceptive appearance lies a vicious and im-placable reality, whose effect on pure ideals and hopes is corrosive. It is both symbol and symptom of the conditions under which man must live that Beatrice comes forward during her trial, not to admit complicity in her father's murder and to explain its necessity, but to deny the parricide in the elaborate and impassioned paradox that restoration of divine order can be no crime. The greater paradox, however, is that societal institutions, themselves organized to impose what is construed to be God's order upon this fallen world, destroy Beatrice through their inflexible machinery. For Beatrice, for Everyman, there is no refuge from the savagery of the world: the logical order descending from the supreme Good does not exist, and all experience thus resolves in paradox.

But a firm distinction separates Beatrice's experience from that of her audience. If she is an existential heroine, confronted with a total ambiguity of values, our vision is larger, less immediate than hers. Shelley allows his audience the perspective Beatrice lacks, and, comprehending design where she sees chaos, we are enabled to resolve the ambiguity. The regulatory principle of human affairs, casually but prophetically enunci-ated by Beatrice in the third scene, is "ill must come of ill" (I,iii,151). An evil act sows the seeds of future evil. Beatrice, who is Cenci's offspring, precipitates her own destruction as he does his, for any human who resorts to evil means unleashes a devastation he cannot control. "Ill must come of ill" is the premise, but beyond that there is no logic to evil either. That Cenci courts his own destruction makes him no more and no less susceptible to it than is Beatrice, who in murdering her father to preserve herself unwittingly brings on the destruction she sought to fore-stall. What is ultimately terrifying about this world, however, is that Beatrice has no choice. Within the perverse framework of this tragedy, to act is to commit evil. The tragic premise admits of a second and less obvious reading: an evil act can only be met by another evil act. Good is by its nature fundamentally passive. The good people of this world are, like Christ, sufferers until made aware that martyrdom is upon them, at which point, if they would live, they must deny their Christian precepts and counter with evil. The single representative of the good who does not follow this pattern is Camillo, who purchases salvation with ignorance. He shuffles through the play, kindly, soothing, a true Christian priest—blissfully unaware that he is the lackey of evil. Because he is a good Christian, he is impotent.

To participate in an evil world is to become, like Cenci, suspicious of the motives of all others, to distrust any impulses but one's own—and, indeed, not even to be certain of these—in effect, to become isolated from human society. Shelley's imagery, as we have seen, emphasizes this at every turn. The world is a nest of Chinese boxes, prison within prison: the evil world, the evil castle, the evil self. But one cannot retreat into that last fortress, because even it is not secure. At every turn there is a treacherous threat to one's integrity. The result is the curiously static milieu distinguishing Shelley's tragedy and often criticized without being understood. The ultimate justification for a drama where there is almost no action is a world where action is necessary, but feared. To impose one's will upon the formless savagery of an irrational world is an absolute imperative, but any such act can precipitate a cataclysm. Thus, the drama poises between the necessity of these isolated figures to establish their will in fact and their fear lest it cannot be accomplished safely, between an agony of decision and an agony of indecision. "What hast thy father done?" asks Lucretia of her ravished daughter. Beatrice, clinging still to the logic of a Christian universe, answers with a question, "What have I done?" (III,i,69). But a few lines later she accepts the demands of the world—"Ay, something must be done" (III,i,86)—which she affirms again during the scene: "Ay, / all must be suddenly resolved and done" (III,i,168-169). The ensuing scene between Orsino and Giacomo ends with the priest's exclamation, "When next we meet may all be done—" to which Giacomo adds a hope impossible of fulfillment in this world—"And all / Forgotten" (III,ii,91–92).

The conspirators are naturally anxious that the murder be accomplished quickly and fearful that Cenci may escape and destroy them all; but this linguistic pattern is not simply confined to that part of the tragedy lying between their resolve and its accomplishment. Orsino ends the second scene of Act II with the assertion that success in his world can only proceed from clever flattery of the dark spirit ruling it—"as I will do" (II,ii,161). This remark, uttered at the end of his soliloquy, stands not only as a reiteration of his resolve, but as the culmination of his self-incitement. The two previous scenes have concluded with a similar imprecation falling from Cenci's lips. He has whetted his appetite with plans for his most insidious crime; he has contemplated his artistry with a relish that he realizes the deed will end; but his delay is caused less by his professed delight in caressing the design than it is by a nameless fear of Beatrice. After confronting and subduing his daughter at the banquet scene, Cenci ends the act by urging himself to the ravishment: "It must be done; it shall be done, I swear" (I,iii,178). But Beatrice, the family's "protecting presence," quells Cenci's resolution, and at the end of Act II, Scene i, he betrays his fear in a second curtain line: "Would that it were done!" (II,i,193). In the Ellis Concordance to Shelley's poems fully half of the citations for the active verb "do" and the past participle "done" come from *The Cenci*. For a drama of so little action, that fact is significant.

In the dark wilderness of *The Cenci* exists a principle of natural selection as inexorable as that of Darwin's primeval rain-forest. The unscrupulous have at least a chance of survival, where the weak must succumb. Man is at once both the savage devourer of his own species and prey to savagery in a cycle of meaningless, endless destruction. Shelley has turned Christian values on end in depicting this world: they survive only in Camillo's ignorance or Beatrice's resolute act of will, both of which are only possible through a denial of the evidence so powerfully documented by experience. Beatrice refuses to accept what everything substantiates and what she herself tentatively poses in the great monologue of the final scene: that the principle upon which this universe is based is evil. The divine trinity that rules her fortunes consists of God the Father, God the Holy Father, and God the Count, whose vindictive power is supported by the scheme of things on earth. The one consolation—and it is scarcely a firm support for the denizens of this world—is that evil is incapable of logical order. Breeding chaos, it is the prey of itself. This, which Beatrice Cenci barely grasps, a second Beatrice, the heroine of Mary Shelley's *Valperga*, totally comprehends: "Destruction is the watchword of the world; the death by which it lives, the despair by which it hopes: oh, surely a good being created all this." Cenci will be murdered; Clement VIII will either die or be destroyed. A new figure will represent the "dark spirit" on earth, himself to fall prey to the bestial disorder. The cycle grinds remorselessly toward infinity.

And toward infinity, too, Shelley pursues the dimensions of this oxymoronic order, perversely rendered like a Miltonic universe from elemental Chaos and ancient Night and issuing in torments without qualification or exception. Isolated in his roof-top terrace in the embroiled summer of personal miseries, Shelley, like Orsino, saw "from a tower, the end of all," compressing his vision into one epitomizing metaphor:

> And we are left,—as scorpions ringed with fire,
> What should we do but strike ourselves to death?
> (II, ii, 70–71)

In popular superstition encircling a scorpion with fire compelled the tail forward until the venomous sting at its tip penetrated the head, causing instantaneous death. Similarly, man carries within him the seed of his own destruction, a poison less of the body than of the mind. As Shelley develops his image in the events of the tragedy, he poses not the conquest of spirit by flesh that it first suggests, but an apocalyptic shattering of all pretensions to an ideal order erupting from the brutal, irrational forces abstracted in Count Cenci. Racked like Lear on a wheel of fire, all men and all men's ideals succumb to the insidious thrust of evil. And from the ashes of that fire no phoenix arises.

Shelley, fresh from the sublime conceptions of *Prometheus Unbound* to which he was again soon to return, could hardly have been insensitive to the iconographical significance of his symbol. His *felo-de-se* is a parody of the "snake / That girds eternity," the *drakōn ouroboros* or tail-eating serpent, which, forming a circle without beginning or end, where the tail of death resolves into the head of life, was a Platonic and Cabalistic emblem for the One, the *hen to pan*. The scorpion is, in truth, an inverted One, the symbol for an eternity of destructive evil, of everlasting hell, as the poet had intimated when he invoked the figure in a previous poem. And if the One, that creative Eternity of pure ideals, is forever beyond the reach of mortal man, this second, Cencian eternity is immediate, admitting no escape short of death (and even that, as Beatrice comes to realize, is uncertain). The line circumscribed by the agonized scorpion's self-destruction is enclosed by a second circle, the wall of fire representing destructive experience. Together, the two interlock with an ultimate geometric precision to form the superstructure of a sphere, the perfect symbolic prison of Beatrice's tragic condition and the only aspect of eternity she has known.

Against this extreme and total vision Shelley's contemporary critics mounted their vituperative attack, castigating the Manichean heresy with which Shelley had invested his tragedy. In retrospect, however, they were too easy on the poet. His heresy was far more radical, if we understand the Manichean belief to be that good and evil are equal forces on earth. James Rieger terms Shelley's conception 'Paterin,' meaning that in this world evil is the dominating force, but even this is, perhaps, inadequate to characterize the extremity of Shelley's vision. In the world of *The Cenci* evil is the only force. Good can exist as a principle, even, like Beatrice, as a presence; but good, transferred into action, into force, as a deterrent to evil, becomes evil. Shelley's curious foray into dark humor, the essay "On the Devil, and Devils," which probably was written shortly after *The Cenci*, explains the principles underlying his tragedy. He notes two main interpretations of the Christian devil, the first bearing the likeness of Cenci—"a fiend appointed to chastise / The offenses" of the world, the sadistic deputy of a sadistic God, the Cenci who serves a "dark spirit." The second interpretation mirrors the relationship of Cenci to his daughter so closely that in his essay Shelley adopts the words in which the Count explained his design (IV,i,85,148). This devil is Shelley's version of Lucifer, like Beatrice a bearer of light who rebelled against an evil Omnipotence:

> . . . The benevolent and amiable disposition which distinguished his adversary, furnished God with the true method of executing an enduring and a terrible vengeance. He turned his good into evil, and, by virtue of his omnipotence, inspired him with such impulses, as, in spite of his better nature, irresistibly determined him to act *what he most abhorred*, and to be a minister of those designs and schemes of which he was the chief and the original victim.

In such terms does Beatrice understand the nature of her father's sexual attack. She can withstand an exterior evil, an exterior assault. But the "clinging, black, contaminating mist" suffuses her, becoming an interior evil that subverts good and subdues the girl to her father's will as long as he exists to exercise it. The incestuous act is both profoundly sexual and profoundly metaphysical: if Beatrice is not to become, like Lucifer, the instrument of evil for a cruel God—and Cenci throughout the fourth act voices this purpose—then she must commit murder. The intense bombardment of the imagery in the third and fourth acts emphasizes the truth of Beatrice's assertion at the trial that she has not committed parricide: her crime is deicide.

This justification for Beatrice's revenge is not simply ingenious intellectualizing on Shelley's part. In the movement of his play Shelley imbeds a subtle distinction dropped from his "Preface," a distinction which every critic—even James Rieger, who approaches far closer to the intellectual center of the tragedy than any other—refuses to acknowledge. The Lucifer-figure of *The Cenci* must confront a graver assault than the Lucifer-figure of *Prometheus Unbound*. The immortal Prometheus, in returning Jupiter's tyrannical oppressions with love, frees the world from the divine tyranny. The fundamental principle on which this universe rests is stated without equivocation by Demogorgon: "All things are enslaved which serve things evil." To rebel against evil is not enough: love must be substituted in its place if man would create a new heaven and earth. Shelley applies the same formula to Beatrice in his "Preface" to *The Cenci*: "Undoubtedly no person can be truly dishonoured by the act of another; and the fit return to make to the most enormous injuries is kindness and forbearance, and a resolution to convert the injurer from his dark passions by peace and love. Revenge, retaliation, atonement, are pernicious mistakes." Shelley here, it must be emphasized, is referring to the Beatrice of history; his premises are inadequate to encompass the character whom he created. She murders her father not out of revenge, but imperative self-defense; not because he raped her body, but because he ravaged her spirit, "poisoning / The subtle, pure, and inmost spirit of life" (III,i, 22–23), turning her "good into evil." In the first two acts of the tragedy Beatrice has returned her father's hatred with fear, but with firm forbearance as well. Like Prometheus, she has suffered; she has been chained in the dungeon, forced to eat putrid food, physically tortured, and, as she tells the guests at the banquet, her answer has been to pray that her father would change or that she would be saved. Prometheus, condemned to his rock in the Caucasus for thirty centuries of torture, suffers no more intensely than Beatrice. His spiritual integrity remains inviolate, however, whereas Beatrice's is destroyed. "Peace and love" have only inflamed her father to commit an outrage that negates the possibility of both. The Cenci legend posed for Shelley a physical situation—perhaps the only possible one—in which good was not merely made to suffer from evil, but was subjected to it so completely that *it literally embodied evil*. Beatrice is thus faced with an ethical dilemma admitting of no solution consonant with her conception of good. To become, like Lucifer, the instrument of evil is the greatest of all possible sins against her Catholic God; to commit suicide is an act of mortal sin for which the Church allows no exception; only by killing her father in line with the principles of divine justice can Beatrice hope for absolution from the evil into which her father has plunged her. But the universe does not respond to her conception of it. Her act creates further evil, from which the only relief is death—if even that is to be a relief. For, at best the after-life she conceives at the play's end will be a void; at its worst, it will be a Hell in which the evil God who rules the universe will at last and eternally commit Beatrice to Luciferian violation.

If this is an admittedly unorthodox view of Shelley's tragedy, the work itself, isolated from the rest of Shelley's poetry, leads to no other conclusion. The poet has denied himself "what is vulgarly termed a moral purpose"—in other words, the dogmatic parable expressed in *Prometheus Unbound*. He has lavished on Beatrice "the restless and anatomizing casuistry" that he asserts her history provokes among all classes of men, exercising it with such skill that he justifies her action by creating an ethical system necessitating it. Thus to condemn Beatrice, we must impose upon her world an ethic foreign to its exigencies, denying the repeated symbolism of the imagery and the carefully balanced structure of characterizations. By an objective ideal she may be wrong, but in the inescapable prison of human events, she is merely and thus profoundly tragic, beyond the realm of simple moral platitudes. One might as well argue the criminality of Cordelia, whose reticence causes fragmentation, war, and bloodshed, as impose the ideals of *Prometheus Unbound* upon this mortal woman, impelled by her fate into a no-man's-land where both action and non-action are evil and where objective ethical standards dissolve into the absurd.

Only one incident in the entire play seems to suggest that Beatrice had no need to take justice into her own hands: the arrival of Savella with a warrant for Cenci's death. It would appear that once again Demogorgon has risen to overthrow Jupiter and release Prometheus from bondage. But on the contrary, that Cenci should be ordered killed by the irrational command of a capricious tyrant who had refused aid to the distraught family only emphasizes again how vicious and illogical this world is. Beatrice, thinking that the Pope had refused her petition, knows that she can expect no relief from that quarter. But we who know that Orsino suppressed the petition are also aware that Camillo presented as strong a plea and saw it denied. And we cannot forget that had Lucretia not drugged her husband in order to make his death easier, Beatrice would have been violated again before Savella arrived with official sanction for Cenci's murder in a warrant whose immorality only intensifies the moral purpose by which Beatrice acts. In this illogical universe where Beatrice is reduced to establishing an existential moral order and where she has no reason to suppose that the Pope will suddenly move against her father, Savella's entrance does not at all obviate the imperative by which Beatrice murders the Count. The cruelest of ironies, the entrance of this hatchetman for *Realpolitik*, merely substantiates the bestial evil of the world. Beatrice, who had reason to kill her father, is arrested for a crime which the Pope, who lacked any rationale, would wantonly have commanded. To presuppose Shelley's intentions in this matter is impossible, but that there is so marked a difference between the action of Demogorgon and the command of the Pope suggests once again the total disparity between the worlds of *Prometheus Unbound* and *The Cenci*.

Is it by accident, one wonders, that the determining act of both *Prometheus Unbound* and *The Cenci* should be sexual? Prometheus' fortitude culminated in his sexual union with Asia in which is symbolized the harmonious regeneration of the world. Beatrice's fortitude ends in a union symbolizing the world's degeneration, its moral cacophony. Sexual union is a metaphor for the most intense of physical and spiritual experiences, and, if we carefully distinguish how very different these worlds are, the metaphors in each drama are of equal symbolic weight. That Shelley wrote the last act of *Prometheus*, the great hymn of joy resolving in union, after he had completed *The Cenci* does not indicate that his tragedy was to be subordinated to the ethical structure of his lyrical drama. We can never know, of course, why Shelley chose to return to the earlier work, but it is likely that it was an act of purgation and relief, designed to round off what was to him a vision of the ideal as he had completed what he called his "sad reality." The two works pose for their readers a problem unique in literature: two masterpieces, works of literary genius and intellectual profundity, written in sequence, which attack perhaps the most difficult of philosophical problems, that of evil, and issue impassioned and totally opposed conclusions.

The relationship between the two poems is of extraordinary complexity, ultimately demanding a full-length analysis beyond the possibilities of this study. But if major questions cannot here be resolved, one pre-eminent one can be redefined. Shelley's theory of good and evil was neither as simple nor as easily systematized as many critics, following Mary Shelley's explanation, have made out. Her elucidation occurs in the 1839 note:

> The prominent feature of Shelley's theory of the destiny of the human species was, that evil is not inherent in the system of creation, but an accident that might be expelled . . . Shelley believed that mankind had only to will that there should be no evil, and there would be none. . . . the subject he loved best to dwell on was the image of One warring with the Evil Principle, oppressed not only by it, but by all, even the good, who were deluded into considering evil a necessary portion of humanity. A victim full of fortitude and hope, and the spirit of triumph emanating from a reliance in the ultimate omnipotence of Good.

This Mary notes as the cardinal principle of *The Revolt of Islam*, Shelley's rambling revolutionary poem, which has lost favor with later audiences as much for its intellectual glibness as for its tedious length. Since Mary is relying on a work which is best seen as the culmination of Shelley's youthful enthusiasm for the immediate reform of the world, her statement may be suspect as applying to the whole of Shelley's thought. Only to a part of Shelley's writings, the earliest and least mature, does Mary do justice.

Shelley's early conception of evil is what attracted him so forcefully to Godwin, and the manifestos he delivered in volume to the gullible Elizabeth Hitchener are little more than free-wheeling Godwinian disquisitions on the perfectability of man. Early in 1812 Shelley compares himself to Southey as "no believer in original sin: he thinks that which appears to be a taint of our nature is in effect the result of unnatural political institutions—there we agree—he thinks the prejudices of education and sinister influences of political institution[s] adequate to account for all the Specimens of vice which have fallen within his observation."

This belief is central to Shelley's precocious apocalyptic vision of the year before, *Queen Mab*, in which he attacks the Judaeo-Christian religion both for perpetuating the fiction of a divine sadist tormenting mankind and for inventing an ultimate model by which to justify earthly tyranny. When the poet tamed his blasphemous vision into the more sophisticated dream-poem, *The Daemon of the World* (1816), he transformed diatribe into theodicy. The Spirit conveys the dreaming Ianthe into space from which they survey a brilliant Dantesque pageant of grotesque horrors on earth, where ignorant mortals raise cries of insult against the ruling Daemon. But the Spirit, Shelley says,

> Serene and inaccessibly secure,
> Stood on an isolated pinnacle,
> The flood of ages combating below,
> The depth of the unbounded universe
>   Above, and all around
> Necessity's unchanging harmony.
>   (286–291)

Ianthe's guide declares that "the Proud Power of Evil / Shall not for ever on this fairest world / Shake pestilence and war" (306–308). The gradual renovation of the earth is implicit in Necessity, through the agency of love, virtue, and fortitude before tyranny.

The Daemon is the same power that in a more personal mode Shelley apostrophizes as the Spirit of Intellectual Beauty in his hymn dating from this same year. "Thy light alone," he affirms, "Gives grace and truth to life's unquiet dream" (32,36). When the Spirit is not immanent, man must exist in "This dim vast vale of tears, vacant and desolate" (17), awaiting the return of the light. But, Shelley argues, this is only just; otherwise, "Man were immortal and omnipotent" (39). In this admission lie the seeds of an elemental ideological strife with which Shelley is faced in poem after poem. In rejecting what he thought to be the vengeful God of the Christians for the beneficent One of the Neo-Platonists, Shelley retained the component common to both, that man inhabits a corrupt world. In his *Speculations on Morals*, written sometime between 1816 and 1819, Shelley reverses his early denial of original sin.

> But wherefore should a man be benevolent and just? The immediate emotions of his nature, especially in its most inartificial state, prompt him to inflict pain, and to arrogate dominion. He desires to heap superfluities to his own store, although others perish with famine. He is propelled to guard against the smallest invasion of his own liberty, though he reduces others to a condition of the most pitiless servitude. He is revengeful, proud and selfish.

Mary Shelley's reduction of the poet's view of good and evil thus errs on a primary level: evil *is* "inherent in the system of the creation." Even in *The Revolt of Islam* Shelley, through Cythna's account of the Genesis, subscribes to this view.

It must not be thought, despite the mythical moralities in which Shelley couched his concern with the problem of evil, that his motivation was purely abstract. "How little philosophy & affection consort with this turbid scene—this dark scheme of things finishing in unfruitful death," he lamented to Mary early in their acquaintance. The urgency with which he sought to reduce so inimical a world to viable philosophical principle mirrors the necessity for such a support in his own life. His biography is a record of disease, injustice, oppression, calumny, ingratitude, scandals without warrant, personal tragedies without meaning, much of it suffered for the sake of principle and endured, at least outwardly, with a Promethean forbearance that altered nothing. The madman of *Julian and Maddalo* —that "nerve o'er which do creep / The else unfelt oppressions of this earth" (449–450)—is Shelley's vision of himself deprived of philosophical support; and the lunatic's query, "What Power delights to torture us?" (320) falls from Shelley's lips. He seemed, as he observed to Peacock after William's death and during the composition of his tragedy, "hunted by calamity." Few poets have so intimately felt the effects of the 'Evil Principle.'

Shelley scholars have long assumed that in *Prometheus Unbound* the poet finally resolved the problem of evil. But, while philosophically more successful and complete than Shelley's earlier statements, his lyric drama is as tentative in its conclusions as those others. In this Manichean universe the power of evil can only be checked by an act of will through which the individual, attuning himself to the universal spirit of harmony, love—that Neo-Platonic "One warring against the Evil Principle"—thus triumphs through forgiveness. But, when Shelley reduces the conflict from the realm of the immortals to a human reality, his One becomes, tragically, one. In *The Cenci* the poet represents a world of endless decay, where the appearance can never ultimately match the reality, where evil is ultimately triumphant. The earthly manifestation of the spirit of harmony can, like all things, be violated.

It is all very well for critics to observe that *The Cenci* is written between the acts of *Prometheus Unbound*; but the fact can only be interpreted as a sign of Shelley's breadth of vision, not as proof that Beatrice was morally culpable because, being human and constrained by a world where all acts are evil, she could not preserve her integrity against the power of evil. It behooves us, indeed, to match the one fact of chronology with another. The final act of the cosmic drama, the ecstatic hymn in praise of harmonious regeneration, follows not one, but two works emphatically representing the world, as far as Shelley scans it, as incapable of regeneration. Universal progress, that local deity of the earth enshrined by the youthful Shelley some years in advance of the Victorian captains of industry, the mature poet rejects as a fiction. The landscape of 1819 does not differ essentially from that of 1599, and in the powerful third section of *Peter Bell the Third* Shelley sketches his own world with a pointed, austere chiaroscuro reminiscent of *The Cenci*:

> Hell is a city much like London—
>   A populous and a smoky city;
> There are all sorts of people undone,
> And there is little or no fun done;
>   Small justice shown, and still less pity.
>   (III, 1–5)

"What a world we make, / The oppressor and the oppressed," says Beatrice; and in this second dark poem Shelley leaves no doubt about the meaning of that world:

> So good and bad, sane and mad,
>   The oppressor and the oppressed;
> Those who weep to see what others
> Smile to inflict upon their brothers;
>   Lovers, haters, worst and best!
>
> All are damned. . . .
>   (III, 106–111)

Among this company even Shelley resides, pictured by himself with amused contempt:

> And some few, like we know who,
>   Damned—but God alone knows why—
> To believe their minds are given
> To make this ugly Hell a Heaven;
>   In which faith they live and die.
>   (III, 96–100)

All men are subject to the one immutable law of the fallen world; and its full impact Shelley confides to doggerel as unique in its weightedness as it is extreme in its despair.

> . . . this is Hell—and in this smother
> All are damnable and damned;
> Each one damning, damns the other;
> They are damned by one another,
> By none other are they damned.
>   (III, 71–75)

This from "the knight of the shield of shadow and the lance of gossamere," from the donnish optimist who believed "that mankind had only to will that there should be no evil, and there would be none." As Shelley realized many years before Sartre, Hell is other people.

Clearly, then, in Shelley's later years he at times embraced the view that the world was inherently evil and incapable of regeneration; but in affirming this, we would do wrong to repeat Mary Shelley's mistake and too easily systematize her husband's thought. At the same time that Shelley wrote *Peter Bell the Third*, he also penned his stirring polemic, *The Masque of Anarchy*, urging the workingmen of England to resist the tyranny imposed by the ruling classes. And two years later, foreseeing in *Hellas* the defeat of the Greek independence movement, Shelley nevertheless subscribed to its idealistic vision of a renewed glory for Greece. But if in such poems we trace the hand of the political and philosophical liberal who wrote *Queen Mab*, in others we see the architect of elemental despair, denying any possibility for progress because man lacks the means to alter the evil condition of himself and his world. The dilemma was natural to such a man. On the one hand he was passionately devoted to ideals of social, economic, and religious justice; on the other, the calamities suffered by one who lived by those ideals seemed no more logical than Savella's entrance into Petrella. If Shelley had been able to resolve the dilemma, it would not have figured so prominently in his poetry. But his political liberalism, which is ultimately Christian, was in basic conflict with that perverse, unorthodox Neo-Platonism which conceived the world outside of man's mind to be degenerate, totally divorced from the good.

How Shelley clings to his unavailing Platonism is documented in all its stark futility in the fable of *The Sensitive Plant* (March, 1820), betrayed by the death of the beneficent Lady who tended the garden:

> When winter had gone and spring came back,
> The Sensitive Plant was a leafless wreck;
> But the mandrakes, and toadstools, and docks, and darnels,
> Rose like the dead from their ruined charnels.
>
> (288–291)

Shelley appends to the poem a "Conclusion" in which he affirms that the Plant and the Lady continue to exist in the realm of metaphor, even as all things earthly pass away; but it is small consolation in the face of this perverted apocalypse, recalling Cenci's last words, in which evil claims the world as its own. The Eden of harmonious order, like good in *The*

Cenci, endures only as an idea—not as a force. Beatrice, in the persistence with which she tears the painted veils from the substance of life, embodies Shelley's own mental process by which he probes beyond the comfortable affirmations of *Prometheus Unbound*. In this mortal world love cannot remove the burden of evil; the most it can do is ease it. And even love, like all other ideals, can become the agency through which one's integrity is assaulted from within. In this respect Shelley's portrayal of Beatrice is an enlarged and more mature version of the dreaming poet of *Alastor*, who sought "in vain for a prototype of his conception. . . . [and] Blasted by his disappointment . . . descend[ed] to an untimely grave." In similar fashion, we could apply to Beatrice—as impassioned for perfect justice as the imaginary *persona* of *Epipsychidion* is for perfect love—the cancelled epitaph from Shelley's original preface to that poem: "He was an accomplished & amiable person but his error was, *thnētos ōn mē thnēta phronein* [being mortal, not to be content with mortal things],—his fate is an additional proof that 'The tree of Knowledge is not that of Life.' " By invoking *Manfred*, Shelley suggests his common accord with Byronic pessimism. The "sad reality" documented in Shelley's vision of Hell is also the theme Byron explored in charting the genesis of mortal Purgatory in *Cain*, "the inadequacy of [man's] state to his conceptions." Indeed, as a theme common to the mature works of both poets, it is never probed more deeply than in the triangular warfare between the self-defeating, absolute conceptions of Cenci, Beatrice, and the Pope.

Shelley's deepening pessimism over the inefficacy of good to affect evil reaches toward its fullest statement in his final, meticulous documentation of the human pageant in *The Triumph of Life*, the second reworking of the materials of *Queen Mab*, this time in a vision where human nature seems hopelessly estranged from the purposes of the Neo-Platonic Spirit. The Chariot of Life moves through past, present, and future with merciless and implacable destruction in which there can be neither joy nor meaning, only despair:

> And much I grieved to think how power and will
> In opposition rule our mortal day,
>
> And why God made irreconcilable
> Good and the means of good.
>
> (228–231)

To take one's place in the human pageant, to accept human society and break the prison of the self, is to sentence oneself to torment and destruction. Rousseau's experience is, in essence, the same as Beatrice's:

> . . . among
> The thickest billows of that living storm
> I plunged, and bared my bosom to the clime
> Of that cold light, whose airs too soon deform.
> (465–468)

The development of Shelley's thought, as recorded both in his poetry and his letters, would suggest that *The Cenci* is not at all the radical departure from the poet's customary ideas that has often been supposed, nor is it ethically subservient to the doctrines and ideals of *Prometheus Unbound*. From the airy heights of the Caucasus Shelley plunged into the dark abyss of *The Cenci*, to survey its depths and to test the surety of the bottom. And there he remained, against his will perhaps, to accept the central principle of mortal life as evil, to ponder its implications, and to strive toward a tragic awareness through which the burden could be endured. Early in 1822, his last year, the poet wrote to Hunt in terms that can leave no doubt of his Cencian view of man: "My firm persuasion is that the mass of mankind as things are arranged at present, are cruel deceitful & selfish, & always on the watch to surprize those few who are not—& therefore I have taken suspicion to me as a cloak, & scorn as an impenetrable shield." In the same letter Shelley confessed that with such a frame of mind he could produce no poetry.

If a despair issuing from the Platonic conception of good unattainable on earth leads to the same end as our modern breed of existential despair, it is in one sense a more lethal *malaise*. Difficult as it is to confront an indifferent universe in which there are no dependable values outside of one's self, it is far harder to face an inimical universe which has placed good forever beyond man's reach and which in the scheme of things has confined him to a sphere where all is corrupt and corrupting, "All are damnable and damned." In this world, too, one must posit one's own values, knowing that the system will be not simply indifferent to them, but actively hostile. Beatrice's greatest moment as a moral being consists in that calm reaffirmation of her belief in the good that her father and the Pope have sought to destroy, a reaffirmation by which she greets death committed to a meaning the universe denies to man. We discern something of that same quality in a letter Shelley addressed to Claire Clairmont in March of 1822, where at last he neither declaims against his wrongs nor despairs of humanity, but offers the counsel of a wise maturity:

> Some of yours & of my evils are in common, & I am therefore in a certain degree a judge. If you would take my advice you would give up this idle pursuit after shadows, & temper yourself to the season; seek in the daily & affectionate intercourse of friends a respite from these

perpetual & irritating projects. Live from day to day, attend to your health, cultivate literature & liberal ideas to a certain extent, & expect that from time & change which no exertion of your own can give you.

Whether such a solution would have resolved the nightmare of *The Triumph of Life* is beyond our knowledge. What would have happened at the climax of that poem rests, like what transpired at the climax of Shelley's life, in a limbo of unanswerable questions. But it is clear that in the spring of 1822 Shelley moved from under the Cencian cloud marking the January letter to Hunt and entered a new creative phase. Except for the Dantesque vision, Shelley's output in 1822 concentrates in a serene and worldly lyricism in which he humanizes the supernal and transfigures the mundane. It is not surprising that the one occasion in his earlier poetry where Shelley had shown such a capacity was in the simple, ecstatic lyricism which constitutes the tragic resolution of *The Cenci*.

HAROLD BLOOM

Shelley and His Precursors

I open as I will close, with the tran-
sumptive image proper, the *Merkabah*, which Milton called the Chariot of
Paternal Deity. This Divine Chariot had a long prehistory in poetic texts
both sacred and secular before it reached Shelley. It came to Shelley
through the sequence that goes from Ezekiel to the Revelation of St. John
to Dante, and onwards in English to Milton. Shelley did not know Blake's
poetry, but I want to trace also the movement of this image from Milton
through Gray to Blake, in order to contrast the image in Shelley and in
Blake. Since I have been resorting to Kabbalistic conceptual images as
paradigms for antithetical interpretation, I want also to make some observations upon the esoteric traditions of the Merkabah, though Shelley
himself knew nothing of them.

The tradition of the Merkabah or Divine Throne in motion as a
Chariot begins with the extraordinary first chapter of the Book of the
Prophet Ezekiel, where the word *Merkabah* does not occur. As a word,
Merkabah is first found in the Bible in I Chronicles 28:18, where we find
also the origin of the emblem of the Covering Cherub:

> And for the altar of incense refined gold by weight; and gold for the
> pattern of the chariot of the cherubims, that spread out their wings, and
> covered the ark of the covenant of the LORD.

The anxiety of visual representation was of course acute among the
ancient Jews. Thorlief Boman is correct in emphasizing that whereas
Greek literature describes the appearances of all man-made artifacts, the
Bible instead substitutes origin and process for appearance, by describing

every appearance through an account showing how the thing was made. It is all the more remarkable that just one visual representation was allowed for the Jews, and this was always that of the images of the cherubim, as the flanked the enclosure containing the tablets of Law, in the ark of the Covenant. The crucial act of poetic revisionism performed by Ezekiel was to assimilate this one visual representation that had escaped prohibition, to Isaiah's vision of God:

> In the year that king Uzziah died I saw the LORD sitting upon a throne high and lifted up, and His train filled the temple. Above him stood the Seraphim . . .

Blake, in a poem like *The Tyger*, follows the Hebraic pattern (as we have seen) by having his speaker describe not so much what confronts him, but the supposed process by which the beast was produced, the origins of the Tyger. Ezekiel also describes the heavenly chariot, the Cherubim and the Enthroned Divinity in motion, but he is curiously less Hebraic than Blake is, by his emphasizing so intensely the iconic aspects of the vision he confronts. When the Book of Ezekiel was accepted into the canon, the great image of the Merkabah was canonized also, which meant that it had to be misread canonically. Long before Kabbalah came into existence, a series of esoteric interpretations of the Merkabah had come into being, to be preserved in Talmud and in Midrash. The orthodox or canonical interpretation that gradually separated itself out from esoteric tradition culminated in the *Guide for the Perplexed* of Maimonides (III,7). Maimonides, with the saving caution of canonical misprision, explained that the closing clause of chapter 1 of Ezekiel was to be interpreted as meaning just the opposite of what esoteric teachings had asserted it meant. Verse 28 reads: "This was the appearance of the likeness of the glory of the LORD," upon which Maimonides commented: "*The glory of the LORD* is different from *the LORD* Himself. All the figures in this vision refer to the glory of the LORD, that is, to the chariot, and not to Him Who rides upon the chariot; for God cannot be compared to anything." By a single interpretative act, Maimonides had undone the esoteric element in Ezekiel and had insisted that the chariot was *not* a trope for God. This brilliant defense against esoteric interpretation can be said to have worked in one sense, and not at all in another. But both these senses can be deferred until we have seen further transformations in the image.

Ezekiel emphasizes what he calls the "Wheels and their Work":

> Now as I beheld the living creatures, behold one wheel upon the earth by the living creatures, with his four faces.

The appearance of the wheels and their work was like unto the colour of a beryl: and they four had one likeness: and their appearance and their work was as it were a wheel in the middle of a wheel.

When they went, they went upon their four sides: and they turned not when they went.

As for their rings, they were so high that they were dreadful; and their rings were full of eyes round about them four.

And when the living creatures went, the wheels went by them: and when the living creatures were lifted up from the earth, the wheels were lifted up.

Whithersoever the spirit was to go, they went, thither was their spirit to go; and the wheels were lifted up over against them: for the spirit of the living creature was in the wheels.

When those went, these went; and when those stood, these stood; and when those were lifted up from the earth, the wheels were lifted up over against them: for the spirit of the living creature was in the wheels.

And the likeness of the firmament upon the heads of the living creature was as the colour of the terrible crystal, stretched forth over their heads above.

And under the firmament were their wings straight, the one toward the other: every one had two, which covered on this side, and every one had two, which covered on that side, their bodies.

And when they went, I heard the noise of their wings like the noise of great waters, as the voice of the Almighty, the voice of speech, as the noise of an host: when they stood, they let down their wings.

And there was a voice from the firmament that was over their heads, when they stood, and had let down their wings.

And above the firmament that was over their heads was the likeness of a throne, as the appearance of a sapphire stone: and upon the likeness of the throne was the likeness as the appearance of a man above it.

And I saw as the colour of amber, as the appearance of fire round about within it, from the appearance of his loins even upward, and from the appearance of his loins even downward, I saw as it were the appearance of fire, and it had brightness round about.

As the appearance of the bow that is in the cloud in the day of rain, so was the appearance of the brightness round about. This was the appearance of the likeness of the glory of the LORD. And when I saw it, I fell upon my face, and I heard a voice of one that spake.

(Ezekiel 1:15–28)

There is one wheel to each four-faced being. The rabbinical commentators identified the wheel with the angel Sandalphon, while the Book of Enoch called the wheels another order of angels, who like the Cherubim and Seraphim attended God. There is a rich confusion, much exploited by the Kabbalists, in calling the Merkabah "the wheels and their work," so that chariot and angels scarcely can be distinguished, and there is an even richer confusion, despite Maimonides and his tradition of canonical interpretation, between God and the Merkabah. We can say that there are three major biblical tropes for God, and these are voice, fire, and chariot, or respectively a metonymy, a metaphor, and a transumption or metaleptic reversal. Voice, not being an image, was favored by canonical traditions of interpretation, while fire and, much more strikingly, the chariot, became the prime images for Jewish Gnosticism and later for Kabbalism. Orthodox or Talmudic Haggadah made an inevitable connection between the two images, by warning that any expounder of the Merkabah would find himself surrounded by flame from heaven. Though Kabbalah tended to substitute meditation upon the more abstract *sefirot* for meditation upon the chariot, there are curious amalgamations of *sefirot* and the chariot in Kabbalistic writings. The Kabbalistic tendency to compound or, in rare cases, identify *sefirot* with "the wheels and their work" helped stimulate the Christian Kabbalah, because of the crucial revision of Ezekiel carried out in the last book of the Christian Bible, the Revelation of St. John the Divine, where in chapter 4:6 a vision is recorded of an enthroned man, Christ, surrounded by the four-faced Cherubim of Ezekiel:

> And before the throne there was a sea of glass like unto crystal: and in the midst of the throne, and round about the throne were four beasts full of eyes before and behind.

What is the canonical mode of interpretation that connects the visions of Ezekiel and of Revelation, and subsequently both of these to the vision of Dante? *Figura*, as expounded by Erich Auerbach, Austin Farrer, A. C. Charity, is certainly the accurate answer. Auerbach traced the change in meaning of *figura*, from its original use as "form" through "model," "copy," "dream image," and trope or rhetorical figure until Tertullian and other Christian writers after him began to use it as a figure of things to come. So Tertullian sees Joshua, the minister of Moses, as a *figura* of whom Jesus Christ was the fulfillment, Joshua and Jesus being the same name. As Auerbach says, "*figura* is something real and historical which announced something else that is also real and historical."

In our terms, we might say that to the ephebe or later poet, the precursor is the *figura*, and the ephebe is the fulfillment, but that would be to share the later poet's self-idealization. Instead, the following can be stated as a basic principle of poetic misprision: *No later poet can be the fulfillment of any earlier poet.* He can be the reversal of the precursor, or the deformation of the precursor, but whatever he is, *to revise is not to fulfill.* Unlike *figura*, poetic misprision must be seen as the troping or erroring it is. But so, of course, *contra* Auerbach and Tertullian, is *figura*, and it is surely time to see that *figura* was always a revisionary mode, and so a lie against time. The Old Testament is far too strong, as poetry, to be fulfilled by its revisionary descendant, the self-proclaimed New Testament. "New" means "Early" here and "Old" means "Late," and precisely what the New Testament lacks in regard to the Old is a transumptive stance, which is why the New Testament is a weak poem. *Figura* is supposed to work by making Joshua late and Jesus perpetually early. This works well enough for Joshua and Jesus, since the prior figure is less central, but would have had more difficulty if Moses had been taken as the *figura*. The entire point of the theory of *figura* must be that the second term or fulfillment is the truth, and the first term or *figura* only a shadowy type of the truth. Here is Auerbach's definitive formulation:

> Figural interpretation establishes a connection between two events or persons, the first of which signifies not only itself but also the second, while the second encompasses or fulfills the first.

Auerbach cites the historical Virgil as a *figura* of Dante's Virgil: "The historical Virgil is 'fulfilled' by the dweller in limbo, the companion of the great poets of antiquity." The distance between *figura* and transumption, we might say, is shown by observing that the historical Rousseau is most certainly *not* "fulfilled" by the Rousseau of *The Triumph of Life*, a notion of fulfillment utterly alien to Shelley. But we may wonder whether the idea of *figura* was ever more than a pious self-deception. Is Ezekiel's chariot-vision a *figura* of the vision of St. John? Unless one believes in Revelation, then there is no doubt whatsoever which is the stronger text. The more complex case is when we compare Ezekiel with Dante's Triumphal Chariot of the Church, for here the texts are equally strong. In Canto XXIX of the *Purgatorio*, Dante explicitly refers his chariot to Ezekiel's as well as to John's, but his chariot is unique in bearing his Beatrice, rather than an enthroned version of God. Singleton, in his commentary, remarks suggestively that this is:

> . . . the kind of two-wheeled chariot used by the ancient Romans in war and in triumphal processions. As will become evident in the symbolism of the procession, this chariot represents the Church. But it is also, in this instance, a triumphal chariot, and as such it is strangely empty! Whose triumph is this?

As Singleton suggests, Dante is being superbly audacious, for if Ezekiel's Enthroned Man is the *figura*, then Beatrice is the fulfillment, the truth of which the Bible's most crucial permitted image of God is only a shadowy type. In our terms, Dante is on the threshold that Milton, with even greater audacity, will cross when a very Miltonic Christ is shown riding the Chariot of Paternal Deity at the climax of the War in Heaven in Book VI. As the great master, indeed the inventor of transumptive allusion, Milton fittingly transumes Dante as well as all other relevant non-biblical precursors in the chariot-vision.

> . . . forth rush'd with whirl-wind sound
> The Chariot of Paternal Deitie,
> Flashing thick flames, Wheele within Wheele, undrawn,
> It self instinct with Spirit, but convoyd
> By four Cherubic shapes, four Faces each
> Had wondrous, as with Starrs thir bodies all
> And Wings were set with Eyes, with Eyes the Wheels
> Of Beril, and careering Fires between;
> Over thir heads a chrystal Firmament,
> Whereon a Saphir Throne, inlaid with pure
> Amber, and colours of the showrie Arch.
> Hee in Celestial Panoplie all armd
> Of radiant *Urim*, work divinely wrought,
> Ascended, at his right hand Victorie.
>
> (VI, 749–62)

The scheme of transumption, as I have demonstrated in *A Map of Misreading*, demands a juxtaposition of three times; a true one that was and will be (here, Ezekiel, Revelation, and Milton himself); a less true one that never was (here, Virgil, Dante, Petrarch); and the present moment, which is emptied out of everything but the experiential darkness against which the poet-prophet struggles (here, the allusion, noted by Verity, in the imagery of lines 840–41, to Milton's pamphlet war against "the proud resistance of carnall, and false doctors"). It is illuminating to juxtapose to Milton's vision of Christ in the Chariot of Wrath, Milton's vision of his own "Zeale" as polemicist in his *An Apology Against a Pamphlet*:

Zeale whose substance is ethereal, arming in compleat diamond ascends his fiery Chariot drawn with two blazing Meteors figur'd like beasts, but of a higher breed than any the Zodiack yields, resembling two of those four which *Ezechiel* and *S. John* saw, the one visag'd like a Lion to express power, high autority and indignation, the other of count'nance like a man to cast derision and scorne upon perverse and fraudulent seducers; with these the invincible warriour Zeale shaking loosely the slack reins drives over the heads of Scarlet Prelats, and such as are insolent to maintaine traditions, bruising their stiffe necks under his flaming wheels. Thus did the true Prophets of old combat with the false; Thus Christ himselfe the fountaine of meeknesse found acrimony enough to be still galling and vexing the Prelaticall Pharisees.

Though this transumption to the present is subtly covert, it is there nevertheless, and hints at one aspect of Milton himself, his "Zeale" for the truth, riding in the chariot with his Christ. More even than Dante, Milton has made the *figura* of the chariot in Ezekiel or Revelation a touch questionable. There is no biblical *figura* that Milton is fulfilling; he has mounted Christ in the Merkabah, made the throne-world into a war machine, and sent Christ out to battle as a larger version of his own self-image as Puritan polemicist burning through the ranks of the bishops and the presbyters. If this is *figura*, then the Milton who was Cromwell's Latin Secretary is the only *figura* involved, which is to overturn the Christian notion entirely. The true interpreter of what Milton has done in his chariot-vision is Gray, in the magnificent misprision of his Pindaric ode, *The Progress of Poesy*, where the starting point of Milton's appearance is an allusion to the Christ of Book VI, line 771: "Hee on the wings of Cherub rode sublime." What Milton discreetly hinted at, Gray makes overt, and so Milton himself dares the Lucretian adventure into the abyss:

> Nor second he, that rode sublime
> Upon the seraph-wings of Ecstasy,
> The secrets of the abyss to spy.
> He passed the flaming bounds of place and time:
> The living throne, the sapphire-blaze,
> Where angels tremble while they gaze,
> He saw; but blasted with excess of light,
> Closed his eyes in endless night.

Like certain sages in esoteric tradition, this Milton compensates frighteningly for his daring, but Gray's emphasis is on Milton's own language, since Milton's blindness here echoes his own "Dark with excessive bright" (*Paradise Lost*, III, 380). It is certainly to Gray's vision of Milton that Blake refers, when Blake dares to see himself, in succession to Milton, ascending the chariot in the introductory quatrains to his own poem, *Milton*:

> Bring me my Bow of burning gold:
> Bring me my Arrows of desire:
> Bring me my Spear: O clouds unfold!
> Bring me my Chariot of fire!

The emphasis is on "my," as Blake moves to be the Enthroned Poet riding the chariot that is at once drawn by, and constituted of, the Four Zoas, the "living creatures" of Ezekiel and Revelation.

We are ready, before passing on to Shelley's transformations of the chariot, to surmise the meaning of the chariot as a trope of transumption.

The image of the Merkabah is one whose reappearances, to men, are troped necessarily by metalepsis, for each fresh epiphany of the chariot is a belatedness made early again. The chariot, whether in Ezekiel, Revelation, Dante, or Milton, moves always in a time that is never present, a time that restores *in illo tempore*, in *that* time, the realm of "there was a time when." The chariot is a metonymy of a metonymy for God, which meant that Maimonides, as he secretly knew, was making a deliberately canonical misreading when he remarked that God "cannot be compared to anything." As a metalepsis for God, the chariot uniquely succeeds in breaking continuity, in substituting itself for nature.

I will illustrate this last observation by returning to the biblical metaphor of the fire of God, and juxtaposing it to the chariot. The fire of God, in the Merkabah mystics and later in the Kabbalists, is Gnostic metaphor and very different from the rather matter-of-fact flame out of which the voice of God emerges. Since Jehovah infinitely transcends the whole of His creation, He disdains any ostentatious or cosmic fires. After all, compared to the Greeks or any other ancient people, the biblical Hebrews were not much interested in the four elements, fire included. God's major fire is His descent upon Mount Sinai, which produces a version of a fair-sized earthquake, but nothing really extraordinary or preternatural. In the calling of Moses, it *is* preternatural that the bush is not consumed, but very little is made of the fire itself. I think that, following Freud, we can speak of the Hebraic image of fire as a sublimation, as a perspectivizing metaphor, that suggests God's respect for the nature he has made. It is not from normative Judaism or from orthodox Christianity, but again from Stoicism, Platonism, Gnosticism, and Kabbalism that the more interesting images of fire in poetic and Romantic tradition derive. But I will defer further discussion of the contrast between the image of fire as metaphor, and of the chariot as transumption, until we confront these images in Shelley.

We have been tracing the Chariot as the image of transumption, and particularly as a poetic ratio transforming the visionary's belatedness into an earliness, from its biblical and esoteric origins through poetic tradition down to Shelley. In his twentieth year, Shelley composed his first attempt at a major poem, *Queen Mab*, a revised fragment of which he salvaged under the title, *The Daemon of the World*, in the *Alastor* volume of 1816, four years after *Queen Mab* was finished. The Daemon descends in Shelley's version of the Merkabah:

> The chariot of the Daemon of the World
>   Descends in silent power:
> Its shape reposed within: slight as some cloud

> That catches but the palest tinge of day
> > When evening yields to night,
> Bright as that fibrous woof when stars indue
> > Its transitory robe.
> Four shapeless shadows bright and beautiful
> Draw that strange car of glory, reins of light
> Check their unearthly speed; they stop and fold
> > Their wings of braided air.

About all that Shelley has done, or could do, this early on, is to appropriate the Miltonic chariot, and give it not to Paternal Deity, but to a spirit of rebellion. In *Prometheus Unbound*, the actual attempt at transuming Milton and Milton's sources is made, and though it does not succeed entirely in capturing the image away from canonical tradition, the attempt is formidable:

> I see a chariot like that thinnest boat,
> In which the Mother of the Months is borne
> By ebbing light into her western cave,
> When she upsprings from interlunar dreams;
> O'er which is curved an orblike canopy
> Of gentle darkness, and the hills and woods,
> Distinctly seen through that dusk aery veil,
> Regard like shapes in an enchanter's glass;
> Its wheels are solid clouds, azure and gold,
> Such as the genii of the thunderstorm
> Pile on the floor of the illumined sea
> When the sun rushes under it; they roll
> And move and grow as with an inward wind;
> Within it sits a winged infant, white
> Its countenance, like the whiteness of bright snow,
> Its plumes are as feathers of sunny frost,
> Its limbs gleam white, through the wind-flowing folds
> Of its white robe, woof of ethereal pearl.
> Its hair is white, the brightness of white light
> Scattered in strings; yet its two eyes are heavens
> Of liquid darkness, which the Deity
> Within seems pouring, as a storm is poured
> From jaggèd clouds, out of their snowy lashes,
> Tempering the cold and radiant air around,
> With fire that is not brightness; in its hand
> It sways a quivering moonbeam, from whose point
> A guiding power directs the chariot's prow
> Over its wheelèd clouds, which as they roll
> Over the grass, and flowers, and waves, wake sounds,
> Sweet as a singing rain of silver dew.
> > > (IV, 206–35)

I have written several commentaries on this vision of Ione, and of the related, more magnificent vision of Panthea that follows it directly. My commentaries have been canonical, not in the sense that I can assert necessarily that they were more definitive as canonical misreadings than those of other Shelley critics (though like all interpreters I aspired, and aspire, to strength) but canonical in that they organized themselves around the assumption that Shelley was in the canon of major poetry in English, and so a vital element of meaning in him had to come out of his counterpointing his vision of mythmaking against his own reception of tradition. That now seems to me too idealizing and optimistic a view of Shelley's, or any poet's, relation to a strong tradition. Poets no more fulfill one another than the New Testament fulfills the Old. It is this carry-over from the tradition of figural interpretation of Scripture to secular literature that has allowed a curious overspiritualization of texts canonized by poetic tradition. Since poets also idealize themselves, and their relations to other poets, there is already an excessive self-regard in poetic and critical tradition. Modern theories of mutually benign relations between tradition and individual talent, including those of T. S. Eliot and of Northrop Frye, have added their idealizations, so that it becomes an enormous labor to clear away all of this noble obfuscation.

I note the observation made by Milton-scholarship that Christ ascends the Chariot of Paternal Deity at the exact, numerological midpoint of the first edition of *Paradise Lost*. Shelley was wary of origins, in an almost Nietzschean way, and he had no patience whatsoever with mid-points, but he had the apocalyptic temperament, as Blake did, and so he was obsessed with the last things. In *Prometheus Unbound*, Shelley attempted a humanistic apocalypse, which may be an oxymoron. To overcome this seeming contradiction, Shelley resorted to his version of the image of the Merkabah, doubtless hoping to redeem the crudity of his early vision of the chariot in *The Daemon of the World*. The visions of Ione and Panthea are meant to humanize the visions of Ezekiel, Revelation, Dante, and Milton. Do they succeed in this extraordinarily difficult aim, or do they collapse back into their orthodox origins? Who controls the meanings in Shelley's courageous attempts to reverse, correct, and "fulfill" tradition?

I return to my earlier attack upon the theory of *figura* as expounded by Auerbach; Shelley, like Blake, seems to seek a use of *figura* against *figura*, but I would argue that no reversal in such a use can be a true reversal, but all too easily itself can be reversed back into its original. I have argued already that Milton seems to have understood this, and that in his schemes of allusion in *Paradise Lost* he replaced *figura* by transumption—not a fulfillment or even a reversed fulfillment of tradition, but a true subversion of tradition that enforced Milton's own earliness while troping tradition into belatedness. I will argue now that Shelley learned this Miltonic lesson only *after* he had completed *Prometheus Unbound*. In *The Triumph of Life*, the Merkabah itself becomes a transumption of transumption, but in *Prometheus Unbound* Milton overcomes his revisionist.

Contrast to Panthea's vision (*Prometheus Unbound*, Act IV, lines 236–318) its Miltonic source in *Paradise Lost*, Book V, line 618–27. God has proclaimed His Son and challenged any recalcitrant angels to disobey this proclamation, and then be cast out. The speech is powerfully provocative, so much so that Empson properly says that God Himself caused all the trouble by being so pugnacious in the first place. A celebratory dance of angels follows, which Milton compares to the Platonic dance of the spheres:

> That day, as other solemn days, they spent
> In song and dance about the sacred Hill,
> Mystical dance, which yonder starry Sphere
> Of Planets and of fixt in all her Wheels
> Resembles nearest, mazes intricate,
> Eccentric, intervolv'd, yet regular
> Then most, when most irregular they seem:
> And in thir motions harmony Divine
> So smooths her charming tones, that God's own ear
> Listens delighted . . .

Does Shelley surmount the peculiar strength of this anterior vision, with its astonishing transumptive victory over Plato's *Timaeus*, a victory accomplished by assimilating Plato's cosmic dance to the Ezekiel and Revelation chariots? Panthea's vision gives us, not a dance that is most regular where it seems most irregular, or a dance that Platonically returns upon itself, but rather a dance that "with the force of self-destroying swiftness," is grinding all substance into the ethereal, into light and air. The Shelleyan question is not: "How can we tell the dancer from the dance?" but "How soon can the dance consume the dancer?" Yet the speed that Shelley relies upon for the orb to be self-destructive is itself the Platonic and Miltonic return of a divine motion upon itself, and Shelley's apocalypse of the physical universe is thus accomplished only through the oddity of identifying the whole of reality with the Miltonic dance of angels, and also with the Miltonic chariot. It is only through becoming more divine, meaning more Miltonic, that nature will undo herself. The sacred dance is sped up by Shelley to a quasi-Dionysiac or Orphic frenzy, but the figuration remains Milton's blend of Plato and the Bible, rather than a trope of Shelley's own invention. Shelley's intended defense is his characteristic and magnificent speed in and at the process of rhetorical substitution, but the defense is a desperate one, and Milton triumphs over his revisionist, because it is Milton's transumptive trope that gives coherence to Shelley's image, rather than the reverse. Milton remains *early*, and Shelley, thrusting towards finality, achieves only a superb *belatedness*, a sense that he has come too late into the poetic cosmos to do more than agree with a structure it has bequeathed him, however much he desires to hasten that legacy into a glorious sublimation. Milton captures and overturns Plato; Shelley is *captured* by Milton, and avoids being overturned only by sending the mythic machinery up into the ethereal as rapidly as he can.

In *The Triumph of Life*, his apparently unfinished last poem, and certainly his greatest achievement, Shelley struggles more with Wordsworth than with Milton, and the struggle is in one sense more successful, in that *The Triumph of Life* manages to transume the *Intimations* Ode in the way earlier Wordsworthian poems by Shelley could not, as a comparison of the *Triumph* with the *Hymn to Intellectual Beauty* would show. But Wordsworth is a dangerous opponent to take on, and we will see that Shelley's victory is equivocal. What he gains from Wordsworth, Shelley loses to time or to language, both of which become more problematic in the *Triumph* than they are in Wordsworth. It is as though a casting-out of Wordsworthian nature demands a compensation, a price exacted both by poetic history and by poetic language.

I turn now to the proof text for this critical discourse, *The Triumph of Life*, one of the crucial antithetical texts in the language. The title itself redefines what "antithetical" means for us, since in isolation the phrase, "The Triumph of Life," seems a victory for the natural man or woman, but in context the Shelleyan phrase means "The pageant or celebratory procession of Death-in-Life over the Imagination," or indeed the triumph of what is antithetical in us.

On the model of our map of misprision, *The Triumph of Life* divides as meaningfully as does its precursor, the *Intimations* Ode, despite the technical status of the *Triumph* as a supposedly "unfinished" poem. But there are, of course, no "unfinished" strong poems; there are only stronger and weaker poems. The idea of a "finished" poem itself depends upon the absurd, hidden notion that reifies poems from relationships into entities. As a poem is not even so much a relationship between entities, as it is a relationship between relationships, or a Peircean Idea of Thirdness, we can say that no relationship between relationships can ever be finished *or* unfinished except quite arbitrarily. A monad presumably can be finished; perhaps a dyad can be left unfinished; but a modern poem is a triad, which is why it begins in a dialectical alternation of presence and absence, and why it ends in a transumptive interplay of earliness and lateness. You can be too early or too late, but it makes no sense to say that you are finally too early or finally too late, unless you are talking about death. Meaning in poems, as Vico first saw or at least said, is always a matter of survival, and so we might say that poems no more can discourse truly of the poet's own death than anyone ever quite dies in his own dreams.

We can map the *Triumph* therefore as the complete poem it is, while remembering that a phrase like "complete poem" is oxymoronic. Here, utilizing my own shorthand, is the mapping:

Lines 1–20, the induction: *clinamen*. Dialectical opposition of sun and stars, as presence/absence of nature/poetry; rhetorical irony of saying "dawn" and meaning "twilight"; reaction-formation on Shelley's part against Wordsworthian natural piety; deeper irony implied (as figure-of-thought) of presence of natural sun and absence of stars (poets) preparing for overwhelming presence of chariot of Life, a presence blanker than any absence.

Lines 21–40, the induction completed: *tessera*. Imagery of recurrence, of vision as part of whole that is repetition of vision; synecdoche of poet's vision for all of reality; psychically a reversal into the opposite as Shelley moves from imaginative activity into passive reception of a vision not his own, and so at least purgatorial of the self.

Lines 41–175, the pageant: *kenosis*. Imagery of emptying-out of captives of Life; metonymy of fiction of the leaves; Life the Conqueror as metonymy of death; Chariot of Life as undoing of Merkabah; dance of victims as undoing of Eros; metonymy of foam for sexual passion, metonymy of shade for death-in-life; psychic defense of undoing Shelley's own vision of love, as in St. Ignatius: "My Eros is crucified."

Lines 176–300, epiphany of Rousseau as surrogate for Wordsworth: *daemonization*. The Sublime collapsed into the Grotesque; litotes as reversed hyperbole, infernal imagery of the depths of degradation; powerful repression of Shelley's own desire to carry through the Rousseau-Wordsworth dream of natural redemption; imagery of the great, those on intellectual heights, thrown down.

Lines 300–411, Rousseau's account of his imaginative genesis, culminating in his yielding to the "Shape all light": *askesis*. Imagery of inside subjectivity and outward nature; sublimation of greater vision to lesser as Rousseau drinks of Shape's cup of Nepenthe; radical metaphor of the poem, the tripartite mataphor of three lights: the original one, the Shape's, Life's.

Lines 412–end, Rousseau's vision after his sublimation, Shelley's own reaction, transumption of *Intimations* Ode: the *apophrades*. Return of Wordsworth, but somewhat in Shelley's own colors; imagery of belatedness; deliberate refusal to bring about metaleptic reversal; death of earliness and joy; introjection of past, and so of Wordsworthian defeat; projection of poetic future, and so abandonment of what has become merely a life-in-death.

Those are the contours of misprision in *The Triumph of Life*; I shall not try to demonstrate them exhaustively in a commentary, but shall move instead to the image of the chariot in the poem, to see how Shelley, on the threshold of his proper greatness, handled the difficult process of troping further upon what we already have seen to be the prime image of transumption in Western tradition. Here is the Shelleyan parody of a transumptive mode, far in spirit but perhaps not far in technique from Nietzschean parody:

> And as I gazed methought that in the way
> The throng grew wilder, as the woods of June
> When the South wind shakes the extinguished day.
>
> And a cold glare, intenser than the noon
>   But icy cold, obscured with light
> The Sun as he the stars. Like the young moon
>
>   When on the sunlit limits of the night
> Her white shell trembles amid crimson air
>   And whilst the sleeping tempest gathers might
>
> Doth, as a herald of its coming, bear
>   The ghost of her dead Mother, whose dim form
> Bends in dark ether from her infant's chair,
>
>   So came a chariot on the silent storm
> Of its own rushing splendour, and a Shape
>   So sate within as one whom years deform
>
> Beneath a dusky hood & double cape
>   Crouching within the shadow of a tomb,
> And o'er what seemed the head, a cloud like crape,
>
>   Was bent a dun & faint aetherial gloom
> Tempering the light; upon the chariot's beam
>   A Janus-visaged Shadow did assume
>
> The guidance of that wonder-winged team.
>   The Shapes which drew it in thick lightnings

Were lost: I heard alone on the air's soft stream

The music of their ever moving wings.
All the four faces of that charioteer
Had their eyes banded . . . like profit brings

Speed in the van & blindness in the rear,
Nor then avail the beams that quench the Sun
Or that his banded eyes could pierce the sphere

Of all that is, has been, or will be done.
(74–104)

Dante and Milton both relate their chariot-visions to the Sun; Shelley parodies both when the cold light of his chariot emits beams that quench the sun, but that still do not avail as a light to guide the chariot properly. The larger parody involved is profound, and has been unexamined in the canonical commentaries of *The Triumph of Life*. What does it mean to substitute the equivocal figure, Life, for the Enthroned Man of Ezekiel, and Beatrice in Dante, and Milton's warlike Christ? What kind of transumptive parody is this, when Death-in-Life becomes the conqueror? Shelley has another precursor here, Spenser, whose Lucifera rides in a triumph that is also a demonic parody of the Ezekiel-tradition, but Shelley's Life is not an allegorical opposition to the enthroned beings of tradition, as Lucifera is. Life is not a lightbearer, a son or daughter of the morning fallen into darkness. Life is merely Life, our Life, everybody's life, natural existence, the repetition we all dubiously enjoy and endure. What is Shelley doing to tradition here?

A. C. Charity, commenting on Dante's quest, compares it to Kierkegaard's program of *becoming a Christian*, which is the positive meaning of "repetition," according to Kierkegaard. Shelley, as always, is not interested in becoming a Christian, but rather in the perpetual struggle of *becoming a poet*, and then remaining a poet, by continually becoming a poet again. It is surprising how much of Shelley's poetry, on close analysis, is obsessed with the careers of Wordsworth and Coleridge, who had ceased to be strong poets at just about the time when Shelley became one. Lamenting Keats, in *Adonais*, it is still clearly Wordsworth and Coleridge that Shelley has in mind when he writes of Keats that:

From the contagion of the world's slow stain
He is secure, and now can never mourn
A heart grown cold, a head grown gray in vain;
Nor, when the spirit's self has ceased to burn,
With sparkless ashes load an unlamented urn.

So much echoes here; Shelley's own cry, at the close of the *Ode to the West Wind*:

> Scatter, as from an unextinguished hearth
> Ashes and sparks, my words among mankind!

Two stanzas before, in *Adonais*, Shelley had chided, as I would interpret it, Wordsworth and Coleridge, by crying out "Thou canst not soar where he is sitting now—" and then contrasting Keats's perpetual glowing in the burning fountain of the Eternal, to the sitters who are told: "thy cold embers choke the sordid hearth of shame." The line, "Thou canst not soar where he is sitting now," echoes Milton's Satan, in Book IV, lines 828–29, declaring himself in Eden to the two angelical sentries, Ithuriel and Zephon, in a passage that Keats had echoed in the *Ode to Psyche*. Satan says:

> Know ye not mee? ye knew me once no mate
> For you, there sitting where ye durst not soar.

So Wordsworth and Coleridge are unkindly but not too inaccurately (in 1821) being viewed as an Ithuriel and Zephon pair, knowing not Keats (or Shelley), but living on with an extinguished poetic hearth and writing sparkless verses. But this had been an obsession of Shelley's poetry ever since its real beginnings in 1815, when he had addressed lyrics to Wordsworth and to Coleridge lamenting them as sell-outs, and when he had anticipated (seven years prematurely) his own death, in *Alastor*, where "those who remain behind" are the two Romantic precursor poets, there dubbed not Ithuriel and Zephon, "But pale despair and cold tranquillity," the former being Coleridge and the latter Wordsworth.

As a transumptive parody, Shelley's vision in *The Triumph of Life* addresses itself more even to Wordsworth and Coleridge than it does to Milton and Dante. Shelley shrewdly implies that the Ezekiel-Revelation chariot contains the contrasting epigraph-emblems of both the *Dejection* Ode and the *Intimations* Ode, the pale despair of the portent of an oncoming storm, and the image of the rainbow, sign that the storm is over, with cold tranquillity ensuing. That is why, in *The Triumph of Life*, the onrushing chariot is heralded by the old moon in the new moon's arms, as in the fragment of *Sir Patrick Spens* that begins Coleridge's Ode, and that begins Ione's vision in *Prometheus Unbound*. And that is why, in *The Triumph of Life*, Rousseau encounters Iris or the rainbow just before confronting Wordsworthian Nature as the "Shape all light," as in the fragment of his own "My heart leaps up" that Wordsworth uses to begin the *Intimations* Ode.

I am suggesting then that there is no mystery about Life in *The Triumph of Life*. Life is precisely what has triumphed over Wordsworth and Coleridge, that is, over their imaginative integrity and autonomy as strong poets. Life is the conqueror of poets, the death-in-life that they sought to fend off by divination. Most certainly, Life in this particular sense is what Shelley had always feared, and clearly it is what he rejects in his sublimely suicidal last poem. Rousseau might just as well be named Wordsworth or Coleridge in the poem, except that Shelley was too tactful and urbane to thus utilize those who were still, technically speaking, alive.

But why then the chariot, as the poem's central trope, since it is hardly a dominant image in Wordsworth or in Coleridge? We return to the paradox of poetic origins; poetry is not an art passed on by *imitation*, but by *instruction*. There is no instruction without a Scene of Instruction, a primal fixation upon a precursor (however composite, however idealized) and such a fixation is also a primal repression, in which what is repressed is the acute demand for divination, the ephebe's sense that his own powers are preternatural and autonomous. Before the winter of 1814–15, Shelley wrote badly; he was a very weak poet. After he read deeply in Wordsworth and Coleridge, particularly Wordsworth, he was able to write *Alastor* and the powerful 1816 poems, including *Mont Blanc*. Becoming a poet had meant accepting a primal fixation upon a quasi-divine precursor. For Shelley, as for so many other poets, the problem of continuity or discontinuity with precursors became merged with the problem of continuity in and with one's own poetic self.

Like other poets, Shelley first tried to achieve a perspectivizing stance in relation to precursors through the limiting trope of metaphor. Fire is the prime perspectivizing metaphor of Romanticism, and to burn through context, the context of precursors and of nature, is the revisionary aim of that metaphor. Fire becomes the "inside" or "subjectivity" while nature becomes the context or the "outside" in this unconvincing but prevalent Promethean trope. That is why Shelley begins *Alastor* by addressing earth, air, and water as though he were one with their brother-element of fire. Behind this, ultimately, is the image of fire that went from Heraclitus to the Stoics and from them to the Gnostic system of Valentinus, which Shelley so strongly and so oddly resembles. For the Stoics, fire was rational; they spoke of "the fiery mind of the universe." But, to the Valentinians, the fire was the dark affection or passion they called "ignorance," which contained within itself the three lesser dark passions that had brought about the Fall into nature: "grief, fear and bewilderment." We can see in Shelley a fearful passage of the image of fire, from *Prometheus Unbound*, where it is essentially rational, to *Adonais*, where it is still Stoic and rational but where an element of Gnostic dark affection or "ignorance" has been admitted into the metaphor. In *The Triumph of Life*, the fire of Eros and the cold, glaring light are no longer rational at all, but are given over wholly to the dark passion of Gnostic "ignorance."

Shelley had learned, for himself, what Milton had illustrated by the career of Satan; the metaphor of fire (which is the Prometheus-phase of poetic quest) must "fail," in that its perspectivism is necessarily self-defeating, for all of its "insides" and "outsides" are endlessly equivocal and reversible. Yet post-Enlightenment poetry, as Shelley understood, was in one phase at least a questing for fire, and the defensive meaning of that fire was discontinuity. "The fire for which all thirst" or burning fountain of *Adonais* may have an ultimate source in Plotinus, but its immediate continuity was with the "something that doth live" in our embers that still gave Wordsworth joy, in the final stanzas of the *Intimations* Ode. Those "embers" of Wordsworth, still smoldering in the *Ode to the West Wind*, flare up for a last time in *Adonais*, and then find their continuity, after Shelley, in what Yeats called the Condition of Fire, which has its flamings in Browning and Pater while en route to Yeats.

When the fire metaphor had failed Shelley, he turned in the *Triumph* back to the transumptive image of the chariot, which we have seen him attempt before in his poetry. The chariot, as a trope, succeeds in breaking continuity, in the sense that continuity equals nature of the *res extensa* of Descartes. The fire is a limitation; the chariot substitutes for it as a representation. The fire is a sublimation; the chariot is an introjection of futurity, and a projection of lost or past time. Shelley was a strong poet and a central poet, and he knew instinctively what Vico knew overtly, that poetic meaning is always concerned with the struggle for poetic survival. To avoid the poetic fate of Wordsworth, he had turned to the image of fire. It had failed him. He turned back therefore from Words-worth to the image of the chariot that the antimythological Wordsworth would not handle. Wallace Stevens is Wordsworthianizing when he says: "The solar chariot is junk." Shelley says, in effect, the solar chariot and all the other chariots are obsolete, all right, as Wordsworth had said, but nevertheless Life came riding along in such a chariot, and triumphed over Wordsworth.

But whether Shelley, in terms of poetic meaning, accomplishes a successful transumption of the fundamental Wordsworthian metonymy of gleam for imagination, is quite another matter. The cold light of the chariot overcomes the light of the Wordsworthian Shape, even as the light of nature overcomes the earlier light of Rousseau, or of the young Words-worth. Yet in what I have called the *apophrades* or final part of Shelley's poem, from the "new Vision" of line 411, until the end, the meaning that returns is wholly a Wordsworthian kind of meaning, and the colors of the return flicker a little uncertainly, so that we cannot tell at times if they are Shelley's transformations, or if they are survivals still very much Wordsworth's own. Let us try a somewhat closer reading of the last two parts of the poem, beginning with Rousseau's account of his origins from line 300 on.

Rousseau's vision describes a Wordsworthian process of imaginative rebirth or restoration, but a process that ends in a catastrophe. He awakens first into the earlier world of "there was a time," by way of a paraody of the *Intimations* Ode. In this awakening, he still beholds the visible trace of a greater imaginative anteriority, "a gentle trace / Of light diviner than the common Sun." In the synaesthetic splendor of a "confusing sense" he sees and hears "A shape all light," whom we may describe as a sublimating metaphor for everything that Wordsworth called "nature." In response to her seductive summons, he yields up to her the metaphoric fire of his poethood, in Shelley's cruellest parody of the Wordsworthian "O joy! that in our embers / Is something that doth live." Seven years of brooding on the imaginative failure of Coleridge and of Wordsworth, that is, of their failure to carry their youthful imagination intact into middle age, culminates in this frightening vision:

> 'And still her feet, no less than the sweet tune
> To which they moved, seemed as they moved, to blot
> The thoughts of him who gazed on them, & soon

> 'All that was seemed as if it had been not,
> As if the gazer's mind was strewn beneath
> Her feet like embers, & she, thought by thought,

> 'Trampled its fires into the dust of death . . .'

This is the end, in Shelley, of the fire of sublimation, the hope that poetic discontinuity or autonomy could be achieved by a radical or Nietzschean perspectivism. With the bursting on sight of the new vision, are we any less in the world of Wordsworth's poetry?

> 'So knew I in that light's severe excess
> The presence of that shape which on the stream
> Moved, as I moved along the wilderness,

> 'More dimly than a day appearing dream,
> The ghost of a forgotten form of sleep,
> A light from Heaven whose half extinguished beam

> 'Through the sick day in which we wake to weep
> Glimmers forever sought, forever lost.
> So did that shape its obscure tenour keep

'Beside my path, as silent as a ghost,
  But the new Vision, and its cold bright car,
With savage music, stunning music, crost

'The forest . . .'

(424–35)

How much, besides the chariot itself, had Shelley added to Wordsworth here? The Wordsworthian equivalent is the poignant (if less sublime):

At length the Man perceives it die away,
And fade into the light of common day.

Only the chariot, transformed from its glorious riders to Life's
destructive vehicle, was Shelley's own, as Shelley clearly knew. After
seven years of struggle with Wordsworth's poetry, Shelley's work still
battled to keep itself from being flooded out by the precursor's. He had
learned, finally and superbly, the Miltonic lesson of transumptive allusion,
yet he could not bring himself to apply it to Wordsworth as he had applied
it to the Bible, Dante, and Milton. Why? Because the primal fixation
upon Wordsworth, and consequent repression of self, was simply too great,
would be my answer, an answer that I would illustrate by citing the most
famous single passage of Shelley's prose, the last paragraph of A *Defence of
Poetry*:

For the literature of England, an energetic development of which has
ever preceded or accompanied a great and free development of the
national will, has arisen as it were from a new birth. In spite of the
low-thoughted envy which would undervalue contemporary merit, our
own will be a memorable age in intellectual achievements, and we live
among such philosophers and poets as surpass beyond comparison any
who have appeared since the last national struggle for civil and religious
liberty. The most unfailing herald, companion, and follower of the
awakening of a great people to work a beneficial change in opinion or
institution, is poetry. At such periods there is an accumulation of the
power of communicating and receiving intense and impassioned conceptions respecting man and nature. The persons in whom this power
resides, may often as far as regards many portions of their nature, have
little apparent correspondence with that spirit of good of which they are
the ministers. But even whilst they deny and abjure, they are yet
compelled to serve, the power which is seated upon the throne of their
own soul. It is impossible to read the compositions of the most celebrated
writers of the present day without being startled with the electric life
which burns within their words. They measure the circumference and
sound the depths of human nature with a comprehensive and all-penetrating
spirit, and they are themselves perhaps the most sincerely astonished at
its manifestations; for it is less their spirit than the spirit of the age. Poets

are the hierophants of an unapprehended inspiration; the mirrors of the gigantic shadows which futurity casts upon the present; the words which express what they understand not; the trumpets which sing to battle, and feel not what they inspire; the influence which is moved not, but moves. Poets are the unacknowledged legislators of the world.

Unquestionably, the poets of whom Shelley is speaking here are not himself, Byron, and Keats, but primarily Wordsworth and secondarily Coleridge. It does not matter, Shelley says, that as men Wordsworth and Coleridge have become Tories in politics, pillars of the established Church in religion, and mere time-servers in literature. "Even whilst they deny and abjure" the imagination, Wordsworth and Coleridge serve its power. Wordsworth is a hierophant or expounder of the mysterious, even though he himself cannot apprehend what he expounds. Wordsworth is a transumptive mirror of futurity, and sings Shelley on to the battle of poetry long after Wordsworth himself is uninspired. And then comes the beautifully summarizing formula: Wordsworth is the unmoved mover, as an *influence*. The famous, much misinterpreted last sentence, "Poets are the unacknowledged legislators of the world," clearly needs to be interpreted in the context of the paradox that Shelley himself calls poetic "influence." The late W. H. Auden had a passionate dislike of Shelley, and once went so far as to interpret the last sentence of the *Defence of Poetry* as meaning that Shelley thought that poets were in league with the secret police. An unacknowledged legislator is simply an unacknowledged influence, and since Shelley equates Wordsworth with the *Zeitgeist*, it is hardly an overestimate to say that Wordsworth's influence created a series of laws for a world of feeling and thinking that went beyond the domain of poetry. Very strong poet that he was, Shelley nevertheless had the wisdom and the sadness of knowing overtly what other poets since have evaded knowing, except in the involuntary patterns of their work. Wordsworth will legislate and go on legislating for your poem, no matter how you resist or evade or even unconsciously ignore him.

I do not want to end on such a tone of realistic sorrow and wisdom, even though the superbly intelligent Shelley is not ill-represented by such a tone. He knew that he could not escape the shadow of Wordsworth, and of and in that knowing he made his own poetry. I end by applying to him the last stanza of his own *Hymn of Apollo*. He would not have wanted us to think of him as the speaker of these lines, but he came as close, I think, as any poet since Wordsworth, down to our present day, to justifying our going beyond his intentions, and hearing the poet himself in this great declaration:

I am the eye with which the Universe
   Beholds itself and knows itself divine;
All harmony of instrument or verse,
   All prophecy, all medicine is mine,
All light of art or nature;—to my song
Victory and praise in its own right belong.

LESLIE BRISMAN

"Epipsychidion"

The dream vision of *Epipsychidion* extends in complex ways two themes of Asia's song: in both poems the movement toward a prophetic future is heralded by intimations of a return back to a lost diviner day; and in both concern with poetic voice is the medium through which redemptive awareness is developed. Asia sings in response to the sweet singing of a Voice in the Air; in *Epipsychidion*, the visionary voice is recalled in response to a problem in the speaker's voice.

To read *Epipsychidion* one must accept two literary conventions about responsiveness. One is the extended address to an idealized beloved or muse, an absent Other regarded as a representative of an eternal Presence. The drama of such a poem depends on the element of suspense in unfolding the past and future of this illusion of presence, including the moments of intermission when the poet addresses his larger audience ("She met me, Stranger," l. 72) or only himself (ll. 123–29, and in a sense the whole history recounted in ll. 160–344). The drama concludes with the moment of reconciliation to absence when the poet speaks to the words that mediate between himself and his fictional Other ("Weak Verses, go, kneel at your Sovereign's feet," l. 592). The second convention is that, popularized by Dante, of regarding a youthful vision as the romantic origin of a transcendent one. The poet is surprised to find "Youth's vision thus made perfect" in Emily (l. 42), and as readers we are repeatedly surprised to find that what seems largely a convention about youth's vision ("the words / Of antique verse and high romance," ll. 209–10) can produce the possibility of beginning anew. To appreciate *Epipsychidion* one must pursue the relation of these two literary conventions about presence or absence and about the belatedness or romantic earliness of dreamy vision.

In *Alastor*, the dream vision of an idealized beloved represents the suspiciously daemonized consciousness of the Poet, reacting against which the narrator himself is daemonized into something like an Alastor or vengeful spirit—an analogy to, or parody of, the fully empowered poet. In *Epipsychidion* the passage corresponding to the dream vision of the idealized beloved occurs relatively late—after two passages which, retrospectively, appear to have revealed feminine forms destined to occupy no place closer to the heart of the poet of *Epipsychidion* than did the Arab maiden to the Poet of *Alastor*. The third passage brings the poet to something like the dream vision in *Alastor* from the Poet's point of view:

> Soft as an Incarnation of the Sun,
> When light is changed to love, this glorious One
> Floated into the cavern where I lay,
> And called my Spirit, and the dreaming clay
> Was lifted by the thing that dreamed below
> As smoke by fire, and in her beauty's glow
> Was penetrating me with living light.
> (ll. 335–41)

The idea of light being changed to love represents an extreme extension of the Miltonic idea of sublimation by which grosser matter is transformed into purer spirit. The rhetoric is hyperbolical because this vision marks an achieved moment of the sublime, a moment when the poet seems most clearly empowered to create out of nothing what the character he represents is said to have merely beheld.

In both *Alastor* and *Epipsychidion* descent from rhetorical height takes the form of a romantic quest. If we say that the major dream passage in ll. 190–216 of *Epipsychidion* corresponds to the central vision of *Alastor* (ll. 140–91), then the whole attempt in *Epipsychidion* to find in mortal forms "the shadow of that idol" corresponds to the long journey of the *Alastor* Poet in pursuit of "that fleeting shade" beyond the realms of dream. But if we see the crossing of solipsism—the definitive turn to the high rhetoric of the sublime—delayed in *Epipsychidion* till the episode cited above (ll. 335–44), then the dream passage of ll. 190–216 appears rather as an elaboration of the prehistory of poetic consciousness described in *Alastor* in the lines, "By solemn vision, and bright silver dream, / His infancy was nurtured" (ll. 67–68). The importance of this correspondence is that it helps us see Shelley lingering over the prehistory of the soul in love to the end that the new soul at its birth or romantic origin ("Then, from the caverns of my dreamy youth / I sprang," ll. 217–18) comes appareled with celestial light.

Like the myth of preexistence which Wordsworth revised as background for the experience of loss in his Intimations Ode, Shelley's history of the soul "in the clear golden prime of [his] youth's dawn" poses as a true spiritual beginning, a dream world elsewhere from whence the soul descends into nature. Though it is crucial to see the soul in line 217 making a new beginning when it springs forth from the dreamy background of the preceding verse paragraph, it is no less interesting to inquire what in the poem impels the appearance of the dream vision of preexistence. Looking at the verse paragraph which begins "There was a Being whom my spirit oft / Met," one is tempted to think of narrative verse paragraphs of *The Prelude* which seems to spring forth without apology for appearing at a given moment in the poem. All the difference between Shelley and Wordsworth might be caught in the juxtaposition of the incident beginning "There was a Being" to Wordsworth's incident "There was a boy" (*Prelude*, V.364–425). Yet there remains something essentially Wordsworthian about presenting dreamy youth as though it were an incident, a single spot of time to be revisited.

The three preceding paragraphs, under the veil of being Emily's wisdom, deliver a polemic against exclusiveness, moving from explicit vituperation against marriage to more abstract argument about division in emotional and intellectual commitments. These verse paragraphs thus concern on a thematic level (in terms of the structure of human relationships) what on a structural level Mr. Bloom calls the romantic lyric's stage of *tessera* or antithetical completion. The third paragraph, immediately preceding the dream vision, ends in a vision of what the Kabbalah calls *tikkun* or restitution of broken rhetorical figurations and a broken world:

Mind from its object differs most in this:
Evil from good; misery from happiness;
The baser from the nobler; the impure
And frail, from what is clear and must endure.
If you divide suffering and dross, you may
Diminish till it is consumed away;
If you divide pleasure and love and thought,
Each part exceeds the whole; and we know not
How much, while any yet remains unshared,
Of pleasure may be gained, of sorrow spared:
This truth is that deep well, whence sages draw
The unenvied light of hope; the eternal law
By which those live, to whom this world of life
Is as a garden ravaged, and whose strife

Tills for the promise of a later birth
The wilderness of this Elysian earth.
(ll. 174–89)

What seems like a rather careless profusion of value words in the first four lines may have been influenced by the argument against the narrow mind which limits its contemplation to one object. A mind not narrowly set in one frame of reference can associate with the idea of a limited object evil, misery, the base, the impure and frail. The next two lines suggest a hypothetical program for making the defects of the object world of nature easier to bear. One can no longer stick to the marriage referent, which would make dividing suffering and dross sound like a plan of social concern in which everyone spends a small number of hours with the sick, the ugly, or the poor in spirit so that no one is long bound to them. But one need not trouble oneself specifying why such a plan would prove impracticable; the speculation remains vague, in the realm of what "may be." On the other hand, the two lines suggesting the division of positive pleasures are extended and move out from the realm of what may be into imagined futurity. Spreading the kingdom of love, Shelley gathers into his fold the sages and believers in orthodox religious accounts who look forward to a time of *tikkun olam*—the restoration of a broken world when the dross of experiential loss will be redeemed under the reign of a God of Love.

Shelley distinguishes himself from the orthodox, "to whom this world of life / Is as a garden ravaged," by posing an alternative, personal myth of shared love. *Epipsychidion* will end in an extended vision of an island paradise, replacing the Christian millennium. It proceeds, at this point, to an alternative to Christian Eden. Perhaps for this reason the last line before the dream vision passage describes the post-Edenic world as "The wilderness of this Elysian earth." The adjective is a counter to the Christian myth, and marks Shelley's isolation from a mainstream of visionary orthodoxy. In Christian terms, or in the metaphor adopted by Mr. Bloom, this stage might be called *kenosis* or the putting off of manifest divinity in the service of this earth. Like the narrator of *Alastor*, who lays aside a transcendentalism and regresses by recounting the Poet's childlike faith in the continuity of nature, the poet of *Epipsychidion* undoes his visionary metaphysics by regressing to the childlike "clear golden prime of my youth's dawn" (l. 192).

Both poems depend on our ability to distinguish the softer antithetical vision of dreamy youth from the radical daemonized vision of the sublime. In *Alastor* Shelley identified the regressive stage with the faith in a Wordsworthian "natural piety," the faith in the metonymic contiguity of nature which allows the face of the earth to be explored the way an infant explores his mother's face. In *Epipsychidion* the *kenosis* of the poet does not exactly return him to a Wordsworthian earth, for the "visioned wanderings" of a spirit met by a Being on faery isles and imagined shores is a far cry from the wanderings lonely as a cloud of a poet whose encounters are wholly of and in the realm of the natural. Shelley regresses not to the romanticism of an earlier generation but to the gentler romanticism of a hypothetically earlier Shelley. The "caverns of dreamy youth" are caverns of Shelley's own dreamwork, birthplaces of the self-generated spirit who, fully awakened to his powers, will return to make those caverns his haunts. Here is the verse paragraph in its entirety:

> There was a Being whom my spirit oft
> Met on its visioned wanderings, far aloft,
> In the clear golden prime of my youth's dawn,
> Upon the fairy isles of sunny lawn,
> Amid the enchanted mountains, and the caves
> Of divine sleep, and on the air-like waves
> Of wonder-level dream, whose tremulous floor
> Paved her light steps;—on an imagined shore,
> Under the gray beak of some promontory
> She met me, robed in such exceeding glory
> That I beheld her not. In solitudes
> Her voice came to me through the whispering woods,
> And from the fountains, and the odours deep
> Of flowers, which, like lips murmuring in their sleep
> Of the sweet kisses which had lulled them there,
> Breathed but of her to the enamoured air;
> And from the breezes whether low or loud,
> And from the rain of every passing cloud,
> And from the singing of the summer-birds,
> And from all sounds, all silence. In the words
> Of antique verse and high romance,—in form,
> Sounds, colour—in whatever checks that Storm
> Which with the shattered present chokes the past;
> And in that best philosophy, whose taste
> Makes this cold common hell, our life, a doom
> As glorious as a fiery martyrdom;
> Her Spirit was the harmony of truth.
>
> (ll. 190–216)

The Spirit sighted here is lost in—or rather at one with—a metonymic sea in which all names, all specificities of time and place, are washed together. "The caves / Of divine sleep" and the "waves / Of wonder-level dream" are not two locales but two attempts at representing a visionary landscape. "Her voice came to me through the whispering woods," less from nature than from the rhetorical effort of personifying nature. Even if we grant that woods and fountains are conventional haunts of nature spirits, we must see that the odors are autocthonically Shelleyan, and the extended simile they inspire (causing her, in this metaphor within metaphor, to be expired or breathed forth) evokes the spirit of love with a power suggestive of songful soul-creation in *Comus*. The impression of richly literary language of creation fades when the next four lines, each beginning with the words "And from," emphasize what look like natural origins. Until one has sorted the parts of the sentence one is perhaps more aware of the "from" then of the voice coming from breeze, rain, birds, and sounds. There is a temptation to rest in the very inquiry after origins—a temptation increased by the fact that one of the *froms* has been elided and we must expand the last line to read, "And from all sounds [and from] all silence." But that last line of ten about the origins of voice confronts us with the largest possible diffusion: all sound and all silence divide between them all possibilities, making of inclusive nature not a source but the general medium of voice. Thus *from*, like the opening *in* or the following *through*, really points to a mediating sense of place, and like the four *ins* of the next sentence leads us not to an original singleness but to shared—what the previous verse paragraph called "divided"—pleasure and love and thought.

The rather abstract line concluding the dream-vision paragraph summarizes the diffusion of Her Spirit and makes of the verse paragraph less a search for origins than a conglomerate original vision. The following lines make this clearer: "Then from the caverns of my dreamy youth / I sprang." With these words the preceding paragraph as a whole comes to represent the caverns of dreamy youth, and the generalized period of life called dreamy youth replaces a more specifiable source in dream visitation. The substitution retains the form of dream experience, however, for the words "I sprang" better describe being roused from a dream than they do the ordinarily gradual process of maturing. What springs forth at this point, as if from a dream rather than from any source in nature, is the first of several increasingly mature versions of the daemonized poetic spirit. As a poet, Shelley represses the distinction between mythological and actual past—just as Wordsworth repressed the distinction between the visionary gleam of childhood and that of mythological preexistence.

For Wordsworth, the substitution by which natural forms stand in a place said to have been originally above nature takes the form of metaphoric language barely noticeable as personification:

> —But there's a tree, of many one,
> A single field which I have look'd upon,
> Both of them speak of something that is gone:

> The pansy at my feet
> Doth the same tale repeat:
> Whither is fled the visionary gleam?
> Where is it now, the glory and the dream?
> (Intimations Ode)

Tree and field speak of the vanished dream—of what was more than nature—but they "speak" in wholly natural terms. Shelley risks more:

> A voice said:—'O thou of hearts the weakest,
> The phantom is beside thee whom thou seekest.'
> Then I—'Where?'—the world's echo answered 'where?'
> And in that silence, and in my despair,
> I questioned every tongueless wind that flew
> Over my tower of mourning, if it know
> Whither 'twas fled, this soul out of my soul.
> (ll. 232–38)

If the questions concluding these two passages are not the same, the difference can only emphasize Shelley's determination to have his myth of loss a personal one. "This soul out of my soul," though it could be called a "visionary gleam," could not be said to come "From God, who is our home." For Shelley the soul is ultimately its own home, though the sense of loss requires a vocabulary of otherness. In place of Wordsworth's mild investiture of the landscape with voice, Shelley boldly appropriates the mechanism ("A voice said") and then demystifies what looks like supernature when voice is reduced to echo. In miniature this passage repeats the exchange *Epipsychidion* carries out between the passages of vision and those of natural quest. In the paragraph of dream vision, "Her voice came to me through the whispering woods"; in the paragraph of loss, the winds are "tongueless." Voice is power, and the search for voice is the quest of the whole poem.

If *Epipsychidion* ended shortly after this point, it could restrict vision to dreamy youth, and like Alastor picture experience stretching downward toward death from the occasion of dream vision. *Julian and Maddalo* gain subtlety in summarily recounting how the dream lady returns for a space to her enraptured love. And in *Prometheus Unbound* the recalled dream, like the resurgent Spirit of the Earth who runs up to Asia in Act III, stands for the ethic and the prophetic vision of recall that form the very subject of the poem. *Epipsychidion* might have been schematically easier with just the one period of dreamy youth, but Shelley required a myth of memory in which both the past recaptured and the moment of sublime presence would be dream visions having no part of nature. The appearance of Emily at the daemonized center of the poem purifies as it restores the concept of dream. Here again are the lines I identify as approaching the apex of the sublime, the point where the history of the past breaks off into apostrophe and eternal presence:

> This glorious One
> Floated into the cavern where I lay,
> And called my Spirit, and the dreaming clay
> Was lifted by the thing that dreamed below
> As smoke by fire, and in her beauty's glow
> I stood, and felt the dawn of my long night
> Was penetrating me with living light.
>
> (ll. 336–42)

The cavern image, important to the prophetic analogue for such experience, recalls "the caverns of my dreamy youth" and makes of life generally, as Plato did in the famous myth, a cave but occasionally visited by light. Almost magically, the passage manages to retain its reservations about the externality of transcendental experience in the very phrases that describe it. The illumination is not from above but from below—internal, as it were—and "the dawn of my long night" is a dawn as much the property of as an interference upon the night of life. The passage ostensibly records that which surpasses and redeems one from dream; but dreamy clay is lifted by "the thing that dreamed below," and dream vision remains the source of transcendence.

Like *Prometheus Unbound*, *Epipsychidion* ends with an extended celebration of prophetic vision that circles round and sees in redeemed time "echoes of an antenatal dream." The paradisal place, which is given an origin "in the world's young prime," returns in a way to the visionary space of the dream passage, "In the clear golden prime of my youth's dawn." It returns also to the source of poetic voice and represents in extended narrative the fluency that marks poetic power. Restored too is the vision of power transcending particular voicings, the vision emphasized in the original dream passage by having the list of sources of voice culminate in "all silence." In the new place talk will be empowered

> until thought's melody
> Become too sweet for utterance, and it die
> In words, to live again in looks, which dart
> With thrilling tone into the voiceless heart,
> Harmonizing silence without a sound.
>
> (ll. 560–64)

Until such time, however, the voiceless heart is too closely allied to vacancy, and words must be the vehicle of all images of the soul's transcendence, just as they prove ultimately "The chains of lead around its flight of fire."

PAUL DE MAN

Shelley Disfigured: "The Triumph of Life"

Like several of the English romantics'
major works *The Triumph of Life*, Shelley's last poem, is, as is well-known,
a fragment that has been unearthed, edited, reconstructed, and much discussed. All this archeological labor can be considered a response to the
questions that articulate one of the text's main structures: ". . . 'And what
is this? / Whose shape is that within the car? and why—' " (ll. 177–78);
later repeated in a more subject-oriented, second-person mode: " 'Whence
camest thou? and whither goest thou? / How did thy course begin,' I said,
'and why?' " (ll. 296–97); finally repeated again, now in the first person:
" 'Shew whence I came, and where I am, and why—. . .' " (l. 398). These
questions can easily be referred back to the enigmatic text they

From *Deconstruction and Criticism*. Copyright © 1979 by Harold Bloom. The Continuum
Publishing Co., 1979.

punctuate and they are characteristic of the interpretive labor associated with romanticism. In the case of this movement, they acquire an edge of urgency which is often lacking when they are addressed to earlier periods, except when these periods are themselves mediated by the neo-hellenism, the neo-medievalism, or the neo-baroque of the late eighteenth and the early nineteenth century. This is not surprising, since they are precisely the archeological questions that prompt us to deduce the present from the identification of the more or less immediately anterior past, as well as from the process that leads from then to now. Such an attitude coincides with the use of history as a way to new beginnings, as "digging in the grounds for the new foundations." Much is invested in these metaphors of architecture and of statuary on which seems to hinge our ability to inhabit the world. But if this curiosity about antecedents has produced admirable philological results and allowed, as in the case of *The Triumph of Life*, for the establishment of texts whose unreliability is at least controlled by more reliable means, the questions which triggered all this industry remain more than ever in suspense: What is the meaning of *The Triumph of Life*, of Shelley, and of romanticism? What shape does it have, how did its course begin and why? Perhaps the difficulty of the answers is prefigured in the asking of the questions. The status of all these where's and what's and how's and why's is at stake, as well as the system that links these interrogative pronouns, on the one hand, to questions of definition and of temporal situation and, on the other hand, to questions of shape and of figure. Such questions allow one to conclude that *The Triumph of Life* is a fragment of something whole, or romanticism a fragment, or a moment, in a process that now includes us within its horizon. What relationship do we have to such a text that allows us to call it a fragment that we are then entitled to reconstruct, to identify, and implicitly to complete? This supposes, among other things, that Shelley or romanticism are themselves entities which, like a statue, can be broken into pieces, mutilated, or allegorized (to use Hardy's alternatives) after having been stiffened, frozen, erected, or whatever one wants to call the particular rigidity of statues. Is the status of a text like the status of a statue? Yeats, one of Shelley's closest readers and disciples, wrote a fine poem about history and form called *The Statues*, which it would be rewarding to read in conjunction with *The Triumph of Life*. But there are more economic ways to approach this text and to question the possibility of establishing a relationship to Shelley and to romanticism in general. After all, the link between the present I and its antecedents is itself dramatized in the poem, most explicitly and at greatest length in the encounter between the narrator and the figure designated by the proper name Rousseau, who has himself much to say about his own predecessors.

The unearthed fragments of this fragment, the discarded earlier versions, disclose that the relationship between Shelley and Rousseau, or between Rousseau and his ancestors, underwent considerable changes as the composition of the poem progressed. Consider, for instance, the passage in which the poet, guided at this moment by Rousseau, passes judgment upon his contemporaries and immediate predecessors, including the openly alluded to Wordsworth, with such vehemence that he condemns them all to oblivion. He is reproached for this by Rousseau who intervenes to assert that he himself, as well as Voltaire, would have ascended to "the fane / Where truth and its inventors sit enshrined," if they had not been so faint-hearted as to lack faith in their own intellectual labor as well as, by implication, that of their ancestors. Those encrypted statues of Truth are identified as "Plato and his pupil" (presumably Aristotle) who "Reigned from the center to the circumference" and prepared the way for Bacon and modern science. Rousseau's and Voltaire's capitulation is not a sheer loss however, since Rousseau has gained insight that he is able to communicate in turn to the young Shelley. Donald Reiman, the editor of *The Triumph of Life*, glosses the passage as follows:

> Rousseau . . . tries to impress on the Poet that it was exactly this attitude toward the past struggle of great men that led him and Voltaire to abandon their reforming zeal and succumb to life. Thus the poet's contemptuous allusion to Wordsworth turns against him as Rousseau endeavors to show the Poet how the mistakes of those who have preceded him, especially idealists like himself, can serve as a warning to him: Rousseau and Voltaire fell because they adopted the contemptuous attitude toward history that the poet now displays; the child *is* father of the man, and Shelley's generation, representing the full mastery of the age that dawned in the French Revolution, can learn from the mistakes of that age's earlier generations (those of Rousseau and Voltaire and of Wordsworth).

Although this is certainly not presented as an interpretation of the entire text, but only of this discarded passage, it remains typical of the readings generally given of *The Triumph of Life*, even when they are a great deal more complicated than this straightforward statement. It is a clear example of the recuperation of a failing energy by means of an increased awareness: Rousseau lacked power, but because he can consciously articulate the causes of his weakness in words, the energy is preserved and recovered in the following generation. And this reconversion extends back to its originators, since the elders, at first condemned, are now reinstated in the name of their negative but exemplary knowledge. The child *is* father of the man, just as Wordsworth lucidly said, both humbling and saving himself in the eyes of his followers. This simple motion can take on considerable dialectical intricacy without altering its fundamental scheme. The entire debate as to whether *The Triumph of Life* represents or heralds a movement of growth or of degradation is part of this same genetic and historical metaphor. The unquestioned authority of this metaphor is much more important than the positive or negative valorization of the movement it generates.

The initial situation of Rousseau—allied with Voltaire and Wordsworth in a shared failure, as opposed to Plato, Aristotle, and Bacon, and as opposed, by implication, to Shelley himself—changes in later versions. In the last available text, itself frozen into place by Shelley's accidental death, the hierarchy is quite different: Rousseau is now set apart quite sharply from the representatives of the Enlightenment (which include Voltaire next to Kant and Frederick the Great) who are condemned with some of the original severity, without Rousseau reproving him for it. No allusion to Wordsworth is included at this point, though Wordsworth is certainly present in other regions of the poem. Rousseau is now classified with Plato and Aristotle, but whereas these philosophers were held up as untarnished images of Truth in the earlier version, they are now fallen and, in the imagery of the poem, chained to the chariot of Life, together with "the great bards of old" (l. 247). The reasons for their fall, as well as the elements in their works and in their lives that both unite and distinguish them from Rousseau, are developed in passages that are not difficult to interpret from a thematic point of view. The resulting hierarchies have become more complex: we first have a class of entirely condemned historical personages, which includes representatives of the Enlightenment as well as the emperors and popes of Christianity (ll. 281 ff.); on a distinctly higher level, but nevertheless defeated, we find Rousseau, Plato, Aristotle, and Homer. As possibly exonerated from this defeat, the poem mentions only Bacon, a remnant from the earlier passage who now has lost much of his function, as well as "the sacred few" (l. 128) who, unlike Adonais in the earlier poem, had no earthly destiny whatsoever, either because, by choice or destiny, they died too early or because, like Christ or Socrates, they are mere fictions in the writings of others. As for Shelley himself, his close proximity to Rousseau is now more strongly marked than in the earlier passage; the possibility of his escape from Rousseau's destiny has now become problematic and depends on one's reading of Rousseau's own story, which constitutes the main narrative sequence of the poem.

Lengthy and complex as it is, Rousseau's self-narrated history provides no answer to his true identity, although he is himself shown in quest of such an answer. Questions of origin, of direction, and of identity punctuate the text without ever receiving a clear answer. They always lead back to a new scene of questioning which merely repeats the quest and recedes in infinite regress: the narrator asks himself " 'And what is this? . . .' " (l. 177) and receives an enigmatic answer (" 'Life!' ") from an enigmatic shape; once identified as Rousseau, the shape can indeed reveal some other names in the pageant of history but is soon asked, by the poet, to identify itself in a deeper sense than by a mere name: " 'How did thy course begin . . . and why?' " Complying with this request, Rousseau narrates the history of his existence, also culminating in an encounter with a mysterious entity, " 'A shape all light . . .' " (l. 352) to whom, in his turn, he puts the question " 'whence I came, and where I am, and why—.' " As an answer, he is granted a vision of the same spectacle that prompted the poet-narrator's questioning in the first place; we have to imagine the same sequence of events repeating themselves for Shelley, for Rousseau, and for whomever Rousseau chose to question in his turn as Shelley questioned him. The structure of the text is not one of question and answer, but of a question whose meaning, as question, is effaced from the moment it is asked. The answer to the question is another question, asking what and why one asked, and thus receding ever further from the original query. This movement of effacing and of forgetting becomes prominent in the text and dispels any illusion of dialectical progress or regress. The articulation in terms of the questions is displaced by a very differently structured process that pervades all levels of the narrative and that repeats itself in the main sequences as well as in what seem to be lateral episodes. It finally engulfs and dissolves what started out to be, like *Alastor, Epipsychidion,* or even *Prometheus Unbound,* a quest (or, like *Adonais,* an elegy), to replace it by something quite different for which we have no name readily available among the familiar props of literary history.

Whenever this self-receding scene occurs, the syntax and the imagery of the poem tie themselves into a knot which arrests the process of understanding. The resistance of these passages is such that the reader soon forgets the dramatic situation and is left with only these unresolved riddles to haunt him: the text becomes the successive and cumulative experience of these tangles of meaning and of figuration. One of these tangles occurs near the end of Rousseau's narration of his encounter with the "shape all light" assumed to possess the key to his destiny:

". . . as one between desire and shame
Suspended, I said . . .

'Shew whence I came, and where I am, and why—
Pass not away upon the passing stream.'

" 'Arise and quench thy thirst' " was her reply.
And as a shut lily, stricken by the wand
Of dewy morning's vital alchemy,

"I rose; and bending at her sweet command,
Touched with faint lips the cup she raised,
And suddenly my brain became as sand

"Where the first wave had more than half erased
The track of deer on desert Labrador,
Whilst the fierce wolf from which they fled amazed

"Leaves his stamp visibly upon the shore
Until the second bursts—so on my sight
Burst a new Vision never seen before.
                                                          (ll. 394–410)

The scene dramatizes the failure to satisfy a desire for self-knowledge
and can therefore indeed be considered as something of a key passage.
Rousseau is not given a satisfactory answer, for the ensuing vision is a
vision of continued delusion that includes him. He undergoes instead a
metamorphosis in which his brain, the center of his consciousness, is
transformed. The transformation is also said to be the erasure of an
imprinted track, a passive, mechanical operation that is no longer within
the brain's own control: both the production and the erasure of the track
are not an act performed by the brain, but the brain being acted upon by
something else. The resulting "sand" is not, as some commentators imply,
an image of drought and sterility (this is no desert, but a shore washed by
abundant waters). "My brain became as sand" suggests the modification of
a knowledge into the surface on which this knowledge ought to be
recorded. Ought to be, for instead of being clearly imprinted it is "more
than half erased" and covered over. The process is a replacement, a
substitution, continuing the substitution of "brain" by "sand," of one kind
of track, said to be like that of a deer, by another, said to be like that of a
wolf "from which [the deer] fled amazed." They mark a stage in the
metamorphosis of Rousseau into his present state or shape; when we first
meet him, he is

. . . what I thought was an old root which grew
To strange distortion out of the hill side . . .

> And . . . the grass which methought hung so wide
> And white, was but his thin discoloured hair,
> And . . . the holes he vainly sought to hide
>
> Were or had been eyes.
>
> (ll. 182–88)

The erasure or effacement is indeed the loss of a face, in French *figure*. Rousseau no longer, or hardly (as the tracks are not all gone, but more than half erased), has a face. Like the protagonist in the Hardy story, he is disfigured, *défiguré*, defaced. And also as in the Hardy story, to be disfigured means primarily the loss of the eyes, turned to "stony orbs" or to empty holes. This trajectory from erased self-knowledge to disfiguration is the trajectory of *The Triumph of Life*.

The connotations of the pair deer/wolf, marking a change in the inscriptions made upon Rousseau's mind, go some way in explaining the presence of Rousseau in the poem, a choice that has puzzled several interpreters. The first and obvious contrast is between a gentle and idyllic peace pursued by violent aggression. Shelley, an assiduous reader of Rousseau at a time when he was being read more closely than he has been since, evokes an ambivalence of structure and of mood that is indeed specifically Rousseau's rather than anyone else's, including Wordsworth's. Rousseau's work is characterized in part by an introspective, self-reflexive mode, which uses literary models of Augustinian and pietistic origin, illustrated, for instance, by such literary allusions as Petrarch and the *Astrée* and, in general, by the elements that prompted Schiller to discuss him under the heading of the contemporary idyll. But to this are juxtaposed elements that are closer to Machiavelli than to Petrarch, concerned with political power as well as with economic and legal realities. The first register is one of delicacy of feeling, whereas a curious brand of cunning and violence pervades the other. The uneasy mixture is both a commonplace and a crux of Rousseau interpretation. It appears in the larger as well as the finer dimensions of his writings, most obviously in such broad contrasts as separate the tone and import of a text such as *The Social Contract* from that of *Julie*. That the compatibility between inner states of consciousness and acts of power is a thematic concern of *The Triumph of Life* is clear from the political passages in the poem. In the wake of the in itself banal passage on Bonaparte, the conflict is openly stated:

> . . . much I grieved to think how power and will
> In opposition rule our mortal day—
>
> And why God made irreconcilable
> Good and the means of good; . . .
>
> (ll. 228–31)

Rousseau is unique among Shelley's predecessors not only in that this question of the discrepancy between the power of words as acts and their power to produce other words is inscribed within the thematics and the structure of his writings, but also in the particular form that it takes there. For the tension passes, in Rousseau, through a self which is itself experienced as a complex interplay between drives and the conscious reflection on these drives; Shelley's understanding of this configuration is apparent in this description of Rousseau as "between desire and shame / Suspended. . . ."

The opposition between will and power, the intellectual goal and the practical means, reappears when it is said, by and of Rousseau, that ". . . my words were seeds of misery—/ Even as the deeds of others . . ." (ll. 280–81). The divergence between words and deeds (by way of "seeds") seems to be suspended in Rousseau's work, albeit at the cost of, or rather because of, considerable suffering: "I / Am one of those who have created, even / If it be but a world of agony" (ll. 293–95). For what sets Rousseau apart from the representatives of the Enlightenment is the pathos of what is here called the "heart" ("I was overcome / By my own heart alone. . . ."). The contrast between the cold and skeptical Voltaire and the sensitive Rousseau is another commonplace of popular intellectual history. But Shelley's intuition of the "heart" in Rousseau is more than merely senti-mental. Its impact becomes clearer in the contrast that sets Rousseau apart from "the great bards of old," Homer and Vergil, said to have ". . . inly quelled / The passions which they sung . . ." (ll. 274–75), whereas Rousseau has ". . . suffered what [he] wrote, or viler pain!" Unlike the epic narrators who wrote about events in which they did not take part, Rousseau speaks out of his own self-knowledge, not only in his *Confessions* (which Shelley did not like) but in all his works, regardless of whether they are fictions or political treatises. In the tradition of Augustine, Descartes, and Malebranche, the self is for him not merely the seat of the affections but the primary center of cognition. Shelley is certainly not alone in thus characterizing and praising Rousseau, but the configuration between self, heart, and action is given even wider significance when Rousseau compares himself to the Greek philosophers. Aristotle turns out to be, like Rousseau, a double structure held together by the connivance of words and deeds; if he is now enslaved to the eroding process of "life," it is because he does not exist singly, as pure mind, but cannot be separated from the "woes and wars" his pupil Alexander the Great in-flicted upon the world. Words cannot be isolated from the deeds they perform; the tutor necessarily performs the deeds his pupil derives from his mastery. And just as "deeds" cause the undoing of Aristotle, it is the "heart" that brought down Plato who, like Rousseau, was a theoretician of statecraft and a legislator. Like Aristotle and like Rousseau (who is like a deer but also like a wolf) Plato is at least double; life "conquered [his] heart" as Rousseau was "overcome by [his] own heart alone." The reference to the apocryphal story of Aster makes clear that "heart" here means more than mere affectivity; Plato's heart was conquered by "love" and, in this context, love is like the intellectual eros that links Socrates to his pupils. Rousseau is placed within a configuration, brought about by "words," of knowledge, action, and erotic desire. The elements are present in the symbolic scene from which we started out, since the pursuit of the deer by the wolf, in this context of Ovidian and Dantesque metamorphoses, is bound to suggest Apollo's pursuit of the nymphs as well as scenes of inscription and effacement.

The scene is one of violence and grief, and the distress reappears in the historical description of Rousseau with its repeated emphasis on suffering and agony, as well as in the dramatic action of defeat and enslavement. But this defeat is paradoxical: in a sense, Rousseau has overcome the discrepancy of action and intention that tears apart the historical world, and he has done so because his words have acquired the power of actions as well as of the will. Not only because they represent or reflect on actions but because they themselves, literally, are actions. Their power to act exists independently of their power to know: Aristotle's or Plato's mastery of mind did not give them any control over the deeds of the world, also and especially the deeds that ensured as a consequence of their words and with which they were directly involved. The power that arms their words also makes them lose their power over them. Rousseau gains shape, face, or figure only to lose it as he acquires it. The enigma of this power, the burden of whatever understanding Shelley's poem permits, depends primarily on the reading of Rousseau's recapitulative narrative of his encounter with the "Shape all light" (ll. 308–433).

Rousseau's history, as he looks back upon his existence from the "April prime" of his young years to the present, tells of a specific experience that is certainly not a simple one but that can be designated by a single verb: the experience is that of forgetting. The term appears literally (l. 318) and in various periphrases (such as "oblivious spell," l. 331), or in metaphors with a clear analogical vehicle such as "quell" (l. 329), "blot [from memory]" (l. 330), "trample" (l. 388), "tread out" (l. 390), "erase" (l. 406), etc. It combines with another, more familiar metaphorical strain that is present throughout the entire poem: images of rising and waning light and of the sun.

The structure of "forgetting," in this text, is not clarified by echoes of a Platonic recollection and recognition (anamnesis) that enter the poem, partly by way of Shelley's own Platonic and Neoplatonic readings, partly by way of Wordsworth's *Immortality Ode* whose manifest presence, in this part of the poem, has misled even the most attentive readers of *The Triumph of Life*. In the *Phaedo* (73) and, with qualifications too numerous to develop here, in Wordsworth's *Ode*, what one forgets is a former state which Yeats, who used the same set of emblems, compares to the Unity of Being evoked in Aristophanes' *Symposium* speech as the mainspring of erotic desire. Within a Neoplatonic Christian tradition, this easily becomes a fitting symbol for the Incarnation, for a birth out of a transcendental realm into a finite world. But this is precisely what the experience of forgetting, in *The Triumph of Life*, is not. What one forgets here is not some previous condition, for the line of demarcation between the two conditions is so unclear, the distinction between the forgotten and the remembered so unlike the distinction between two well-defined areas, that we have no assurance whatever that the forgotten ever existed:

> "Whether my life had been before that sleep
> The Heaven which I imagine, or a Hell
>
> Like this harsh world in which I wake to weep
> I know not."
>
> (ll. 332–35)

The polarities of waking and sleeping (or remembering and forgetting) are curiously scrambled, in this passage, with those of past and present, of the imagined and the real, of knowing and not knowing. For if, as is clear from the previous scene, to be born into life is to fall asleep, thus associating life with sleep, then to "wake" from an earlier condition of non-sleeping into "this harsh world" of life can only be to become aware of one's persistent condition of slumber, to be more than ever asleep, a deeper sleep replacing a lighter one, a deeper forgetting being achieved by an act of memory which remembers one's forgetting. And since Heaven and Hell are not here two transcendental realms but the mere opposition between the imagined and the real, what we do not know is whether we are awake or asleep, dead or alive, forgetting or remembering. We cannot tell the difference between sameness and difference, and this inability to know takes on the form of a pseudoknowledge which is called a forgetting. Not just because it is an unbearable condition of indetermination which has to be repressed, but because the condition itself, regardless of how it affects us, necessarily hovers between a state of knowing and not-knowing, like the symptom of a disease which recurs at the precise moment that one remembers its absence. What is forgotten is absent in the mode of a possible delusion, which is another way of saying that it does not fit within a symmetrical structure of presence and absence.

In conformity with the consistent system of sun imagery, this hovering motion is evoked throughout the poem by scenes of glimmering light. This very "glimmer" unites the poet-narrator to Rousseau, as the movement of the opening sunrise is repeated in Rousseau's encounter with the feminine shape, just as it unites the theme of forgetting with the motions of the light. The verb appears in the opening scene:

> . . . a strange trance over my fancy grew
> Which was not slumber, for the shade it spread
>
> Was so transparent that the scene came through
> As clear as when a veil of light is drawn
> O'er the evening hills they *glimmer*; . . .
> (ll. 29–33, emphasis added)

and then again, later on, now with Rousseau on stage:

> The presence of that shape which on the stream
> Moved, as I moved along the wilderness,
>
> More dimly than a day appearing dream,
> The ghost of a forgotten form of sleep,
> A light from Heaven whose half extinguished beam
>
> Through the sick day in which we wake to weep
> *Glimmers*, forever sought, forever lost.
> So did that shape its obscure tenour keep. . . .
> (ll. 425–32, emphasis added)

It is impossible to say, in either passage, how the polarities of light and dark are matched with those of waking and sleep; the confusion is the same as in the previously quoted passage on forgetting and remembering. The light, in the second passage, is said to be like a dream, or like sleep ("the ghost of a forgotten form of sleep"), yet it shines, however distantly, upon a condition which is one of awakening ("the sad day in which we wake to weep"); in this light, to be awake is to be as if one were asleep. In the first passage, it is explicitly stated that since the poet perceives so clearly, he cannot be asleep, but the clarity is then said to be like that of a veil drawn over a darkening surface, a description which necessarily connotes covering and hiding, even if the veil is said to be "of light." Light covers light, trance covers slumber and creates conditions of optical confusion that resemble nothing as much as the experience of trying to read *The Triumph of Life*, as its meaning glimmers, hovers, and wavers, but refuses to yield the clarity it keeps announcing.

This play of veiling and unveiling is, of course, altogether tantalizing. Forgetting is a highly erotic experience; it is like glimmering light because it cannot be decided whether it reveals or hides; it is like desire because like the wolf pursuing the deer, it does violence to what sustains it; it is like a trance or a dream because it is asleep to the very extent that it is conscious and awake, and dead to the extent that it is alive. The passage that concerns us makes this knot, by which knowledge, oblivion, and desire hang suspended, into an articulated sequence of events that demands interpretation.

The chain that leads Rousseau from the birth of his consciousness to his present state of impending death passes through a well-marked succession of relays. Plato and Wordsworth provide the initial linking of birth with forgetting, but this forgetting has, in Shelley's poem, the glimmering ambivalence which makes it impossible to consider it as an act of closure or of beginning and which makes any further comparison with Wordsworth irrelevant. The metaphor for this process is that of "a gentle rivulet . . . [which] filled the grove / With sound which all who hear must needs forget / All pleasure and all pain . . ." (ll. 314–19). Unlike Yeats's, Shelley's river does not function as the "generated soul," as the descent of the transcendental soul into earthly time and space. As the passage develops, it enters into a system of relationships that are natural rather than esoteric. The property of the river that the poem singles out is its sound; the oblivious spell emanates from the repetitive rhythm of the water, which articulates a random noise into a definite pattern. Water, which has no shape of itself, is molded into shape by its contact with the earth, just as in the scene of the water washing away the tracks, it generates the very possibility of structure, pattern, form, or shape by way of the disappearance of shape into shapelessness. The repetition of the erasures rhythmically articulates what is in fact a disarticulation, and the poem seems to be shaped by the undoing of shapes. But since this pattern does not fully correspond to what it covers up, it leaves the trace which allows one to call this ambivalent shaping a forgetting. The birth of what an earlier Shelley poem such as Mont Blanc would still have called the mind occurs as the distortion which allows one to make the random regular by "forgetting" differences.

As soon as the water's noise becomes articulated sound it can enter into contact with the light. The birth of form as the interference of light and water passes, in the semi-synaesthesia of the passage, through the mediation of sound; it is however only a semi-synaesthesia, for the optical and auditory perceptions, though simultaneous, nevertheless remain treated in asymmetrical opposition:

> A shape all light, which with one hand did fling
> Dew on the earth, as if she were the Dawn
> Whose invisible rain forever seemed to sing
>
> A silver music on the mossy lawn,
> And *still* before her on the dusky grass
> Iris her many coloured scarf had drawn.
>   (ll. 352–57, emphasis added)

The water of the original river here fulfills a double and not necessarily complementary action, as it combines with the light to form, on the one hand, Iris's scarf or rainbow and, on the other hand, the "silver music" of oblivion. A traditional symbol of the integration of the phenomenal with the transcendental world, the natural synthesis of water and light in the rainbow is, in Shelley, the familiar "dome of many coloured glass" whose "stain" is the earthly trace and promise of an Eternity in which Adonais' soul is said to dwell "like a star." As such, it irradiates all the textures and forms of the natural world with the veil of the sun's *farbiger Abglanz*, just as it provides the analogical light and heat that will make it possible to refer to the poet's mind as "embers." The metaphorical chain which links the sun to water, to color, to heat, to nature, to mind, and to consciousness, is certainly at work in the poem and can be summarized in this image of the rainbow. But this symbol is said to exist here in the tenuous mode of insistence, as something that *still* prevails (l. 356) despite the encroachment of something else, also emanating from water and sun and associated with them from the start, called music and forgetting. This something else, of which it could be said that it wrenches the final statement of *Adonais* into a different shape, appears in some degree of tension with the symbol of the rainbow.

The entire scene of the shape's apparition and subsequent waning (l. 412) is structured as a near-miraculous suspension between these two different forces whose interaction gives to the figure the hovering motion which may well be the mode of being of all figures. This glimmering figure takes on the form of the unreachable reflection of Narcissus, the manifestation of shape at the expense of its possession. The suspended fascination of the Narcissus stance is caught in the moment when the shape is said to move.

> . . . with palms so tender
> Their tread broke not the mirror of its billow, . . .
>   (ll. 361–62)

The scene is self-reflexive: the closure of the shape's contours is brought about by self-duplication. The light generates its own shape by means of a mirror, a surface that articulates it without setting up a clear separation that differentiates inside from outside as self is differentiated from other. The self that comes into being in the moment of reflection is, in spatial terms, optical symmetry as the ground of structure, optical repetition as the structural principle that engenders entities as shapes. "Shape all light" is referentially meaningless since light, the necessary condition for shape, is itself, like water, without shape, and acquires shape only when split in the illusion of a doubleness which is not that of self and other. The sun, in this text, is from the start the figure of this self-contained specularity. But the double of the sun can only be the eye conceived as the mirror of light. "Shape" and "mirror" are inseparable in this scene, just as the sun is inseparable from the shapes it generates and which are, in fact, the eye, and just as the sun is inseparable from itself since it produces the illusion of the self as shape. The sun can be said "to stand," a figure which assumes the existence of an entire spatial organization, because it stands personified

> amid the blaze
> Of his own glory, . . .
>   (ll. 349–50)

The sun "sees" its own light reflected, like Narcissus, in a well that is a mirror and also an eye:

> . . . the Sun's image radiantly intense
> Burned on the waters of the well that glowed
> Like gold, . . .
>   (ll. 345–47)

Because the sun is itself a specular structure, the eye can be said to generate a world of natural forms. The otherness of a world that is in fact without order now becomes, for the eye, a maze made accessible to solar paths, as the eye turns from the blank radiance of the sun to its green and blue reflection in the world, and allows us to be in this world as in a landscape of roads and intents. The sun

> threaded all the forest maze
> With winding paths of emerald fire. . . .
>   (ll. 347–48)

The boldest, but also the most traditional, image in this passage is that of the sunray as a thread that stitches the texture of the world, the necessary and complementary background for the eye of Narcissus. The water and pupil of the eye generate the rainbow of natural forms along which it dwells in sensory self-fulfillment. The figure of the sun, present from the beginning of the poem, repeats itself in the figure of the eye's self-erotic contact with its own surface, which is also the mirror of the natural world. The erotic element is marked from the start, in the polarity of a male sun and a feminine shape, eye or well, which is said to

> bend her
> Head under the dark boughs, till like a willow
> Her fair hair swept the bosom of the stream
> That whispered with delight to be their pillow.
> (ll. 363–66)

Shelley's imagery, often assumed to be incoherent and erratic, is instead extraordinarily systematic whenever light is being thematized. The passage condenses all that earlier and later poets (one can think of Valéry and Gide's Narcissus, as well as of the *Roman de la Rose* or of Spenser) ever did with light, water, and mirrors. It also bears witness to the affinity of his imagination with that of Rousseau, who allowed the phantasm of language born rhapsodically out of an erotic well to tell its story before he took it all away. Shelley's treatment of the birth of light reveals all that is invested in the emblem of the rainbow. It represents the very possibility of cognition, even for processes of articulation so elementary that it would be impossible to conceive of any principle of organization, however primitive, that would not be entirely dependent on its power. To efface it would be to take away the sun which, if it were to happen to this text, for example, would leave little else. *And still,* this light is allowed to exist in *The Triumph of Life* only under the most tenuous of conditions.

The frailty of the stance is represented in the supernatural delicacy which gives the shape "palms so tender / Their tread broke not the mirror of [the river's] billow" and which allows it to "glide along the river." The entire scene is set up as a barely imaginable balance between this gliding motion, which remains on one side of the watery surface and thus allows the specular image to come into being, and the contrary motion which, like Narcissus at the end of the mythical story, breaks through the surface of the mirror and disrupts the suspended fall of its own existence. As the passage develops, the story must run its course. The contradictory motions of "gliding" and "treading" which suspended gravity between rising and falling finally capsize. The "threading" sunrays become the "treading" of feet upon a surface which, in this text, does not stiffen into solidity. Shelley's poem insists on the hyperbolic lightness of the reflexive contact, since the reflecting surface is never allowed the smooth stasis that is necessary to the duplication of the image. The water is kept in constant motion: it is called a "billow" and the surface, although compared to a crystal, is roughened by the winds that give some degree of verisimilitude to the shape's gliding motion. By the end of the section, we have moved from "thread" to "tread" to "trample," in a movement of increased violence that erases the initial tenderness. There is no doubt that, when we again meet the shape (ll. 425 ff.) it is no longer gliding along the river but drowned, Ophelia-like, below the surface of the water. The violence is confirmed in the return of the rainbow, in the ensuing vision, as a rigid, stony arch said "fiercely [to extoll] the fortune" of the shape's defeat by what the poem calls "life."

This chain of metaphorical transformations can be understood, up to this point, without transposition into a vocabulary that would not be that of their own referents, not unlike the movement of the figure itself as it endeavors to glide incessantly along a surface which it tries to keep intact. Specifically, the figure of the rainbow is a figure of the unity of perception and cognition undisturbed by the possibly disruptive mediation of its own figuration. This is not surprising, since the underlying assumption of such a paraphrastic reading is itself one of specular understanding in which the text serves as a mirror of our own knowledge and our knowledge mirrors in its turn the text's signification. But we can only inadequately understand in this fashion why the shaped light of understanding is itself allowed to wane away, layer by layer, until it is entirely forgotten and remains present only in the guise of an edifice that serves to celebrate and to perpetuate its oblivion. Nor can we understand the power that weighs down the seductive grace of figuration until it destroys itself. The figure of the sun, with all its chain of correlatives, should also be read in a non-phenomenal way, a necessity which is itself phenomenally represented in the dramatic tension of the text.

The transition from "gliding" to "trampling" passes, in the action that is being narrated, through the intermediate relay of "measure." The term actively reintroduces music which, after having been stressed in the previous scene (ll. 354–55), is at first only present by analogy in this phase of the action (ll. 359–74). Measure is articulated sound, that is to say language. Language rather than music, in the traditional sense of harmony and melody. As melody, the "song" of the water and, by extension, the various sounds of nature, only provide a background that easily blends with the seduction of the natural world:

. . . all the place

Was filled with many sounds woven into one
Oblivious melody, confusing sense
Amid the gliding waves and shadows dun; . . .
(ll. 339–42)

As melody and harmony, song belongs to the same gliding motion that is interrupted only when the shape's feet

> to the ceaseless song
>
> Of leaves and winds and waves and birds and bees
> And falling drops moved in a measure new. . . .
>
> (ll. 375–77)

The "tread" of this dancer, which needs a ground to the extent that it carries the weight of gravity, is no longer melodious, but reduces music to the mere measure of repeated articulations. It singles out from music the accentual or tonal punctuation which is also present in spoken diction. The scene could be said to narrate the birth of music out of the spirit of language, since the determining property is an articulation distinctive of verbal sound prior to its signifying function. The thematization of language in *The Triumph of Life* occurs at this point, when "measure" separates from the phenomenal aspects of signification as a specular *representation*, and stresses instead the literal and material aspects of language. In the dramatic action of the narrative, measure disrupts the symmetry of cognition as representation (the figure of the rainbow, of the eye and of the sun). But since measure is any principle of linguistic organization, not only as rhyme and meter but as any syntactical or grammatical scansion, one can read "feet" not just as the poetic meter that is so conspicuously evident in the *terza rima* of the poem, but as any principle of signification. Yet it is precisely these "feet" which extinguish and bury the poetic and philosophical light.

It is tempting to interpret this event, the shape's "trampling" the fires of thought "into the dust of death" (l. 388), certainly the most enigmatic moment in the poem, as the bifurcation between the semantic and the non-signifying, material properties of language. The various devices of articulation, from word to sentence formation (by means of grammar, syntax, accentuation, tone, etc.), which are made to convey meaning, and these same articulations left to themselves, independently of their signifying constraints, do not necessarily determine each other. The latent polarity implied in all classical theories of the sign allows for the relative independence of the signifier and for its free play in relation to its signifying function. If, for instance, compelling rhyme schemes such as "billow," "willow," "pillow" or transformations such as "thread" to "tread" or "seed" to "deed" occur at crucial moments in the text, then the question arises whether these particularly meaningful movements or events are not being generated by random and superficial properties of the signifier rather than by the constraints of meaning. The obliteration of thought by "measure" would then have to be interpreted as the loss of semantic depth and its replacement by what Mallarmé calls "*le hasard infini des conjonctions*" (*Igitur*).

But this is not the story, or not the entire story, told by *The Triumph of Life.* For the arbitrary element in the alignment between meaning and linguistic articulation does not by itself have the power to break down the specular structure which the text erects and then claims to dissolve. It does not account for the final phase of the Narcissus story, as the shape traverses the mirror and goes under, just as the stars are conquered by the sun at the beginning of the poem and the sun then conquered in its turn by the light of the Chariot of Life. The undoing of the representational and iconic function of figuration by the play of the signifier does not suffice to bring about the disfiguration which *The Triumph of Life* acts out or represents. For it is the alignment of a signification with any principle of linguistic articulation whatsoever, sensory or not, which constitutes the figure. The iconic, sensory or, if one wishes, the aesthetic moment is not constitutive of figuration. Figuration is the element in language that allows for the reiteration of meaning by substitution; the process is at least twofold and this plurality is naturally illustrated by optical icons of specularity. But the particular seduction of the figure is not necessarily that it creates an illusion of sensory pleasure, but that it creates an illusion of meaning. In Shelley's poem, the shape is a figure regardless of whether it appears as a figure of light (the rainbow) or of articulation in general (music as measure and language). The transition from pleasure to signification, from the aesthetic to the semiological dimension, is clearly marked in the passage, as one moves from the figure of the rainbow to that of the dance, from sight to measure. It marks the identification of the shape as the model of figuration in general. By taking this step beyond the traditional conceptions of figuration as modes of representation, as polarities of subject and object, of part and whole, of necessity and chance or of sun and eye, the way is prepared for the subsequent undoing and erasure of the figure. But the extension, which coincides with the passage from tropological models such as metaphor, synecdoche, metalepsis, or prosopopoeia (in which a phenomenal element, spatial or temporal, is necessarily involved) to tropes such as grammar and syntax (which function on the level of the letter without the intervention of an iconic factor) is not by itself capable of erasing the figure or, in the representational code of the text, of drowning the shape or trampling out throught. Another intervention, another aspect of language has to come into play.

The narrative sequence of Rousseau's encounter, as it unfolds from the apparition of the shape (l. 343) to its replacement (l. 434) by a "new vision," follows a motion framed by two events that are acts of power: the sun overcoming the light of the stars, the light of life overcoming the sun. The movement from a punctual action, determined in time by a violent act of power, to the gliding, suspended motion "of that shape which on the stream / Moved, as I moved along the wilderness" (ll. 425–26) is the same motion inherent in the title of the poem. As has been pointed out by several commentators, "triumph" designates the actual victory as well as the *trionfo*, the pageant that celebrates the outcome of the battle. The reading of the scene should allow for a more general interpretation of this contradictory motion.

We now understand the shape to be the figure for the figurality of all signification. The specular structure of the scene as a visual plot of light and water is not the determining factor but merely an illustration (*hypotyposis*) of a plural structure that involves natural entities only as principles of articulation among others. It follows that the figure is not naturally given or produced but that it is posited by an arbitrary act of language. The appearance and the waning of the light-shape, in spite of the solar analogon, is not a natural event resulting from the mediated interaction of several powers, but a single, and therefore violent, act of power achieved by the positional power of language considered by and in itself: the sun masters the stars because it *posits* forms, just as "life" subsequently masters the sun because it posits, by inscription, the "track" of historical events. The positing power does not reside in Rousseau as subject; the mastery of the shape over Rousseau is never in question. He rises and bends at her command and his mind is passively trampled into dust without resistance. The positing power of language is both entirely arbitrary, in having a strength that cannot be reduced to necessity, and entirely inexorable in that there is no alternative to it. It stands beyond the polarities of chance and determination and can therefore not be part of a temporal sequence of events. The sequence has to be punctured by acts that cannot be made a part of it. It cannot begin, for example, by telling us of the waning of the stars under the growing impact of the sun, a natural motion which is the outcome of a mediation, but it must evoke the violent "springing forth" of a sun detached from all antecedents. Only retrospectively can this event be seen and misunderstood as a substitution and a beginning, as a dialectical relationship between day and night, or between two transcendental orders of being. The sun does not appear in conjunction with or in reaction to the night and the stars, but of its own unrelated power. *The Triumph of Life* differs entirely from such Promethean or titanic myths as Keats's *Hyperion* or even *Paradise Lost* which thrive on the agonistic pathos of dialectical battle. It is unimaginable that Shelley's non-epic, non-religious poem would begin by elegiacally or rebelliously evoking the tragic defeat of the former gods, the stars, at the hands of the sun. The text has no room for the tragedy of defeat or of victory among next-of-kin, or among gods and men. The previous occupants of the narrative space are expelled by decree, by the sheer power of utterance, and consequently at once forgotten. In the vocabulary of the poem, it occurs by *imposition* (l. 20), the emphatic mode of positing. This compresses the prosopopoeia of the personified sun, in the first lines of the poem, into a curiously absurd pseudo-description. The most continuous and gradual event in nature, the subtle gradations of the dawn, is collapsed into the brusque swiftness of a single moment:

> Swift as a spirit hastening to his task
> . . . the Sun sprang forth
> . . . and the mask
>
> Of darkness fell from the awakened Earth.
>
> (ll. 1–4)

The appearances, later in the poem, of the Chariot of Life are equally brusque and unmotivated. When they occur, they are not "descendants" of the sun, not the natural continuation of the original, positing gesture but positings in their own right. Unlike night following day, they always again have to be posited, which explains why they are repetitions and not beginnings.

How can a positional act, which relates to nothing that comes before or after, become inscribed in a sequential narrative? How does a speech act become a trope, a catachresis which then engenders in its turn the narrative sequence of an allegory? It can only be because we impose, in our turn, on the senseless power of positional language the authority of sense and of meaning. But this is radically inconsistent: language posits and language means (since it articulates) but language cannot posit meaning; it can only reiterate (or reflect) it in its reconfirmed falsehood. Nor does the knowledge of this impossibility make it less impossible. This impossible position is precisely the figure, the trope, metaphor as a violent—and not as a dark—light, a deadly Apollo.

The imposition of meaning occurs in *The Triumph of Life* in the form of the questions that served as point of departure for the reading. It is as a questioning entity, standing within the pathos of its own indetermination, that the human subject appears in the text, in the figures of the narrator who interrogates Rousseau and of Rousseau who interrogates the shape. But these figures do not coincide with the voice that narrates the poem in which they are represented; this voice does not question and does not share in their predicament. We can therefore not ask why it is that we, as subjects, choose to impose meaning, since we are ourselves defined by this very question. From the moment the subject thus asks, it has already foreclosed any alternative and has become the figural token of meaning, *"Ein Zeichen sind wir / Deutungslos . . ."* (Hölderlin). To question is to forget. Considered performatively, figuration (as question) performs the erasure of the positing power of language. In *The Triumph of Life*, this happens when a positional speech act is represented as what it resembles least of all, a sunrise.

To forget, in this poem, is by no means a passive process. In the Rousseau episode, things happen because the subject Rousseau keeps forgetting. In his earliest stages, he forgets the incoherence of a world in which events occur by sheer dint of a blind force, in the same way that the sun, in the opening lines, occurs by sheer imposition. The episode describes the emergence of an articulated language of cognition by the erasure, the forgetting of the events this language in fact performed. It culminates in the appearance of the shape, which is both a figure of specular self-knowledge, the figure of thought, but also a figure of "thought's empire over thought," of the element in thought that destroys thought in its attempt to forget its duplicity. For the initial violence of position can only be half erased, since the erasure is accomplished by a device of language that never ceases to partake of the very violence against which it is directed. It seems to extend the instantaneousness of the act of positing over a series of transformations, but this duration is a fictitious state, in which "all . . . seemed as if it had been not" (l. 385). The trampling gesture enacts the necessary recurrence of the initial violence: a figure of thought, the very light of cognition, obliterates thought. At its apparent beginning as well as at its apparent end, thought (i.e., figuration) forgets what it thinks and cannot do otherwise if it is to maintain itself. Each of the episodes forgets the knowledge achieved by the forgetting that precedes it, just as the instantaneous sunrise of the opening scene is at once covered over by a "strange trance" which allows the narrator to imagine the scene as something remembered even before it could take place. Positing "glimmers" into a glimmering knowledge that acts out the aporias of signification and of performance.

The repetitive erasures by which language performs the erasure of its own positions can be called disfiguration. The disfiguration of Rousseau is enacted in the text, in the scene of the root, and repeats itself in a more general mode in the disfiguration of the shape:

> . . . The fair shape waned in the coming light
> As veil by veil the silent splendour drops
> From Lucifer, amid the chrysolite
>
> Of sunrise ere it strike the mountain tops—
> (ll. 412–15)

Lucifer, or metaphor, the bearer of light which carries over the light of the senses and of cognition from events and entities to their meaning, irrevocably loses the contour of its own face or shape. We see it happen when the figure first appears as water music, then as rainbow, then as measure, to finally sink away "below the watery floor" trampled to death by its own power. Unlike Lycidas, it is not resurrected in the guise of a star, but repeated on a level of literality which is not that of meaning but of actual events, called "Life" in Shelley's poem. But "Life" is as little the end of figuration as the sunrise was its beginning. For just as language is misrepresented as a natural event, life is just as falsely represented by the same light that emanates from the sun and that will have to engender its own rainbow and measure. Only that this light destroys its previous representation as the wolf destroys the deer. The process is endless, since the knowledge of the language's performative power is itself a figure in its own right and, as such, bound to repeat the disfiguration of metaphor as Shelley is bound to repeat the aberration of Rousseau in what appears to be a more violent mode. Which also implies, by the same token, that he is bound to forget him, just as, in all rigor, *The Social Contract* can be said to erase *Julie* from the canon of Rousseau's works, or *The Triumph of Life* can be said to reduce all of Shelley's previous work to nought.

The persistence of light imagery, in the description of the Chariot of Life as well as in the inaugural sunrise, creates the illusion of a continuity and makes the knowledge of its interruption serve as a ruse to efface its actual occurrence. The poem is sheltered from the performance of disfiguration by the power of its negative knowledge. But this knowledge is powerless to prevent what now functions as the decisive textual articulation: its reduction to the status of a fragment brought about by the actual death and subsequent disfigurement of Shelley's body, burned after his boat capsized and he drowned off the coast of Lerici. This defaced body is present in the margin of the last manuscript page and has become an inseparable part of the poem. At this point, figuration and cognition are actually interrupted by an event which shapes the text but which is not present in its represented or articulated meaning. It may seem a freak of chance to have a text thus molded by an actual occurence, yet the reading of *The Triumph of Life* establishes that this mutilated textual model exposes the wound of a fracture that lies hidden in all texts. If anything, this text is more rather than less typical than texts that have not been thus truncated. The rhythmical interruptions that mark off the successive episodes of the narrative are not new moments of cognition but literal events textually reinscribed by a delusive act of figuration or of forgetting.

In Shelley's absence, the task of thus reinscribing the disfiguration now devolves entirely on the reader. The final test of reading, in *The Triumph of Life*, depends on how one reads the textuality of this event, how one disposes of Shelley's body. The challenge that is in fact present in all texts and that *The Triumph of Life* identifies, thematizes, and thus tries to avoid in the most effective way possible, is here actually carried out as the sequence of symbolic interruptions is in its turn interrupted by an event that is no longer simply imaginary or symbolic. The apparent ease with which readers of *The Triumph of Life* have been able to dispose of this challenge demonstrates the inadequacy of our understanding of Shelley and, beyond him, of romanticism in general.

For what we have done with the dead Shelley, and with all the other dead bodies that appear in romantic literature—one thinks, among many others, of the "dead man" that " 'mid that beauteous scene / Of trees, and hills and water, bolt upright / Rose with his ghastly face; . . ." in Wordsworth's *Prelude* (V.470–72)—is simply to bury them, to bury them in their own texts made into epitaphs and monumental graves. They have been made into statues for the benefit of future archeologists "digging in the grounds for the new foundations" of their own monuments. They have been transformed into historical and aesthetic objects. There are various and subtle strategies, much too numerous to enumerate, to accomplish this.

Such monumentalization is by no means necessarily a naive or evasive gesture, and it certainly is not a gesture that anyone can pretend to avoid making. It does not have to be naive, since it does not have to be the repression of a self-threatening knowledge. Like *The Triumph of Life*, it can state the full power of this threat in all its negativity; the poem demonstrates that this rigor does not prevent Shelley from allegorizing his own negative assurance, thus awakening the suspicion that the negation is a *Verneinung*, an intended exorcism. And it is not avoidable, since the failure to exorcize the threat, even in the face of such evidence as the radical blockage that befalls this poem, becomes precisely the challenge to understanding that always again demands to be read. And to read is to understand, to question, to know, to forget, to erase, to deface, to repeat—that is to say, the endless prosopopoeia by which the dead are made to have a face and a voice which tells the allegory of their demise and allows us to apostrophize them in our turn. No degree of knowledge can ever stop this madness, for it is the madness of words. What *would* be naive is to believe that this strategy, which is not *our* strategy as subjects, since we are its product rather than its agent, can be a source of value and has to be celebrated or denounced accordingly.

Whenever this belief occurs—and it occurs all the time—it leads to a misreading that can and should be discarded, unlike the coercive "forgetting" that Shelley's poem analytically thematizes and that stands beyond good and evil. It would be of little use to enumerate and categorize the various forms and names which this belief takes on in our present critical and literary scene. It functions along monotonously predictable lines, by the historicization and the aesthetification of texts, as well as by their use, as in this essay, for the assertion of methodological claims made all the more pious by their denial of piety. Attempts to define, to understand, or to circumscribe romanticism in relation to ourselves and in relation to other literary movements are all part of this naive belief. *The Triumph of Life* warns us that nothing, whether deed, word, thought, or text, ever happens in relation, positive or negative, to anything that precedes, follows, or exists elsewhere, but only as a random event whose power, like the power of death, is due to the randomness of its occurrence. It also warns us why and how these events then have to be reintegrated in a historical and aesthetic system of recuperation that repeats itself regardless of the exposure of its fallacy. This process differs entirely from the recuperative and nihilistic allegories of historicism. If it is true and unavoidable that any reading is a monumentalization of sorts, the way in which Rousseau is read and disfigured in *The Triumph of Life* puts Shelley among the few readers who "guessed whose statue those fragments had composed." Reading as disfiguration, to the very extent that it resists historicism, turns out to be historically more reliable than the products of historical archeology. To monumentalize this observation into a *method* of reading would be to regress from the rigor exhibited by Shelley which is exemplary precisely because it refuses to be generalized into a system.

JEAN HALL

"Adonais"

Like *Epipsychidion*, *Adonais* consists of three transformational sections: stanzas I through XVII, in which the mourning poet sees the entire world as a decaying material hulk; stanzas XVIII through XXXV, in which the world seems to him split into the eternally self-sustaining cycle of natural process and its opposite, the finite linear career of the human spirit; and stanzas XXXVI through LV, in which the world is again seen whole, this time as a material body capable of redemption by the imagination.

Although Wasserman gives a similar structural description of the poem, his emphasis upon the configuration of images in *Adonais*, which he sees striving toward the "most nearly perfect order of which they are capable," creates the impression that the poem is writing itself. But the various world-views expressed in *Adonais* come from a completely interested and personal viewpoint: the perspective of the poem's speaker, who is contemplating his dead comrade's body, repeatedly sees the entire world transformed into the image of that body—a transformation which becomes at once a statement of the human condition and a forecast of his own future.

Shelley finds precedent for this fascination with the corpse in one of the two classical pastoral elegies he used as models for his poem, Bion's "Lament for Adonis." That poem luxuriates in the death of Adonis, again and again showing how "round his navel was floating dark blood: crimson from his thighs grew his chest, and purple beneath it Adonis' breasts that once were snowy," and granting "Adonis, a dead body now," the bed of

From *The Transforming Image: A Study of Shelley's Major Poetry.* Copyright © 1980 by the Board of Trustees of the University of Illinois. University of Illinois Press, 1980.

his goddess lover because "Fair even in death is he . . . Lay him down in the soft coverlets wherein he used to rest when through the night he wrought with thee in holy sleep." In section one of *Adonais* this eroticism of death is transformed by Shelley into a horror of death and of dead bodies. By a principle of antipathy the corpse becomes the focal point of the speaker's world, which against his wishes invades everything he sees and transforms all into images of deathliness. Although this is an inversion of the last world of *Epipsychidion*, where the lovers' bodies become the sympathetic "type and expression" of a world of ideal love, the governing principle of the two poems is the same: man's perception of his world depends upon possible transformational relationships between the human body and the world's body.

The dead Adonais was not only a human being but also a poet, as is the speaker who mourns him. Therefore another body, the body of poetry, enters into the symbolic complex of *Adonais*. In this connection, Shelley transforms the myth of Venus and Adonis that figures in the classical elegies which are his poetic models. The goddess who mourns his Adonais becomes the dead poet's mother rather than his lover, and her name becomes Urania rather than Venus because she is the muse of poetry. That her transformation from lover to mother is related to her identification with poetry is a revealing clue to the speaker's general idea of the poetic enterprise. In section one of *Adonais* the body of poetry is seen as ideally being a kind of protection, a deserved parental nurturing, for young poets—who, unlike the imaginative lover of *Epipsychidion*, presumably are not yet ready to assume adult roles. The reproachful speaker asks Urania, "Where wert thou, mighty Mother, when he lay . . . pierced by the shaft which flies/ In darkness?" (9–11). This is the answer he imagines:

> With veilèd eyes,
> 'Mid listening Echoes, in her Paradise
> She sate, while one, with soft enamoured breath,
> Rekindled all the fading melodies,
> With which, like flowers that mock the corse beneath,
> He had adorned and hid the coming bulk of Death.
> (13–18)

Unlike the island paradise in *Epipsychidion*, which is the imagination's bold and sophisticated transformation of reality, Urania's Paradise is a refuge from reality, a poetical retreat wherein the Mother herself is mothered by the false consolations of a decorative poetry. The songs of this Paradise are "like flowers that mock the corse beneath," for they "adorned and hid the coming bulk of Death."

Apparently, then, at this level poetry is an ornate creation of surfaces—a verbal cosmetic designed to conceal horror. Once we see this, it becomes evident that section one of *Adonais* is just that kind of poem. The elaborate pathetic fallacy of this section—nature's fulsome weeping and mourning—what does it accomplish but to delay the inevitable moment when death must be recognized? The poet invites us to Adonais' bier because we must see the body "while still/ He lies, as if in dewy sleep he lay" (60–61), as though the false appearance of life were a consolation. Morning's tears "Dimmed the aëreal eyes that kindle day" (123), and "Grief made the young Spring wild, and she threw down / Her kindling buds, as if she Autumn were" (136–37), paralyzing time, with the ambivalent result that Adonais' corpse remains freshly preserved but completely lifeless. The temporal texture of section one suggests that poetry creates a false eternity or paradise which we cling to for agonizing comfort as long as we possibly can.

But our grasp inevitably must fail; for ornate poetic formulas are an unsatisfactory substitute for the true body of poetry, which for the speaker of section one is the body of the poet himself. This becomes clear when Adonais' Splendours, "The quick Dreams,/ The passion-wingèd Ministers of thought,/ Who were his flocks" (73–75), pay a memorial visit to his bier. Shelley's friend John Taafe pointed out in his annotations of *Adonais* that the term "Splendour" comes from Dante and signifies "any kind of immaterial substance." These Splendours surround the body, and as one kneels to kiss its mouth, "the damp death / Quenched its caress upon his icy lips," making the Splendour "pass to its eclipse" (104–8). The spiritual fire of the poet's creation is absorbed by the damp body of his death, suggesting that the life of poetry can last only as long as the life of its poet. This explains why time has stopped in section one of *Adonais*: the speaker, himself a poet, grieves not only for Adonais' death but also for his own. He creates an artificial poetic eternity not only to preserve Adonais' corpse, but to prolong his own life and song. But he achieves this result at the cost of sorrow. His lyric world necessarily must be an eternity of grief, forever paralyzed by the sense of his past loss and the dread of his future death.

Just as the uncontrolled lyric flight in the first section of *Epipsychidion* involved the creation of a void which destroyed the singer's efforts and forced him to transform his song into another form, so also this ambivalent poetic eternity of *Adonais* at length must disintegrate, compelling this poet to seek new consolations. In *Adonais*, the simple progression of natural time accomplishes this. At the beginning of section two we find that "Winter is come and gone,/ But grief returns with the revolving year"

(154–55). Presumably then, a year has passed since the grieving Spring of section one threw down her buds; although the poet still stands by Adonais' bier, by this time the corpse has been decently interred and the earth over it is covered with new flowers.

As the poet knows, this yearly natural cycle, which grants Adonais a rebirth in the form of the flowers on his grave, would comprise such poetic consolation as seems possible for the classical elegist whose form he is following. In Bion's "Lament for Adonis," Cytherea's tears mingle with Adonis' blood and both "are turned to flowers; of the blood are roses born, and of the tears anemones." But the poem's last statement is, "Cease thy laments, today Cytherea; stay thy dirges. Again must thou lament, again must thou weep another year." The elegy so ends because this kind of transformation—man into flower—offers not so much the consolations of immortality as the eternally recurring memory of grief. Although the flower may remind Cytherea of her slain lover, the flower is not itself the man, and indeed, serves only to vividly recall her loss.

So the cyclical resolution of the classical elegy is not really very different from the artificial poetic eternity of *Adonais'* section one. Although the one is an unnatural prolongation of time and the other is a submission to the seasonal recurrences of natural time, both serve to perpetuate grief: one kind of time preserves a corpse and the other kind creates a memorial flower, but neither can re-create the lost unique human being. As Moschus says, in his "Lament for Bion": "Alas, when in the garden wither the mallows, the green celery, and the luxuriant curled anise, they live again thereafter and spring up another year, but we men, we that are tall and strong, we that are wise, when once we die, unhearing sleep in the hollow earth, a long sleep without end or wakening." In section two of *Adonais* the speaker concurs with Moschus. Himself bathed in the vitality of spring, he sees that Adonais' "leprous corpse, touched by this spirit tender,/ Exhales itself in flowers of gentle breath" (172–73). Such exhalation pointedly is not the breath of the man's life. The organic tenderness of spring produces the loves and births of cylical vitality, but this creation is based upon the previous winter's deaths. The flowers grow out of humus; their superficial beauty is nourished by the deep horror of "The leprous corpse." Nature's creations in section two are really not so different from poetry's creations in section one: there the decorative veneer of poetry, "like flowers that mock the corse beneath,/ . . . adorned and hid the coming bulk of death"; here, actual flowers "illumine death / And mock the merry worm that wakes beneath" (175–76).

Just as the distinction between the eternal cycles of nature and this artificial eternity of poetry turns out to be a distinction without a real difference, so the Urania of section two, who is unlike the paradise-dwelling Urania of section one because she comes out into the world and is bound to natural time's cycle, turns out to be a new Urania only insignificantly different from the old. As she cries to her dead poet, "I would give/ All that I am to be as thou now art!/ But I am chained to Time, and cannot thence depart!" (232–34). Because she is chained to natural time, this Urania tends to take a cyclical view of poetry. She thinks of poets as timebound beings who attain full power only by developing through their "full cycle" and spiritually filling their "crescent sphere" (241–42). There is a moment of optimum greatness for poetry, then, and that is during the mature phase of poets' lives.

In describing the nature of this greatness, Urania draws upon the part of the Venus and Adonis myth that portrays Adonis as an unseasoned hunter killed by the boar he stalks. For her the poet's art is analogous to the hunter's, and so Adonais was killed by prematurely daring "the unpastured dragon in his den" (238)—by speaking out freely before he had strength to cope with the inevitably ensuing attacks. Her best advice to the dead poet is that he should have exercised greater caution, should have restrained his blow, until his powers filled their "crescent sphere." The prudent preservation of life, rather than the creation of poetry, is Urania's first concern. This follows from her view of time, to which she is chained and from which she cannot depart. For if the natural cycle of life is all there is, then at any cost we must maximize the time nature grants us. This is a strategy doomed to ultimate failure, however, for the simple reason that eventually everyone must die. Like the paradise-enchanted Urania of section one, the prudent Urania of section two at best only can delay death for a time. Even her powerful mature poets, those capable of daring dragons, are "godlike mind[s]" soaring forth like the sun, "in [their] delight / Making earth bare and veiling heaven," only to sink at last below the evening horizon, abandoning the living to "the spirit's awful night" (258–61). Because Urania knows that her poetry is an artifice that only temporarily delays the inevitable, her world is suffused with the same qualities of grief and dread as the world of section one. These poems do manage a kind of lyric life, but inevitably, it is a life of pain.

To this point, then, Adonais has created two worlds that turn out to offer distinctions bereft of real difference. At every turn the poet's maneuverings for a new vision, a new possibility of freedom, have been cancelled by the ubiquitous presence of death. He has envisioned two variations of nature, two Uranias, and two processions of mourners beside Adonais' bier—the Splendours in section one, and now the company of Adonais' fellow poets in section two. If the poem were to run true to its previous form, these new mourners should be an insignificant variation upon the previous group.

Instead, the poet here at last finds his opening to freedom. Somewhat apart from the other mourners he sees a "Stranger" (303) who turns out to be—himself. This self-portrait often has been considered a piece of unforgivably indulgent self-pity. But if we place it within the context of the dramatic lyric, it becomes evident that this is a transforming image which permits self-examination. The image functions as do the transforming images of Jupiter and Christ encountered by Prometheus: it is the poet's self, but made into a stranger whom he must confront. It is clothed as a hunter and a devotee of Dionysus, whose animal is that "pardlike Spirit" the leopard, and whose followers carry the thyrsus, a "light spear topped with a cypress cone" (280, 291). Here is appropriate dress for section two of *Adonais*, in which poetic genius seems equivalent to the strength of life's prime, and the making of poetry involves the hunting of one's foes. But it seems that to be a hunter has deranged this particular poet. Like the frenzied followers of Dionysus, his passions have possessed him. He is like Actaeon; for having "gazed on Nature's naked loveliness" and been driven mad, he wanders "With feeble steps o'er the world's wilderness,/ And his own thoughts, along that rugged way,/ Pursued, like raging hounds, their father and their prey" (275–79). It is the story of the *Alastor* Poet again. This wandering "Stranger" is a stranger to himself because he is his own destroyer. At once, he plays the roles of pursuer and pursued, hunter and quarry.

This is the classic Shelleyan poetic pathology, and as in *Prometheus Unbound*, *Adonais* shows this condition to be rooted in unexamined aggressive impulses. When Prometheus cursed Jupiter he also indirectly cursed himself, creating his own proper world of hatred. Likewise, in hating the attackers of Adonais, this hunter-poet has created a world in which poetry is used aggressively, to overpower its detractors—at least that is the intention. But in fact, the poet's aggressions have overcome himself, leading to the weakness and depression evident everywhere in the first two worlds of *Adonais*. This Stranger's "ensanguined brow" bears marks "like Cain's or Christ's" (306), just as Prometheus became by turns the images of Jupiter and Christ, because both Prometheus and the poet of *Adonais* are at once the murderer and the murdered, the crucifier and the crucified— their bodies are the worlds within which their aggression is both meted out and suffered. The poet inhabits a world of death not really because of Adonais' death, but because he has been one "Who in another's fate . . . wept his own" (300). The attacks on Adonais' poetry have mattered less to him than the attacks on his own, and his response has been a rage that indirectly has polluted his soul.

In stanza XXXVII he abandons his attack upon the critics, leaving them to inhabit the worlds they create for themselves, which in his opinion, is a just and entirely ample punishment: "be thyself and know thyself to be!" Adonais' critic remains in the cyclical world of section two, a viper whose venom overflows "ever at thy season," creating a "Remorse and Self-contempt" which "shall cling to thee." The self-inflicted poisoning suffered by the poet of section two is left for the critic, while the poet himself goes on to better things. He copes with his aggression by transforming its energy into a new form. In the new poem he creates in section three of Adonais, the emotional power previously devoted to hatred and dread is converted into an expression of imaginative joy.

This is the turning point of Adonais. Hitherto, the transforming image dominating the poem has been the body of death; but by encountering himself as a stranger, the poet has discovered that this body of death was not Adonais but himself. It is "We" who "decay/ Like corpses in a charnel" (348) when we live a life of hatred. The surprise of Epipsychidion was that the real transforming image of the poem was not Emily but the divine sexual body of her poet; similarly, the surprise of Adonais is that the poet has created his own world of death and therefore equally well could create his own world of immortality. All this is within his power because the world he sees is a transformation of his own image, his own body. In section three of Adonais the poetic energies that hitherto had been turned morbidly inward will be radiated outward by the changed poet. He is freed to live, to feel joy, to sing.

But his immortal world is not to be construed literally. After all, Adonais is a poem of immortality written by an atheist; we must be careful in specifying the nature of its affirmations. Shelley's remarks about death and immortality in the Essay on Christianity provide clarification. This essay depicts Christ as a poet who created a liberal imaginative vision of life and death to counter the narrow view that "Men shall die and their bodies shall rot under the ground. . . . There is a time when we shall neither hear nor see, neither be heard or be seen by the multitude of beings like ourselves by whom we have been so long surrounded. . . . It appears that we moulder to a heap of senseless dust, a few worms that arise and perish like ourselves" (VI, 235). This picture of the leprous corpse, so strikingly similar to the views of the first two sections of Adonais, and like them, the product of a "gloomy and cold imagination," is countered by Christ's poetic vision of a future wherein "Another and a more extensive state of being, rather than the complete extinction of being, will follow from that mysterious change which we call death. . . . The unobscured irradiations from the fountain-fire of all goodness shall reveal all that is mysterious and unintelligible until the mutual communications of knowledge and of happiness throughout all thinking natures constitute a harmony of good that never varies and never ends. This is Heaven, when pain and evil cease, and when the benignant principle unt[rammel]led and uncontrolled, visits in the fulness of its power the universal frame of things" (VI, 235–36). Shelley's reaction to these images (which, as we shall see, anticipate the imagery of section three of *Adonais*) is of great interest: "How delightful a picture even if it be not true! How magnificent & illustrious is the conception which this bold theory suggests to the contemplation, even if it be no more than the imagination of some sublimest and most holy poet, who impressed with the loveliness and majesty of his own nature, is impatient and discontented, with the narrow limits which this imperfect life and the dark grave have assigned for ever as his melancholy portion" (VI, 236). Apparently, Shelley does not quite cease to believe in the leprous corpse; instead, he denies it. The limits of mortality are narrow, and he thinks it well to replace them with the expansiveness of the imagination. If on the one hand we know that death does set our limits, on the other, if we have experienced imaginative joy, we know it to be equally true that the human spirit can have its moments of infinity.

Consequently, section three of *Adonais* aims at giving both the singer and the reader the *experience* of imaginative expansiveness, which will constitute the immortality of this poem. The poem affirms not an objective truth, but an action—the act of imaginative creation. This explains why it is so much more moving than "The Sensitive Plant," Shelley's other major poem about death, which in the end expresses a wistful longing for immortality but is unable to imaginatively release an experience of deathless joy within the confines of the poem. As in *Epipsychidion, Adonais* finally acts out a completely poetic reality rather than making an impossible effort to reach some *Ding an sich* outside its own lyric universe. Here is not God's Heaven but "an Heaven of Song" (413). This self-created heaven can be ideal, for although it comes from the poet it also expands beyond him. It is simultaneously his own human creation and the immortal vision seen by his best imaginative self. The whole of *Adonais* enacts an ideal episode of self-development, beginning with the poet's fear of death and ending with his joyous creation of an imaginative immortality.

He begins by imaginatively embracing the world's body:

Who mourns for Adonais? Oh, come forth,
Fond wretch! and know thyself and him aright.
Clasp with thy panting soul the pendulous Earth;
As from a centre, dart thy spirit's light
Beyond all worlds, and until its spacious might
Satiate the void circumference

(415–20)

This echoes the poet's questions in section one ("I weep for Adonais . . . Where wert thou, mighty Mother?"); but instead of calling for Urania's help, here in section three he abandons dependence upon the goddess in order to become his own poet. Consequently, Urania vanishes from the poem—she is an authority no longer needed. As this passage suggests, the paradise created by this poet will not be the poetic retreat of section one, but the everyday world of life and death, transformed, irradiated, enlarged, into his own proper paradise. By clasping the earth he transforms it into a radiating center that darts spiritual light into the "void circumference," creating the fulfilled sphere of the imagination, the sovereign circle of the lyric. Like the island paradise of *Epipsychidion*, this is a realm in which the world and the human body remain themselves, but through imaginative redemption exhibit their ideal potential.

When he releases this world-creating joy the singer at last can see through the deathly "shadow of our night" (352) that hitherto has dominated his perceptions; without denying the presence of night, he sees that the black "void circumference" is irradiated by stars. To the redeemed imagination, each of these is a projective "centre," a testament of poetry. It is here that Adonais legitimately belongs, in a cluster inhabited by "the inheritors of unfulfilled renown" (397)—Chatterton, Sidney, Lucan— poets who died, as Urania would have said, before their "crescent sphere" was filled. As Shelley's translation of his epigraph from Plato runs,

Thou wert the morning star among the living,
    Ere thy fair light had fled;—
Now, having died, thou art as Hesperus, giving
    New splendour to the dead.

Adonais, the fading morning star, is one and the same as Adonais, the emerging star of evening. Here the cyclical universe of section two falls away to reveal eternity, which is a moment of poetic truth disclosed in the perception of its singer. The lyricist sees that Urania was wrong in believing that poets should remain prudently silent until their maturity. Age is irrelevant; the mission of the poet is fearlessly to sing of eternity whenever he sees it. Because this poet now does so, he can cease to mourn the early death of Adonais. Adonais was a true singer, and so there is no reason to regret his passing. It is not the length of the poet's life that matters; it is the way in which it has been lived. Furthermore, if the dead have sung well in life, the living will take up their song and continue it, which happens here. In this final section of *Adonais* the dead poet is reborn in the song of the living one.

This transmission of the poetic tradition, another version of that "great poem" discussed in the *Defence*, "which all poets, like the co-operating thoughts of one great mind, have built up since the beginning of the world," is embodied in this poet's song by a striking image. He sees that the aggregate of heaven's poetic stars forms a "burning fountain" whose fire shoots downward to the earth's core and crests there, only to reverse direction and flow upward to its source, carrying along with it whatever "pure spirit" (338–39) it encounters in the earth. Such a fire-fountain inverts the vector of earth's water-fountains; it follows that its processes poetically reverse the processes of earth's mortal decay. The poetic fire "Sweeps through the dull dense world" and resurfaces, in the process, "Torturing th' unwilling dross that checks its flight / To its own likeness" (382, 384–85). Things that grow out of the earth—"trees and beasts and men" (387)—become forms which reveal the transformations of the upward-stressing poetic fire. The unity of this fiery "one Spirit" (381) is not neoplatonic or theistic; it is the oneness of the imagination— the transformational power of the world's poets, living and dead. Once again, Shelley's heaven emerges as the heaven of culture, the collective mind of civilization. But this is not an object with a real existence; it is a faith rekindled and transmitted through the song of the living.

Within this heaven of culture that embraces the living and the dead, the body of Adonais at last may be seen aright. When the singer returns for the third time to the grave, what he is aware of is not the "leprous corpse" but "a slope of green access/ Where, like an infant's smile, over the dead / A light of laughing flowers along the grass is spread" (439–41). That consolation uneasily affirmed by the classical elegy—man's transformation into flower—finally is seen in the comprehensive cultural context which those elegies failed to provide. The laughing flowers are indeed Adonais because they are part of the poetic one Spirit that everywhere grows out of the earth and joyously bursts upward, imagina-tively redeeming the world's body.

This perception is expanded and enriched by the poet's vision of the environment surrounding Adonais' grave, which in his narrow concen-tration on the "leprous corpse" he never before had really appreciated. Adonais lies in the Protestant Cemetery in Rome, becoming the avatar of the imagination's empire who has invaded and possessed the very heart of the old Roman Empire. That was an empire of the world, chained to time and secured by mortal strength and mortal weapons—enjoying the very mortal power that in section two Urania wished for poetry. But time's cycles have destroyed Rome, which becomes "at once the Paradise,/ The grave, the city, and the wilderness" (433–34). This place simultaneously reveals the imaginative truth of worldly power's inevitable failure and culture's immortality, as does the landscape of "Ozymandias." The pyramid of Caius Cestius, champion of the Roman people, stands near Adonais' grave "Like flame transformed to marble" (437), eternally bursting upward into heaven's light and so becoming the one monument of decaying Rome that has the same imaginative vitality as the new Adonais-flowers. These champions of the spirit, old and new, "waged contention with their time's decay,/ And of the past are all that cannot pass away" (431–32).

But if culture transcends the human generations, still, the individual human being does not. That was the dual perception of "Ode to the West Wind," and the poet of *Adonais* also cannot avoid seeing it. In the last five stanzas of the poem he realizes that the heavenly "burning fountain" of poetry is countered by "the fountain of [his] mourning mind" (454). Break the seal of that mortal fountain, and the tears and bitterness of section one will return. His "Heaven of Song" may have a kind of permanence insofar as it is carried on by civilization, but he himself cannot indefinitely sustain a song of such rapture. As with the orgasmic conclusion of *Epipsychidion*, the all-out commitment of the individual's energy necessarily implies its eventual exhaustion. This poet knows that he cannot forever transform death into immortality; sooner or later his poetic rapture must dwindle, leaving his "mourning mind" again to confront the world of death.

As in *Epipsychidion*, when his rapture encounters its limits he must choose the mode of its dying. Is he now to conserve himself, or to go on? In terms of the moral insights of *Adonais*, conserving himself would be a regression because it would be a return to Uranian prudence—a valuing of mere longevity over imaginative immortality. The only authentic way for this poet to go is forward, to incandescently extinguish himself, to die of happiness. In choosing to so die the singer achieves the climax of his self-development, for he transcends the self-centeredness that has trammeled his vision in the first two sections of the poem, and dies in rapture, by reaching out unendurably beyond himself toward the starry Adonais. As in *Epipsychidion*, the climax of his poem also must be its death. However, both poems have demonstrated the paradox that a generous death may be the fullest form of life.

This ending has been seen as an unforgivable destruction of the poem. Indeed, it certainly is the suicide of the imagination. But the question is, could the poem end any other way? Is there really any other choice, given the assumptions of *Adonais*? Shelley shows his awareness of the question by the resemblance he suggests between the mortal waters of his poem and the waters of *Lycidas*. In Shelley's poem Milton is "third among the suns of light," a poetic sun still shining although he himself "went, unterrified,/ Into the gulf of death" (35–36), that same "amorous Deep" (25) into which the starlike Adonais also has sunk. This is reminiscent of the Miltonic "remorseless deep" that swallowed Lycidas. And the conclusion of Shelley's poem is both reminiscent of, and pointedly different from, the conclusion of Milton's. Here is the final fate of Lycidas:

> Weep no more, woeful Shepherds weep no more,
> For *Lycidas* your sorrow is not dead.
> Sunk though he be beneath the wat'ry floor,
> So sinks the day-star in the Ocean bed,
> And yet anon repairs his drooping head,
> And tricks his beams, and with new-spangled Ore,
> Flames in the forehead of the morning sky:
> So *Lycidas*, sunk low, but mounted high,
> Through the dear might of him that walk'd the waves,
> Where other groves, and other streams along,
> With Nectar pure his oozy Locks he laves,
> And hears the unexpressive nuptial Song,
> In the blest Kingdoms meek of joy and love.

Like the risen Adonais, the risen Lycidas is symbolized by the morning and evening star. But Milton handles this material in a way very different from Shelley's. The Miltonic method is paradoxical: Lycidas is "sunk low, but mounted high." This sense of paradox is necessary because the resolution of the conflict, which is God's, passes beyond our understanding and can be registered there only as a mystery. God's harmonies become our miracles; "the dear might of him that walk'd the waves" restores Lycidas from the remorseless deep, although the speaker never recovers Lycidas's body or actually sees the Heaven where Lycidas' soul dwells. His poetic attempts to imagine God's world finally must be transcended through his religious faith. Therefore this rustic swain ends by rising from his poetic isolation in order to return to the normal round of life—"Tomorrow to fresh Woods and Pastures new." He can leave his moment of grief to return refreshed to his own daily business because he is sustained by the faith that God also will be going about His.

But there is no God to support the poetic vision of *Adonais*. Just as *Epipsychidion* referred to Spenser and Dante as models, *Adonais* refers to

Lycidas; and in both cases, the Shelleyan poem creates a self-made lyrical world of the moment whereas the models exist within a Christian framework. In this perspective, the Shelleyan refusal either to hold back personal energy or to pretend that such energy can be infinite, emerges as a form of religious humility. This poet will not falsify the conditions of his being by pretending that his powers are the equivalent of God's. He has created a world of song, but that world is a transformation of life, not life itself. The poet may have godlike world-creating powers, but by accepting his own death at the poem's conclusion, he emphasizes that he is not literally God. He cannot create an eternal world; his utmost power is to create a poem that within its own terms contains everything because it implies its own beginning, development, and end. God's heaven is forever, but the poet's heaven is for the moment only; God creates reality, but the poet creates the fleeting experience of ecstasy. So poetry has both its transcendences and its limitations, and by insisting upon this, Shelley continues the feature of skeptical conclusions that figures prominently in his major poetry.

PAUL FRY

Shelley's "Defence of Poetry" in Our Time

There is no evidence that any of the major Romantics read Longinus at all carefully. Coleridge appears to have known him best, but even his judgment is perfunctory. Shelley's lone reference to Longinus vaguely supposes him to be hostile—like any other reviewer—to the free enterprise of poetry: "Poetry and the art which professes to regulate and limit its powers cannot subsist together. Longinus could not have been the contemporary of Homer, nor Boileau of Horace [i.e., Horace the writer of lyric poems]." It is hard to decide, on the evidence of this passage, whether Shelley read Longinus or not, but it is plain that he did not read him carefully. Whatever the case may be, however, Shelley is closest in spirit to Longinus of all the Romantic critics, including Coleridge.

One might say that Shelley was *at liberty* to be more Longinian than Coleridge—less given to formalization, that is—because Shelley was never much affected by the holistic aesthetics of Kant. There is little evidence in his critical thinking of the plastic "multëity in unity" that appears everywhere in Coleridge. There are times when Shelley too supposes that form must be the standard of art, but whenever he does so he finds the conventional notions of decorum and internal consistency to be quite sufficient. In this vein of commonplace Shelley describes what is "harmonious and perfect" in Greek art as "a whole, consistent with itself," while in the *Defence of Poetry* he observes that the Athenian drama was practiced most "according to the philosophy of it" and preserved "a beautiful proportion and unity."

In this and a few other particulars, the influence of Aristotle can be found in Shelley—whose approach to poetry, however, is fundamentally very different. As Shelley's critics have always pointed out, there is little or nothing of a specifically aesthetic nature in his writing. He frequently adverts to the idea of unity and harmony in the universe or in the "great mind" that animates the universe, but that sort of unity can only be approximated, as he also says, in the domain of physical objects and works of art. What is most typically "poetical" for Shelley is the fragment, or moment. Even the most perfectly sustained compositions are best viewed as fragments of a "cyclic poem." To this "poem" alone Shelley's concept of unity can be applied, as we shall see. His emphasis similarly falls on discontinuity in the relationship between part and whole: "The parts of a composition may be poetical, without the composition as a whole being a poem. A single sentence may be considered *as a* whole, though it be found in a series of unassimilated portions; a single word even may be found in a series of unassimilated portions; a single word even may be the spark of inextinguishable thought." Everywhere in Shelley there recurs the idea, in itself naive and undisciplined by dialectic, that essences are liberating while forms are oppressive: hence the conflict between freedom and institutional restraint in politics or between impulse and ceremony in morals. In his poetics this contrast is fortunately more complicated but it remains instrumental.

Just as the sublime was transmitted from soul to soul in Longinus, so it is, in Shelley, with the poetic "spark." In the early days of electricity and galvanism literary sparks flew freely. Byron's poetry is full of them. Most of all in Shelley, though, in such passages as this one from the *Defence*, they resemble the oratorical thunderbolt of Longinus: "Poetry is a sword of lightning, ever unsheathed, which consumes the scabbard that would contain it." Volatility thus heatedly imagined defies form, as when the "strain" of a poetic mind like that of Bacon "distends, and then bursts the circumference of the hearer's mind." Because Shelley was inclined to believe that light is a fluid and not a particle, his mind could move easily from the thrust of lightning to its devastation without distinguishing cause and effect; lightning itself is the overflow, as from a fountain, that it causes. Thus because Dante was the "Lucifer" of a "starry flock" in Republican Italy, each of whose words is "a spark, a burning atom . . . pregnant with a lightning which has yet found no conductor," it follows that a "great poem" like the *Commedia* is a fountain that will shed—with the help of a conductor—"its divine effluence" on the auditor. The sliding of these figures from stars to lightning to streams to conduits closely resembles Longinus's rendering of the "vapours" that are transmitted from "the men of old" to "the souls of those who emulate them," vapors that "we may describe as *effluences*."

The result of this flooding, Shelley says, is that we become "a portion of that beauty which we contemplate." Just so, the effect of this experience on the auditor in Longinus is the pleasing illusion that the soul "had itself produced what it has heard." Both writers imagine a conductor, then, through which the poetic spark can be passed to many persons in turn, each in turn fancying himself to be its originator. So Shelley writes: "The pleasure resulting from the manner in which [poets] express the influence of society or nature upon their own minds, communicates itself to others, and gathers a sort of *reduplication* from the community." The word I have italicized suggests the production of a facsimile as well as increase in general. For Shelley as well as for Longinus, surprisingly enough when one considers how vague the ideas of both of them appear to be, the function of inspiration is, quite precisely, to reproduce itself. I shall discuss this point in more detail elsewhere.

So much, then, for the affinities of Shelley and Longinus. A much broader and more generalized comparision is obviously possible: I have only wanted to stress one or two of the issues that have been recurrent themes in this book. To turn now to a more unlikely pairing, Shelley and Dryden. They have been contrasted as the very antipodes of poetry in famous essays by T. S. Eliot and C. S. Lewis, and certainly in most respects their sensibilities and talents have nothing in common. Shelley loathed "the reign of Charles II." Because he took it for granted, with Longinus, that political and sensual tyranny always coexist, Shelley could never have sympathized with Dryden, whose personality was, for the most part, that of his age. Here Shelley differs markedly from Hazlitt—and from Keats, who studied Dryden carefully in 1819 and in whose casual criticism there is more of the chameleon poet than the virtuous philosopher. And yet, with all this said, Shelley and the Dryden of the "Preface to *Fables*" still share important ideas. What I want to emphasize, in this case also, is the similarity of their attitudes toward the flow of inspiration.

Dryden more than once wrote of the "Almighty Poet" who deter-mines our actions whether we know it or not, much as a narrator determines the actions of a character. Part of what determines us, espe-cially if we are poets, is this Poet's preexisting language; in writing of the "lineal descent" of poets and the "transfusion" of translation, Dryden indicates that every poem is directed by the language that comes before it. Shelley nearly always stresses the contrast between creation and transla-tion—as when he tells Leigh Hunt that he, Hunt, was "formed to be a living fountain and not a canal however clear"—but at bottom his view of originality in fact resembles Dryden's. His version of Dryden's "lineal descent" is, again, the "great cyclic poem," the first chaotic fragments of which anticipate everything to come. In the characteristic phrasing of both Longinus and Dryden the difference between inspiration and inspiring language is very slight, and this is true also in Shelley. His cyclic poem is closely equivalent to, and sometimes identical with, the concepts of "Power" and "Mind" that would be complementary to a poem of any kind in normal usage. These matters will receive a large share of attention in the present chapter.

Dryden and Shelley also take similar views of poetic craft. Dryden appears to have decided by 1700, following Hobbes, that "thoughts . . . have always some connexion" and therefore need not, perhaps cannot, be composed with exhaustive care. Shelley too, in a draft of the first paragraph of the *Defence*, defined the imagination as a force that promotes associations. In his published revision Shelley avoided the mechanistic overtones of this definition, but I think that his changed wording makes little or no practical difference. Throughout the *Defence* the imagination, dictating unpremeditated verse, remains inseparable from the Muse. The "birth and recurrence" of poetry have "no necessary connexion with consciousness or will." Here again Shelley differs substantially from Coleridge, whose Secondary Imagination coexists "with the conscious will."

Both Shelley and the later Dryden oppose systematic thinking about literature. (Herein Shelley most resembles Byron, who declared that "when a man talks of system, his case is hopeless.") Indeed, Shelley mistrusted complex theories in any field (religion, say, or "political economy") as defects of feeling. He read the literary journals but remained aloof, until he read Peacock, from any and all controversies that had no direct bearing on politics. He never mentioned Hazlitt's critical ideas, perhaps because he disliked him in person and as a journalist; he thought of Jeffrey, Gifford, Wilson, Southey, and the rest solely as creatures of party faction; and to Byron's feud with Bowles over Pope his first reaction was simply indifference. He read and borrowed from Wordsworth's "Preface" and from Coleridge, especially the *Biographia* and *The Statesman's Manual*, but he nearly always severed what he borrowed from its original close-knit context. Unlike Coleridge, Shelley lacked patience to develop qualified viewpoints. His taste in philosophy ran to the simplicity of extremes, whether of materialism or idealism, and he was inclined, as M.H. Abrams has remarked disapprovingly, to encourage "a general annulment of distinctions." It is just this tendency, though, that I find myself admiring and wishing to defend in *A Defence of Poetry*, which Yeats declared, largely in tribute to its unqualified stance, to be "the profoundest essay on the foundations of poetry in English."

I

In late February 1821 Shelley wrote his publisher that in his *Defence* he would "expose the inmost idol of [Peacock's] error." But in the first half-paragraph of his *Defence*, and from time to time later, Shelley himself comes close to sharing the error. For the next few pages I shall hover around that first half-paragraph with the purpose of identifying this error fully. Having done that, I will be able to show just where Shelley actually follows Peacock and where, in turning against him, he makes his most important contribution to poetics.

Two of the "poets" most conspicuously celebrated in the *Defence* are Plato, whose *eidola*, or false images in a cave, are said to be the poet's only materials in the *Republic*, and Bacon, another disparager of poetry and of the "idols of the cave." So, in harboring an "inmost idol," according to Shelley's witty expression, Peacock has been taken in by appearances and thus joins company with the poets he abuses. But he also joins the philosophers whose views he shares: it is at once Shelley's compliment to Peacock and the essence of his refutation that by allusion he unites his friend with other writers whose vigorous imaginations belie their complicity with the image-makers. But just how far is Shelley himself, prior to the *Defence* and even within it, taken in by the idol he exposes in Peacock? Quite far, apparently, if he chooses to begin his essay by assigning special but only limited tasks to that rather petty faculty, the image-ination, over which Peacock has triumphed. To speak of image-making is to suppose the accessibility of some reality that will be obscured by images. The attacks of Peacock and Plato and Bacon all depend on their enforcement of this contrast, which appears to be upheld, in turn, by Shelley's first remarks on the imagination and the reason.

"Poetry," Peacock had written memorably in "The Four Ages of Poetry," "is the mental rattle that awakened the attention of intellect in the infancy of society." In other words, by fostering the savage's eye for resemblances, poetry helped him to begin organizing his experience. Because all their neighbors were engrossed in "robbing and fighting," the poets were at first the sole makers and guardians of their culture, "not only historians but theologians, moralists, and"—as Shelley noted in particular— "legislators." Imagination, in short—and this is the key point to have in mind—precedes reason in the evolution of the human faculties, but then with the perfecting of reason the imagination becomes vestigial and should properly fall into disuse. Reason and only reason contributes to scientific progress. It affords "the philosophic mental tranquillity which looks round with an equal eye on all external things, collects a store of ideas, discriminates their relative value, assigns to all their proper place," and in general subserves "the real business of life" (Shelley could have capitalized on all these untimely allusions to Wordsworth). "Poetry," by contrast, "cannot travel out of the regions of its birth, the uncultivated lands of semi-civilized men." Because it is necessarily figurative and twisted into meter ("language on the rack of Procrustes"), poetry is unfit for "pure reason and dispassionte truth. . . , as we may judge by versifying one of Euclid's equations." Poetry "can never make a philosopher, nor a statesman, nor in any class of life an useful or rational man."

Unquestionably Peacock somewhat exaggerates his position for effect. Although it is difficult to agree with his early editor that his attitude toward scientific rationalism is actually "ironic," he undoubtedly did believe, being a writer himself, that literature has its place. Thus he probably agreed in advance, at least to some small extent, with Shelley. And Shelley, on the other hand, although he believed that his friend was "a nursling of the exact and superficial school of poetry" and thus far in league with those reviewers who were real enemies, could still agree with Peacock in some ways. Peacock's point of view, however cavalierly expressed, was in many respects that of Plato, and it also coincided with Shelley's own favorable attitude toward experimental science and progressive politics. Nevertheless, Peacock's *Four Ages* had to be answered. There was still that "inmost idol" to be exposed.

When Peacock writes that "the savage . . . lisps in numbers," Shelley agrees in response that "the savage (for the savage is to ages what the child is to years) is naturally a poet." This opinion they both inherit from nearly all the Enlightenment theorists of the origin of language. By and large, however, these writers (who include Rousseau, Herder, and Monboddo) anticipate Peacock rather than Shelley in arguing that for better or worse society has outgrown the kind of knowledge that depends on figures of speech. On this significant point Shelley parts company with practically everyone: He agrees that imagination precedes reason in the development of thought, but he goes on to insist that the imagination has not therefore been left behind by the grand march of intellect. On the contrary, imagination must pave the way for the reason in every new venture of thought or else the mind will atrophy and fail to keep pace with the need for change in society. Moreover, reason has no useful function that is independent of, or different from, the function of the imagination. Insofar as it is valuable, reason "in her most exalted mood" simply *is* the imagination. Hence for any praiseworthy human endeavor there is only one faculty, not two of them dividing the labor.

This is Shelley's most radical and effective position. We have noted, though, that the opening sentences of the *Defence* promise nothing so extreme. There Shelley discriminates between reason and imagination as though they were equal in value, and he does so in terms that would almost have satisfied Peacock. Shelley's first definition of reason, "mind contemplating the relations borne by one thought to another, however produced," seems roughly the same as the descripton by Peacock of the rational philosophic mind that I have already quoted. And imagination viewed as "mind acting on those thoughts so as to colour them with its own light" seems to be just the sort of subjectivity, ornamental at best and a distortion of accurate thought at worst, that the scientific approach to the world is said to have outmoded. So far there are really no grounds for challenging Peacock. These first sentences themselves are so cumbrously pseudoscientific in manner that they seem an unconscious parody of Coleridge in certain registers and of Shelley's own tractarian prose. From this point on, in both argument and tone, Shelley's personal view will begin to take over, but for the moment he seems to be invoking his own earlier philosophy of mind, the philosophy he still held when he last spoke with Peacock in England.

As an apprentice Godwinian and admirer of Paine's *Age of Reason*, Shelley had believed that reason would prevail in the world. That was his faith—although "faith" itself he held in distaste as a superstition, as a product of imagination to which the mind obstinately clings. Reason was then, to him, "a thing independent and inflexible [i.e., incorruptible]." The imagination, by contrast, is enamored of unrealities. In a fragment on religion of 1814 Shelley calls the belief in miracles "a creative activity of imagination," and in the "Fragment on Miracles" of the same period he declares that "logic and dialectics" are better than the imaginative adherence to "a doctrine pretending to be true." There is no difference between these opinions and Peacock's contrast between rational enlightenment and the poet's reliance on "the superstitions which are the creed of his age." In Peacock's view, and the earlier Shelley's, imagination is a backward faculty that is ranged against innovation; it consists merely in "a crude congeries of traditional phantasies."

Even as late as 1819 (in the *Philosophical View of Reform*), when Shelley no longer idolized the Reason of the Enlightenment, he still evidently thought that although neither faculty was obsolete, "the cultivation of the imagination and the cultivation of scientific truth" were separate but equal enterprises. The position implied here is the one that anyone not given to extremes will be likely to take: Poetry and science each have their sphere, and each has a useful cultural function as long as it is not considered to be a substitute for the other. This is the position of I. A. Richards, for example, who maintains that our "intellectual beliefs" and "emotional beliefs" depend on efficient communications issuing from the reason and the imagination, respectively. But in Richards's designation of poetry as "pseudo-statement" there still appears the bias that marks the attitude of a Peacock. In thinking of this kind, however evenhanded it may seem, rhetoric is viewed as a special kind of language that is the natural enemy of logic. Figural language that is not candidly fictive in its designs upon us will try to pass itself off as the "literal" language of science. At one time this was the earnestly held opinion of Shelley himself. Writing—as it happens—of the poetry of Peacock in 1812, the young Shelley warns himself against its siren call: "I have rigidly accustomed myself not to be seduced by the loveliest eloquence or the sweetest strains."

Probably as long as one accepts the validity of the distinction between the figural and the literal, one is likely to be wary lest poetry exceed its bounds and poach in the preserves of prose: "The best way, on topics similar to these, is to tell the plain truth, without the confusion and ornament of metaphor." That is Shelley addressing the Irish in 1812, complaining of what he was later to describe, in his *Treatise on Morals*, as "the abuse of a metaphorical expression to a literal purpose." Now, one cannot be brought to reconsider this invidious contrast without first coming to question whether the notion of "metaphor," or transfer of sense, is indeed only intelligible, as it has been said to be, in opposition to the "literal," or proper sense. Two different ideas are commonly proposed as to what the literal might be. According to the first and etymologically legitimate idea, a word is used literally if it corresponds to its accepted definition. The second concerns a word that is used in accordance with its normative connection to an object. It is this latter, less cautious sense of the "literal" that Shelley contrasts with metaphor in his *Treatise on Morals*.

In so doing he parallels the contrast he makes elsewhere in the same essay between two fundamental types of philosophy, one of which deals with fact and the other with words (called "logic" here but surely including the philosophies of rhetoric and grammar): "Metaphysics may be defined as the science of all that we know, feel, remember, and believe inasmuch as our knowledge, sensations, memory, and faith constitute the universe considered relatively to human identity. Logic, or the science of words, must no longer be confounded with metaphysics or the science of facts. Words are the instruments of mind whose capacities it becomes the metaphysician to know, but they are not mind, nor are they portions of mind." It will be noticed that although Shelley may insist that "the science of things is superior to the science of words," he takes it for granted almost from the beginning that "things" are *mental*. This idea gains in importance in his later work, but it is there very early. "Nothing exists but as it is perceived" is Shelley's Berkeleyan dictum in "On Life" and elsewhere; hence his "facts" should not be confused with things in themselves. He will often write "things" when he means "thoughts" (in the opening sentences of the *Defence* there are two manuscript changes from "things" to "thoughts"), but that is simply because the nominalist habit of expression is difficult to get over and too handy to do without.

The subtler distinction, with which for a long time Shelley continues to sustain the conventional contrasts of science and poetry or reason and imagination, is the distinction between thought and words. Although even in the *Defence* he glances in passing at "those who cannot distinguish words from thoughts," this distinction too is more typical, I think, of an earlier period. It is most frequently and polemically urged in the disputatious prose of 1812, when he says, for example, that "words are only signs for ideas." To come to an end of this survey of Shelley's early thinking about the idols of the cave, my point is that in the *Defence* almost for the first time Shelley went some way toward giving up the idol of the idols—the notion that appearances make up half of a pair, the other half being fact, or reality—in order to succeed in exposing the "inmost idol" of Peacock's "error." In the "Four Ages" Peacock had written that "the reason and the understanding are best addressed in the simplest and most unvarnished prose." This had been Shelley's own opinion, and it seems to survive, in both style and theme, in the first sentences of the *Defence*.

II

The business of the imagination, Shelley adds to these sentences, is "to colour [thoughts] with its own light, . . . composing from them, as from elements, other thoughts, each containing within itself the principle of its own integrity." The "thoughts" that are thus colored, the same thoughts that are also contemplated by the reason, are what the philosophers of the Empirical tradition called "impressions"; they are given to the mind, either by sense or by unknown causes. Empiricists like Hume contrast thoughts such as these with the compound thoughts, or "ideas," that are forged exclusively by the imagination, because there is no demonstrable basis in reality for the arrangement of impressions in a connecting pattern. "Reason alone," writes Hume in the *Treatise of Human Nature*, "can never give rise to any original idea." Shelley follows Hume very closely but he does not normally consider impressions, understood as sense-data, to be "thoughts." His normal attitude is expressed most clearly in his *Treatise on Morals:* "The most astonishing combinations of poetry, the subtlest deductions of logic and mathematics are no other than combinations which the intellect makes of sensations according to its own laws." Thus, since the function of combining is performed solely by the imagination, it must be concluded that *all* thoughts, including those contemplated by the reason, are furnished by the imagination, which alone is independent from the contingency of the real. In other words, science does not offer unmediated representations of the world; like poetry, science is mind obeying "its own laws."

Most broadly considered, the coloring of imagination is the filter of self that veils perception. It is what causes Sir William Drummond, the disciple of Hume and Berkeley whom Shelley admired, to speak of "the painted field of my vision." Shelley rather curiously describes this distortion as an anthropomorphosis: "We see trees, houses, fields, living beings in our own shape, and in shapes more or less analogous to our own." This is eccentric; even solipsism and psychosis, we assume, will project themselves in images that partly disguise the self. But the general meaning is clear. With perhaps only slight exaggeration, a recent commentator on the *Defence* has written that Shelley regards "the world as a mind-made poem in which metaphor is tantamount to metamorphosis and imagination is the agent of transformation in human nature." Reason, on the other hand, is inert and lacks any vital principle of its own. Calculating machine that it is, it lacks the self-consciousness it would need even to be aware of its own achievement or to perceive the significance of its information: "We want the creative faculty to imagine that which we know." By the time Shelley has said this, the gathering force of his argument has long since driven reason from the field. At the end of the first paragraph, after it had seemed that the two faculties would divide the useful arts equally between themselves, Shelley violently tilts the bias in his series of contrasting definitions: "Reason is the enumeration of quantities already known; imagination is the perception of the value of those quantities, both separately and as a whole. Reason respects the differences, and imagination the similitudes of things. Reason is to the imagination as the instrument to the agent, as the body to the spirit, as the shadow to the substance."

In this passage reason is most drastically curtailed as the "instrument to the agent." It is a tool with operations that have no independence from the force that puts it to work. It repeats the gestures of what wields it just as a hammer extends the movement of an arm. Thus, Shelley's victory over Peacock comes about not simply from his having asserted the inferiority of reason but from his having first insinuated and then asserted that reason is not really a separate faculty at all, but only the echo, or ape, of imagination, mechanically reproducing acts of mind that were once, and only once, creative. This assertion is reflected in the symbols Shelley uses to describe the relationship of the two faculties in the second draft of the letter to his publisher that was to have been the *Defence*: "[Peacock] would extinguish Imagination which is the Sun of life, & grope his way by the cold & uncertain & borrowed light of . . . the Moon he calls Reason,— . . . the watery [*light*] orb which is the Queen of his [*cold*] pale Heaven." Readers of Nabokov's *Pale Fire*, if not of *Timon of Athens*, will recognize Shelley's source, which provides these metaphors with some of their polemical strength: "The moon's an arrant thief, / And her pale fire she snatches from the sun" (Timon has just said that the sun is also a thief—of which more below). Shelley's conceit is the more pointed in that traditionally, and most notably in Shakespeare, it is the imagination that was compared with the moon. For Shelley the imagination becomes a sun that creates its world by making it visible. Heating up the cool terminology of Hume, Shelley in such passages becomes a hierophant of "the Magian worship of the sun as the creator and preserver of the world."

With this main point established, Shelley can then devise still more daring expressions that reach out to encompass the old and lesser idea of imagination as well as his new one. Wordsworth in the "Preface" says finely that poetry is "the breath and finer spirit of all things," but then seems content for it to serve the scientist merely as an ornament or a means of popularization, better perhaps than the poetry of Erasmus Darwin but not fundamentally different from it. Shelley is bolder. He insists that imagination—"poetry"—presides over both the humanization *and* the conceptual groundwork of science. Thus it is both "the root and blossom of all other systems of thought; it is that from which all spring, and that which adorns all." It governs every phase of the scientific method, from the inmost bulwark of deduction to the furthest horizon of speculation, being "the center and circumference of knowledge; . . . that which comprehends all science, and that to which all science must be referred."

All this is more carefully thought through than may appear. Even for the scientist, Shelley's hyperboles in defense of mythopoeic knowledge do not overstep the bounds of the plausible. In thinking of science, Shelley is likely to have had in mind the laws of "natural science" and the principles of moral and political utility. Setting the latter aside for the moment, one can speak, not very fancifully, of the poetic origins of the laws of physical science. *Gravity*, a word Shelley himself often uses metaphorically for "attraction," was intuited first by the poets. The author of *The Witch of Atlas* could point to Aristophanes' myth of the hermaphrodites in the *Symposium*; he would have known, in any case, of the elder Darwin's opinion that life in its infancy passed through a hermaphroditic stage. Or, citing a more narrowly gravitational principle, "Everything that rises must fall," one could argue that this idea was first conceived imaginatively as the Elizabethan Wheel of Fortune. Yet further, as Douglas Bush notes somewhat disapprovingly, there is Shelley's own "linking of love with electricity in a thought-created world." There are likewise poetic anticipations of the Conservation of Energy, e.g., Milton's account of creation from Chaos, the balance of destruction and preservation mirrored forth in the Hindu zodiac, and many others. These examples do not resemble "the versifying of one of Euclid's equations," but they will serve to explain what Shelley means. Geometry itself, in any case, does not offer an escape from subjectivity. As Hilary Putnam writes, "The overthrow of Euclidean geometry was not *just* an overthrow of a theory of space. Euclidean geometry was the paradigm of certainty, attained through a priori reasoning, and more than that, the paradigm held up to the moral philosopher by Plato as well as by Spinoza." Even at this extreme, then, it is not the hyperbolic Shelley but the scientific Peacock who is involved in a fallacy.

The greatest apparent weakness of Shelley's position concerning science is the fact that even the most prescient of intuitions cannot in themselves prove anything. If the imagination does supply the reason with hypotheses, it is left for the reason to devise the experiments that will verify them. But verification and proof are not the same thing. Verification, the strict ascertainment of what is true, is generally thought to be impossible; even the most retrenched objectivists believe that what is true must be determined negatively, i.e., by the falsification of alternatives. Proof, a more practical affair that certainly is possible, can be established only with respect to more or less changeable and relative contexts. The principles that dictate an experiment subtly anticipate its success or failure. Far more than Bacon, for one, supposed, what Thomas Kuhn has called "paradigms" of thought shape and determine each experimental phase in the history of science until new paradigms arise, making what had hitherto been proved newly limited in its application or even irrelevant to the new aims of science. (I only refer here to the strongest results of science, to what really has in one sense or another been proved, and not to such phantoms temporarily sustained by experiment as phlogiston, atmospheric ether, and the like.)

This idea of science is the one supported by Shelley: the operations of reason do not differ in kind from those of imagination but only repeat them in ever narrower applications because the horizons of reason are governed by general conceptions that are not its own. Our tendency to forget that the facts in our possession have been preselected by our attitudes is fully accounted for in Shelley's observation that "the poetry in [utilitarian thought] is concealed by the accumulation of facts and calculating processes." No defender of poetry or criticism, not even Aristotle, can deny Plato's charge that the poets and rhapsodes (who are also critics, like Ion) tell lies. Plotinus tried, but he referred the whole matter to an isolated, transcendent sphere to which Shelley is much less serenely devoted than he is often said to be. What a defense of poetry *can* do, and this is what Shelley's *Defence* does, is to claim that although poetry distorts the truth, science distorts it just as much and in just the same way. Science too, at its most "poetic" and least self-oblivious, nothing affirms and therefore never lieth. It need only divest itself of the omniscience that Peacock accorded to Euclidean geometry and admit that the poetical faculty alone, as Shelley says, "creates new materials for knowledge."

The dynamic thinking of the imagination becomes static when it is repeated by the reason, inevitably so without the intercession of new "poetry." "Ethical science," for example, "arranges the elements which reason has created." The crystallization of classes and systems, suspended in space—as we conceive of them—rather than successive through time, resembles the change from the vital sciences of the nineteenth century to the structural ones of the twentieth as it is described by Foucault. During the course of this period the paradigmatic science for other scientists was first biology, then economics, then linguistics; and within these three sciences over the same period the focus of attention shifted from the processual to the formal: from function to norm in biology, from conflict to rule in economics, and from signification to system in linguistics. Shelley would argue that shifts of this kind are what poetry must guard against or, if need be, reverse. What begins as a vital sense of resemblance, a link forged by sympathy, ends all too soon as an enforcement of uniformity, whether by government, religion, or mere mental habit.

III

The notion that the thinking of one faculty loses vitality when repeated by another suggests an equivalent notion that must pertain to language. If poetic language is "vitally metaphorical," the language of reason must consist of dead metaphors, including equations, laws, and identifications, all bearing traces of their figural origins that are almost too faint to notice. Although considerations of this sort would imply that there is a very close relationship between thought and language, Shelley is most frequently inclined not to accept this implication. In some places he thinks that his contrast between imagination and reason must itself reflect the immemorial contrasts between the spirit and the letter. At the same time, however, his coup against rationalism does entail the supposition that imagination and reason are not generically distinct and that the materials with which they function differ only in being alive or dead. In that case the opposition between spirit and letter is by no means absolute.

Without always quite wishing to, Shelley reveals in the argument of the *Defence* that the activity of the imagination is not ineffable but can be understood as a kind of language. "The coloring of imagination" is an expression that Shelley uses in common with Wordsworth and many others. It is a rhetorical as well as a psychological process, *colors* being a traditional term for rhetorical devices. Shelley's poetry had been abused for its surfeit of "colouring epithets," and if only for this reason it is safe to assume that, although he was no great reader of rhetoric manuals, he was aware of this sense of his term. Wordsworth intends to discriminate at least slightly, in the 1800 "Preface," between the "colouring of imagination" and the "selection" of everyday language that gets colored, but this distinction in itself shows that the metaphorical and the literal share a common medium. Shelley uses the notion of "color" with much the same result. Instead of enforcing the contrast between spirit and letter, he turns out to have questioned it.

The image-making faculty is itself an image, the "Spirit of BEAUTY, that dost consecrate / With thine own hues all thou dost shine upon / Of human thought or form" ("Hymn to Intellectual Beauty"). It is at this strange point of overlap between cause and effect that one encounters Shelley's figure of the veil: "Oh, that words . . . / Were stripped of their thin masks and various hue" ("Ode to Liberty," 234–37). In contrasting the spirit and the form of a work, Shelley likes to think of the latter, its "accidental vesture," as a raiment that includes language and conceals "the beauty of [poets'] conceptions in its naked truth and splendour." And yet, as the 1816 "Hymn" declares, the imagination itself, the creative sun, is what supplies those colors that the poet wants to strip away from his expression—in order to reveal the colorless transparency of his imaginings. Even if one attempts to resolve the paradox by saying that a concrete expression is like a prism, or "dome of many colored glass," that refracts "the white radiance" of the imagination—even then, the spirit and the letter are still intermixed in their common light.

On many occasions, as we have seen, Shelley wishes to preserve the notion of language that had prevailed almost universally since its exposition by Locke, namely, that words are arbitrary signs that obscure the pure essence of thoughts. But the position taken up by Shelley in the *Defence* reveals that words and thoughts are very similar to each other. Here in full is Shelley's description of the movement from living to dead metaphor in expressions that derive from "poetry": "[The poets'] language is vitally metaphorical; that is, it marks the before unapprehended relations of things and perpetuates their apprehension, until the words which represent them, become, through time, signs for portions or classes of thoughts instead of pictures of integral thoughts; and then if no new poets should arise to create afresh the associations which have been thus disorganized, language will be dead to all the nobler purposes of human intercourse." This passage leaves no place for thought. Language itself supplies what Hume calls ideas, or the combination of impressions. Apart from that innovation, Shelley here follows nearly all the theorists of the origin of language by supposing that in being repeated language grows inflexible because it is less and less immediately connected with archetypal impressions and more and more determined, therefore, by its internal relations as a system. From the scientific point of view this development is a good thing: only in being abstracted from immediate impressions can language serve the purposes of generalization. But for Shelley, as for Blake, generalization is mere lunacy, a pale fire stolen from a forgotten original: "The copiousness of lexicography and the distinctions of grammar are the works of a later age, and are merely the catalogue and form of the creations of poetry."

In implying that language at its origin was and is, in Eliot's phrase, "as immediate as the odor of a rose," Shelley can uggest that it is at once bodily, or concrete, and quintessentially distilled, or abstracted, without being merely a formal sign of either condition. Poetic language, in short, is dynamic and has no arbitrary structure: "The grammatical forms . . . are convertible with respect to the highest poetry without injuring it as poetry." Now, it is in this respect most obviously that poetry "in a general sense" ("the expression of the imagination") differs from poetry "in a more restricted sense." The latter from the outset must all too closely anticipate the expression of the *reason* in that it expresses "arrangements of language" that differ from rational utterances only in being more delicate. Far from being convertible without injury, then, the verbal arrangements of poetry in the restricted sense cannot be translated at all whereas the highest poetry, Shelley has wanted to say, has nothing verbal about it. It is at once the inspiration and the eternal meaning of poetry in the restricted sense and of all the other art forms. Again a wedge appears to have been driven between spirit and letter.

Well and good, but how can the realm of concepts, even of universals, be shown to exist at all, short of being the One indivisibly, if it does not itself participate in some medium that is concrete enough to allow for, nay, to *forge*, differentiation? If it contains all colors, even the white radiance itself must therefore be a system of signs. That this conclusion at least sometimes governs Shelley's own thought may be shown with reference to his concept of "allegory." Only one kind of allegory can plausibly be defined as a form referring to something ineffable, and that, of course, is the story told by religion: "All original religions are allegorical, or susceptible of allegory, and, like Janus, have a double face of false and true." Here the dualism is explicit and neat, but in any less purely theistic allegory, when interpretation is a matter of finding parallels for certain figures, then plainly the hidden sense is not ineffable but a para*phrase* that has its own definite shape and purport. To this effect Shelley quotes with approval from the *Vita Nuova* in his Advertisement for *Epipsychidion* (1821): "Great were his shame, who should rhyme anything under a garb of metaphor or rhetorical colour [*sotto vesta di figura o di colore rettorico*], and then, being asked, should be incapable of stripping his words of this garb so that they might have a veritable meaning [*e poscia . . . non sapesse denudare le sue parole da cotale vesta, in guisa che avessero verace intentimento*]" (Shelley slightly misquotes the Italian, which I have here interspersed with Rossetti's translation as given by Clark). In general, therefore, allegory does not uphold the duality of language and pure thought. Rather it refers from one sentence to another. The difference in degree between the two sentences, between concealment and exposure, is just the difference—and no more—between Shelley's "restricted" and "general" senses of poetry.

IV

The Italian of the passage quoted above may have furnished some of the language of the *Defence*: "vesture," "colour," "naked truth." An anomaly in all of Shelley's work that has frequently been noticed concerns the question of what covers what: "The veil of error and the figured curtain of imagination," writes one commentator, "have a mutuality that is ambivalent: sometimes ironic, sometimes liberating." In part this is simply a question of relative values: what is mundane and dreary needs dressing up, what is celestial and bright needs to be unveiled. Shelley himself is sure that from this point of view his veil-symbol is not anomalous: "Whether [poetry] spreads its figured curtain, or withdraws life's dark veil from before the scene of things, it equally creates for us a being within our being." As in the case of allegory, the anomaly obtrudes itself only if one attempts to identify nakedness with ineffability or transcendence. Shelley speaks of "the scene of things," and again he says that by lifting "the veil," poetry "makes familiar objects be as if they were not familiar." This is perfectly intelligible; it is Wallace Stevens's making "the visible / A little hard to see," and it anticipates the "defamiliarization" of the early Russian Formalists. Yet in all these instances the similarity between surface and subsurface is greater than the contrast: something specific, concrete, and quotidian is torn aside to reveal something specific, concrete, and unusual. We have to do with either a language-event or an object-event, but never, given the logic of these figures, with a transformation of language into matter or spirit. Either appearances are bottomless or else they are realities; the deep truth is not imageless but an image.

Two passages from the *Defence* are illuminating in this regard, even though each of them does little more in intent, perhaps, than to rehearse a commonplace of empirical psychology in a lyrical vein. The first passage recalls the psychology of Hume: "A word, or a trait in the representation of a scene or a passion, will touch the enchanted chord, and reanimate, in those who have ever experienced these emotions, the sleeping, the cold, the buried image of the past." In Hume, the memory houses lingering and resonating impressions that may be reactivated by some kindred impulse. This is of course the process of association. The memory for Shelley is a "lyre [that] trembles and sounds after the wind has died away." Unless reanimated by a new note of "poetry," the chord in the memory simply dies away until its echo becomes reflexive—and is then claimed, we may add, as an a priori truth by the reason. Now, Shelley's associative "madeleine," his catalytic word, can take effect only if in some sense it resembles what it reanimates. The resemblance cannot be the resemblance of a sign to a corresponding "thought," furthermore, because that which is lodged in the memory, the "chord," already belongs within the system of the sign that is added to it. A new sound gives renewed life to an old sound and not to some forgotten signification either of the old sound or of itself.

Thus Shelley's "word, or trait" establishes a connection between signs and not between a sign and a thought.

At this point, when it is no longer possible to avoid terms that will seem anachronistic, it will be reassuring to glance at a theoretical challenge to the empiricist view of language that Shelley himself had read as early as 1813, Horne Tooke's *Diversions of Purley* (1786–98). In a rarely discussed passage in the *Treatise on Morals*, Shelley delivers his opinion of this work: "The discoveries of Horne Tooke in philology do not, as he has asserted, throw light upon metaphysics: they only render the instruments requisite to its perception more exact and accurate. Aristotle and his followers, Locke and most of the modern philosophers gave logic the name of metaphysics" (as we noted earlier, "metaphysics" for Shelley is the science of subjective "facts"—i.e., of thoughts—and logic is the science of words). Concerning Aristotle, Shelley may have in mind the *Categories*, which has often been criticized for having founded its distinctions in language, not reality; concerning Locke, Shelley is in fact echoing Tooke himself, who advises us to reread Locke and "substitute the composition &c. of *terms*, wherever he was supposed a composition &c. of *ideas*." Tooke adds in this place that Locke actually wished, too late, to recast his *Essay* as a study of the linguistic determination of thought.

Tooke begins his treatise with a surprising observation that would be of interest to Shelley's Demogorgon: "Truth, in my opinion, has been improperly imagined at the bottom of a well: it lies much nearer to the surface." He takes his stand against the then universally accepted premise, after Aristotle and Locke, that words are "the signs of *ideas*." Tooke's own position, shored up by vast learning in sundry alphabets, closely anticipates not only the view of Saussure but also, even in phrasing, that of Jacques Lacan. Words are signs of *sounds*, says Tooke (viz., Saussure's "acoustic images"), and then he continues: "There may be not only signs of sounds; but again, for the sake of abbreviation [i.e., short-cuts in thinking], signs of those signs, one *under another* in a continued progression" (italics mine). It is significant that Shelley apparently accepts this much of Tooke's argument; that is what is implied, in any case, by the word *discoveries* in the *Treatise on Morals*. What Shelley does not then proceed to accept is Tooke's further claim that "Hermes has blinded Philosophy" and that his own researches will discredit "all the different systems of Metaphysical Imposture." But if Shelley has accepted the premise, he can reject the conclusion only with the greatest difficulty. There is nothing implicitly materialistic about Tooke's argument, however it may have appeared to Shelley or to Tooke himself. On the contrary, reading Tooke may encourage one to take the *Logos* literally. What Tooke will not accommodate, though, is the possibility of any ideation that is transcendent in the sense of being beyond, or other than, signs.

In the third Book of the *Essay*, Locke introduces the idea of "general signs," or words for classes of thoughts. By Shelley's day this idea comprised the standard explanation, variously attached to theories of progress and decline, of how language forgoes the direct reliance on things that was said to have characterized its earliest stage of development. Both Wordsworth's "Preface" and Shelley's *Defence* react against the prevalency of general signs by calling for a return to the natural signs of language at its origin. Coleridge in the *Biographia* undermined Wordsworth's "real language of men" by pointing out that the *lingua communis* even of rustics is never prompted directly by nature but is always mediated either by reading, especially of the Bible, or by spoken models like that of the parish priest. Hence, he concludes wittily and truly, the language of nature began in the Schools. Not Coleridge, however, but a kind of undertow from within is what breaks down Shelley's Wordsworthian idea, similarly derived from the Enlightenment literature on the origin of language, that "in the infancy of society language itself is poetry." All such formulas aim at the subordination of language to thought: in the beginning was the sense-impression. Wordsworth's position is at least consistent in that he takes the original language to have been plain-spoken, nonfigurative. For Shelley, on the other hand, if the originary language is "vitally metaphorical," then the first word was already, somehow, a transfer of sense from one word to another. Thus, Shelley's view of language, held in spite of himself at times but at other times deliberately worked out, is ultimately that of Tooke and of Coleridge's refutation of Wordsworth, not that of Locke and Wordsworth. While wishing to preserve the truths of metaphysics, he is obliged to admit that their formulations are dead metaphors.

A second passage in the *Defence* which has the effect of bringing the deep truth to the surface is a commonplace made available to Shelley by the currency of such studies of ancient language and myths as Anathase Kircher's *Polygraphia Nova* (1663), Warburton's *Divine Legation of Moses* (1737–41), and, most recently, Drummond's *Oedipus Judaicus*. Poets both ancient and modern, writes Shelley, "have employed language as the hieroglyphic of their thoughts." Here, in seeking a Romantic analogue, we find Coleridge on the side of natural signs after all; language at its origin is already arbitrary, yes, but used by the poet it *becomes* a repository of natural signs like the hieroglyphic Symbol which, in *The Statesman's Manual*, "always partakes of the reality which it renders intelligible." Coleridge's Symbol and Shelley's hieroglyphic are invoked with the purpose of elevating language to a plane that is above its normal one. Both have the opposite effect, however, which consists in drawing the universe of reference down onto the plane of language. Shelley's hieroglyphic makes a sign of thought rather than the other way around.

Shelley's writings harbor plenty of other challenges to the binary concept of expression. There are the "signs" of Cythna which have already been noticed in this context by Yeats and Earl Wasserman, signs devised for making "a subtler language within language." And there is also the rarely noticed passage in the "Essay on Life" in which Shelley comes close to imagining the universe itself as a system of signs. Speaking solely of "the misuse of words and signs," he nevertheless offers a description of the world as it is perceived to which exceptions would be hard to find: "By signs, I would be understood in a wide sense, including what is properly meant by the term, and what I peculiarly mean. In this latter sense, almost all familiar objects are signs, standing not for themselves but for others in their capacity of suggesting one thought which shall lead to a train of thoughts." I do not mean to overlook the qualification expressed in "almost all familiar objects"; it is just these from which, in *The Statesman's Manual*, the Symbol redeems us and from which, in the *Defence*, the language of poetry lifts the veil. It should be clear by now, though, that for Shelley more continuously and graphically than for Coleridge, the lifted veil discloses another veil of like texture.

V

Shelley's idea of poetry "in a general sense," then, which is most often thought to derive unrevised from Wordsworth's "breath and finer spirit of all things," is not altogether vague; it can be understood with some precision as a colored region behind the colors of expression. Carefully considered, the difficult passage on the superiority of verbal poetry to the poetry of stone, sound, and so forth will support this view:

> Language, colour, form, and religious and civil habits of action, are all the instruments and materials of poetry; they may be called poetry by that figure of speech which considers the effect as a synonyme of the cause. But poetry in a more restricted sense expresses those arrangements of language, and especially metrical language, which are created by that imperial faculty, whose throne is curtained within the invisible nature of man. And this springs from the nature itself of language, which is a more direct representation of the actions and passions of our internal being, and is susceptible of more various and delicate combinations, than colour, form, or motion, and is more plastic and obedient to the control

of that faculty of which it is the creation. For language is arbitrarily produced by the imagination and has relation to thoughts alone; but all other materials, instruments, and conditions of art, have relations among each other, which limit and interpose between conception and expression. The former is a mirror which reflects, the latter is a cloud which enfeebles, the light of which both are mediums of communication.

When the mimetic mirror is trained inward, as it is here, and not upon phenomena, as it still is in the *Republic* and to some extent in *Hamlet*, the binary concept of expression is apt to be undermined rather than confirmed. The idea that thoughts could mirror things had been an unobtrusively figurative premise of the realistic tradition in English philosophy before Locke. But to suggest that language can mirror thought, especially when the clarity of the reflection in that case is contrasted with the fogging of the mirror by everything else, is to suggest in turn that language reflects itself, or else something that closely resembles it.

But still, *all* the media are said here to participate, to a lesser extent, in thought. By a metonymy of cause and effect, says Shelley, they are all "poetry." Presumably, again, Shelley's "figure of speech" can be valid only if there is something poetry-*like* about the imagination, something that is itself a system of signification; similarly all the nonlinguistic media are also systems of signification, like the "things" of the *Treatise on Morals*. Their drawback, in contrast with language, is that even as systems they can only partly reflect the system of mind. Because as materials they can never be wholly transformed into conception, they continue to share the nature of what they represent more than that of what shapes them. Pigments taken from the earth are needed to paint a landscape; clay is used to mold a Venus whose human model has feet of clay herself, and so on. Thus in his "Notes on Sculptures in Rome and Florence" (1819; editor's title), Shelley looks at a statue representing Sleep and regrets that "the hardness of the stone does not permit the arriving at any great expression."

Poetry in the more restricted sense, on the other hand, touches upon the quasi-material world of dead metaphor called "fact" only insofar as it has ceased to be poetry in the general sense. As a linguistic medium it is in direct and exclusive communion with the power that is enthroned within and curtained from view. Thus it is most concealed just where it is most truly poetry, and for this reason its meaning can never be confidently uncovered by the interpreter. The imagination reveals different aspects of its hidden nature to different eras, but there is another kind of partiality involved as well: one or another worn-out code of perception will distort even that which is revealed. The spirit of revenge, "self-conceit," chivalry, and sensuality are four such codes, or frames of reference, that Shelley mentions. Each fresh insight shrivels and dries up the instant it is exposed, as it were, to the air and must be peeled away in its turn. Shelley hopes that this process will prove to have been cumulative but its admitted endlessness makes one wonder: "Veil after veil may be undrawn, and the inmost naked beauty of the meaning never exposed." Two other sorts of nonprogressive distortion are guaranteed, in any case, by the passage of time. The first results from the failure of the historian to retain the whole truth concerning the facts, or non-poetry, of the past, and the second results, again, from the limitless partiality with which the imagination declares itself: "Time, which destroys the beauty and the use of the story of particular facts, stript of the poetry which should invest them, augments that of Poetry, and for ever develops new and wonderful applications of the eternal truth which it contains."

VI

Evidently for Shelley, as for Longinus, the reader who is engaged in the crucial, although imperfect, transmission of "eternal truth" from generation to generation plays the role of poet. A new facet of this truth must be presented as poetry at every new turn of history, otherwise the vitality of what is known and considered morally, scientifically, or legislatively binding will soon dwindle. Shelley hopes, again, that these changes will be progressive. Despite his clichés about the origin of language, he is no primitivist, as his "Essay on Christianity" makes clear: "Later and more correct observations [than those of the ancient mourners for the Golden Age] have instructed us that uncivilized man is the most pernicious and miserable of beings and that the violence and injustice which are the genuine indications of real inequality obtain among these beings without mixture and without palliation." To come to Shelley's most famous hyperbole: The progress the culture owes to poetry and that poetry in turn partakes in consists in the forging of ever new and better legislation. Shelley's favorite example of how this progress works is the literature of "chivalry" in the Middle Ages, mainly that of Dante, which advanced the condition both of slaves and of women toward equality.

Shelley thus agrees with Peacock concerning the progress of society, differing only as to its causes. Institutionalized laws, whether scientific, moral, or political, cannot change, in his view, because they are inert. They can be altered only from without, by revolution or by some kind of revolutionary poetry. Wishing to discover this process at large in the world, the startlingly misinformed Shelley wrote late in 1819, in *A Philosophical View of Reform*, that in America "there is a law by which the constitution is reserved for revision every ten years." Poetry is also a law that repeals laws. So when Shelley writes of reactionaries who "are willing to think things that are rusty and decayed venerable," he is thinking at the same time of a mental state in which language has become an inflated currency, "dead to all the nobler purposes of human intercourse," that is revered more and more as the repository of ceremonial forms and unimportant facts. It is in this spirit that Nelson Goodman asks, "Is a metaphor . . . simply a juvenile fact and a fact simply a senile metaphor?"

Poetry "creates anew the universe, after it has been annihilated in our minds by the recurrence of impressions blunted by reiteration," and thus poetry constantly struggles against the senescence of culture. It is with this purpose in mind that Shelley adopts the Renaissance conceit of the poet as creator. With Sidney in the background and a quotation from Tasso ready to hand (*Non merita nome di creatore, se non Iddio ed il Poeta*), Shelley turns this idea to his own use. We have seen that the poet's "creation" replaces an old set of *eidola* with new ones which in turn must be renewed. For this reason Shelley's poet-creator is not exactly the secondary god of the Neoplatonists. He is much closer to the God of Descartes, a God who must sustain the universe by recreating it at every minute. Although Shelley appears not to have been familiar with Descartes, he seems to have known him, and perhaps Spinoza, by osmosis. In a place where he cites Machiavelli so vaguely that scholars have not been able to find the reference, he says something decidedly Cartesian: "All language institution and form, require not only to be produced but to be sustained: the office and character of a poet participates [*sic*] in the divine nature as regards providence, no less than as regards creation."

Of necessity poetry resembles revolution, and T. S. Eliot rightly identifies the *Defence* as "perhaps the first appearance of the kinetic or revolutionary theory of poetry." The risorgimento that poetry affords must be iconoclastic and offer violence of some sort to existing orders. The "great secret of morals" may be Love, and love may indeed prove to be the poet's positive contribution to social history, but there is still, first and last, the present fabric of things to be undone, a veil to be *torn* aside. The innovation required of the poet is technical, furthermore, as well as prophetic: "Every great poet must inevitably innovate upon the example of his predecessors in the exact structure of his peculiar versification." The need for variety is so pressing that most regular meters should be avoided, and the rhythm of prose writers who qualify as poets will scarcely amount to a prosody at all: "[Plato] forebore to invent any regular plan of rhythm which should include, under determinate forms, the varied pauses of his style." Thus whereas for Peacock versification, or "harmony," was a reactionary, precivilized kind of violence—"language on the rack of Procrustes"—versification for Shelley is a radical kind of violence carried out against the tyranny of the past. It is an aspect of the poet's adversary attitude toward his own age and toward the poets of the past.

Here recurs another theme of Longinus. Among other inspiring enemies the poet wrestles, as Longinus pointed out and Dryden repeated, with the mighty dead. The posture of the poet in Shelley is still more complex. On the one hand he represents the world, especially its "language, gesture, and . . . imitative arts," which thus "become at once the representation and the medium"; while on the other hand that same world, whether as the arena of language or as a language itself ("almost all familiar objects are signs"), is just what the poet must set out to destroy in the course of transforming it. "Sounds as well as thoughts," writes Shelley further on, "have relation both between each other and towards that which they represent." In other words, poetry is the record both of its stimulus and of its response, which latter must be, to some extent at least, a reaction-formation. The recorded stimulus, consisting of all influences including those of the past, comprises the continuity of poetry with the past, while the recorded response is the answer of the individual to those influences. This has always been so, even where the answer is not violent but only a playful emulation: "A child at play by itself will express its delight by its voice and motions; and every inflexion of tone and every gesture will bear exact relation to a corresponding antitype [i.e., proto-type, not opposite] in the pleasurable impressions which awakened it; it will be the reflected image of that impression; and as the lyre trembles and sounds after the wind has died away, so the child seeks, by prolonging in its voice and motions the duration of the effect, to prolong also a consciousness of the cause."

Poetry reveals its influences by reacting to them, not by replicating them, but it always does reveal them. It is never isolated and independent. When Shelley writes in the Preface to *Prometheus Unbound* that "one great poet is a masterpiece of nature which another not only ought to study but must study," he seems to believe that study of this kind is a compulsion depriving duty of its merit. Apparently the great poet, being part of nature, can no more be resisted than the light of day. Quite frequently Shelley brackets nature and art with such equal attention that although they are supposed to be opposites, alternatives, they become in effect interchangeable, just as they were for Longinus. In choosing the best language, for example, one must be "familiar with nature" as well as "with the most celebrated productions of the human mind" because, as we have seen, nature is a kind of language and language poetically used has the palpability of nature.

In this way the poet takes an adversary stance toward both nature and art. Even in descriptions that are solely aesthetic Shelley stresses the part played by resistance: "There is a principle within the human being, and perhaps within all sentient beings, which acts otherwise than in the lyre, and produces not melody alone, but harmony, by an internal adjustment of the sounds or motions thus excited to the impressions which excite them." There is an element of salutary discord in this harmony; what is at issue for Shelley in such passages, as also for Socrates when he takes up the metaphor of "attunement" in the *Phaedo*, is nothing less than the autonomy of the "soul," or poetic faculty. The "internal adjustment" that makes a more complicated music possible has as its deeper function the manifestation of freedom. Hence true poetry by its very existence symbolizes the moral and political condition to which humanity can aspire. It is really for this reason, then, that the reaction of poetry to any and all impressions is in part adversary, "promethean." Poetry alone, apparently, can contradict the refrain of Shelley's metaphysical fragments, that "mind . . . cannot create, it can only perceive." However, this is a point that Shelley can never resolve, much as he would like to. The same argument may be used to deny the originality of poets that Shelley had often used, in his youth, to deny the divine origin of the universe: There must be "an infinity of creative and created gods, each more eminently requiring an intelligent author of his being than the foregoing."

It is interesting that Shelley's liveliest expressions of cordiality toward the contributions of both nature and art to the poet appear in the "Preface" to the poem that most vividly dramatizes the tyranny of external and internal forces, *Prometheus Unbound*. Jupiter is a patriarchal tyrant, and only the assertion of the enchained Prometheus that Jupiter exists by his sufferance, that the tyrant is a created embodiment of his own mind, can change the existing order. Thus although Jupiter plays the father, Prometheus the Titan is really the older of the two. This conflict over precedence seems at first to be a stalemate, leaving the two gods as coevals sustaining each other with their mutual hate. Displacing his unusually intense dislike of fathers, Shelley tends in general to concentrate on fraternal rivalries for the palm of originality. Thus it is not the past but the present that makes a poet: "A poet is the combined product of such internal powers as modify the nature of others; and of such external influences as excite and sustain these powers; he is not one, but both.

Every man's mind is, in this respect, modified by all the objects of nature and art. . . . Poets, not otherwise than philosophers, painters, sculptors, and musicians, are, in one sense, the creators, and in another, the creations, of their age."

Or, as he had put it in the earlier Preface to *Laon and Cythna*, each poet is, like Prometheus, "in a degree the author of the very influence by which his being is pervaded." Shelley's treatment of the freedom of the poet is always thus ambivalent. He can write about "Visionary rhyme,—in joy and pain / Struck from the inmost fountains of my brain," but the figure is not persuasive. What is the source of the fountains? "Internal powers" are given, after all, as much as "external influences." In *Prometheus Unbound*, beyond all rivalries for preeminence there stands Demogorgon in the role of Necessity.

WILLIAM KEACH

Shelley's Last Lyrics

"**I** have suffered what I wrote," says
Rousseau in *The Triumph of Life*,

> "And so my words were seeds of misery—
> Even as the deeds of others."
>
> (280–1)

These words may mean that Rousseau's writing gave expression to sufferings
he had actually lived through—this is certainly what we would expect the
author of *The Confessions* to claim. But they may just as well mean that
he, and others, eventually lived through sufferings brought about by, or
first expressed theoretically and fictively in, his writing. Words can be
'seeds of misery' both because they are sown by and because they sow
suffering. Count Maddalo offers a similarly equivocal pronouncement in
commenting on the 'wild language' that he and Julian have heard the
madman utter:

> Most wretched men
> Are cradled into poetry by wrong,
> They learn in suffering what they teach in song.
>
> (544–6)

Unless he is drawing a contrasting and not a summarizing maxim from
what they have observed in the asylum, it is perverse, even for Maddalo,
to say that the madman has been 'cradled' by wrong into his tormented
discourse. Be that as it may, Maddalo at first seems to place 'wrong' deeds
in a clearly anterior position to poetry. But the indeterminate grammar of

---

that last line obscures any sense of even provisional clarity. We expect the line to say that men teach in 'song' what they have already learned in 'suffering', and such a reading is gramatically plausible. But the syntax also encourages a reverse reading: men learn in 'suffering' what they have already taught in 'song' (and notice that the phrase 'what they teach in song' may be the direct object either of 'learn' or of 'suffering'). Like Rousseau, Maddalo holds open the possibility that the words of poetry may be 'seeds of misery'— / Even as the deeds of others'.

I begin with these troubled, uncertain broodings about words and deeds, song and suffering, by way of introducing a critical perspective that has been consciously set aside or underplayed [elsewhere], where the aim has been to give priority to the formal features of Shelley's writing and to concepts and attitudes characteristic of his own way of thinking about poetic language. If the advantages of that approach are at all apparent by now, so too is one disadvantage: it has inevitably isolated the poems from historical and biographical pressures that often, we may assume, had as much to do with their coming into being as did Shelley's compositional will and verbal resourcefulness. This is not a matter of apologetic reverence for 'biographical criticism'—of nostalgia for what a deconstructive reader of Wordsworth has called 'mimetical trivia'—but rather of allowing one's primary concern with the work and play of language in the text to remain open to whatever context the text itself makes pertinent. So I want to look at a group of poems in which Shelley's stylistic choices and performances are inextricably enmeshed in the choices and performances of living.

I

While there is a great deal of critical interest now in The Triumph of Life, probably written in May and June of 1822, much less has been said about the shorter poems. Shelley wrote during the six months before his death on 8 July. Some have found it easy to dismiss these lyrics as 'slight pieces', 'ariettes' (as Shelley himself once called them) that show us little more than that he could be urbane and melancholy at the same time. Those who have taken the poems more seriously, on the other hand, have sometimes done so in a slightly misleading way. Here is Harold Bloom in The Oxford Anthology of English Literature: 'Shelley's heart, when he died, had begun to touch the limits of desire, as his final love lyrics show. A tough but subtle temperament, he had worn himself out, and was ready to depart.' This sort of elegiac despair seems apter to Adonais than to the lyrics of 1822; it is an attitude that makes itself felt in these poems, but only in relation to other quite different, even nostalgic, impulses.

For six months Jane Williams was Shelley's muse, lyric focus and—with her husband Edward—primary audience. Four of the 1822 lyrics refer 'to Jane' in their titles; five others are less explicitly, but no less centrally, about her. The Williamses had come to Pisa in January 1821 at the suggestion of Shelley's cousin, Thomas Medwin; in January 1822 they were living directly below the Shelleys in a building called the Tre Palazzi di Chesa, on the north side of the Arno. They were married only in common law. Jane Cleveland (her maiden name) had been left by a first husband with whom she was apparently unhappy; since living with Williams, a retired lieutenant in the army of the East India Company, she had given birth to two children, the second one after arriving in Pisa in March 1821. Her relationship with Shelley has of course been the subject of much scholarly sleuthing and speculation. When he first met them, Shelley preferred Edward: he was more literary and intellectual (for a time he was taking down daily dictation of Shelley's translation of Spinoza's *Tractatus Theologico-Politicus*), and being an experienced sailor, he was a good companion for Shelley's boating expeditions on the Arno. Shelley at first found Jane 'extremely pretty & gentle' but 'apparently not *very* clever'. Yet even in this letter to Claire Clairmont (16 January 1821) he confessed, having 'only seen her for an hour', that 'I like her very much'. He continued to have reservations, at least when writing to Claire: 'W. I like & have got reconciled to Jane' (14 May 1821). But by January 1822 the reservations had given way to warmly intimate and idealizing affection. He described her to John Gisborne as 'more amiable and beautiful than ever, and a sort of spirit of embodied peace in our circle of tempests', adding 'So much for first impressions!' (12 January 1822).

Just how intimate Jane Williams and Shelley became during the last half-year of his life has been much disputed. Walter E. Peck claimed to have seen an unpublished letter from Shelley to Byron in which Shelley says that he made love to her one evening after they had gone together to a local *festa* near San Terenzo. The letter has never been found or substantiated. More recently, G.M. Matthews has used a combination of literary and biographical inference to argue that Shelley's serious intimacy with Jane Williams 'developed late and very rapidly at San Terenzo towards a crisis', that they became lovers during the latter part of June, and that this was 'the most profoundly disturbing personal experience of Shelley's whole maturity'. Matthews' argument has been countered in extensive detail by Donald Reiman, who insists that there is no evidence from Shelley's writing or from his life to justify our concluding the relationship with Jane Williams was ever anything but idealizing and 'Platonic'. Others who have looked at the evidence, most notably Judith Chernaik, think that Shelley was in love with her by spring 1822 but that exactly what that love came to must remain a matter of speculation. There are multiple unintended ironies, then, in Newman Ivey White's saying that 'The only authentic record of the high-water mark of Shelley's attraction to Jane Williams is Shelley's own poems.' Poetic fictions lead beyond themselves to actual events and circumstances, which in turn lead back to the poems as our 'only authentic record'. Words themselves may be deeds, it would seem, as well as the seeds of deeds.

While Jane Williams stands at the center of the 1822 lyrics, other figures from what Shelley calls 'our circle of tempests' haunt these poems in ways which have never been taken adequately into account. One of these is certainly Mary Shelley; another is Claire Clairmont. Shelley's relationship to Mary had been under repeated, almost constant strain since the death of their daughter Clara in September 1818, which Mary partly blamed, and with some justification, on a grueling amount of travel designed to put Shelley and Claire in touch with Byron and Allegra in Venice. One source of the strain was Claire herself, whose ambiguous closeness to Shelley had always made Mary uneasy. That uneasiness was sharply exacerbated in August 1821 by the so-called 'Hoppner scandal': Mary learned in a letter from Shelley that Richard Hoppner, British consul-general at Venice, and his wife had been spreading the story 'that Claire was my mistress' and that in the winter of 1818–19 'Clare was with child by me—that I gave her the most violent medicines to procure abortion—that . . . this not succeeding she was brought to bed & that I immediately tore the child from her & sent it to the foundling hospital.' Mary did not believe that Claire had given birth to Shelley's child. But that Claire had been his lover Shelley himself did not explicitly deny ('that is all very well & so far there is nothing new: all the world has heard so much & people may believe or not believe as they think good'). The Hoppner scandal revived Mary's worries about Shelley and Claire just when Shelley's fascination with Emilia Viviani had run its course (her arranged marriage finally took place 8 September 1821).

Mary's alienation from Shelley, which he complained about but also seems to have resigned himself to, is not only understandable but surprisingly temperate, given the circumstances. It was one thing to accept Shelley's principles of non-exclusive love, as Mary seems to have done; it was another to be almost continuously pregnant or nursing while moving from one place to another in a foreign country (she was pregnant five times during the seven years between 1815 and 1822), and then to find herself depicted symbolically in *Epipsychidion* as the 'cold chaste Moon' whose 'soft yet icy flame . . . warms not but illumines' (281–5). Shelley, for his part, could not have turned poetically to Jane Williams without thinking of what it implied about his commitments to Mary—and less directly to Claire Clairmont, whose correspondence with Shelley was often kept secret from Mary during these months.

Then there was Byron, whose shadow is superimposed on those of Mary Shelley and Claire Clairmont in the lyrics of 1822. Mary wrote to Maria Gisborne on 30 November 1821:

> So here we live, Lord B just opposite to us in Casa Lanfranchi. . . . Pisa you see has become a little nest of singing birds—You will be both surprised and delighted at the work just about to be published by him. . . . It made a great impression upon me, and appears almost a revelation from its power and beauty—Shelley rides with him—I, of course, see little of him.

The mixture of subdued sarcasm and admiration in this letter is intensely suggestive of the situation in Pisa during the winter of 1821–2. The focus, 'of course,' is on Byron, who had arrived on the scene at the beginning of November and whose presence exerted an enormous pressure on what Shelley wrote at this time—and more tellingly perhaps, on what he did not write.

Shelley was remarkably open to Byron's talent and power, in spite of the fact that they had come increasingly to threaten his own personal and poetic self-confidence. This was the fourth time Shelley had lived in Byron's presence: each time his estimation of Byron's greatness grew, along with the sense of his own comparative inadequacy. If we look backwards and forwards chronologically from 1 November 1821, when Byron arrived in Pisa, over equal stretches of Shelley's career, we find that this date marks a striking drop in productivity. The nine months before Byron arrived, from February through October 1821, are filled with major projects conceived and written to completion; *Epipsychidion*, *A Defence of Poetry*, *Adonais*, *Hellas*, along with more than thirty lyrics. The 'Sonnet to Byron', probably written in November shortly after Byron's arrival, marks the interface between this extraordinary fecundity and a time of relative barrenness. It begins with what turned out to be a prophetic conjecture:

> If I esteemed you less, Envy would kill
> Pleasure, and leave to Wonder and Despair
> The ministration of the thoughts that fill
> The mind which, like a worm whose life may share

A portion of the unapproachable,
Marks your creations rise as fast and fair
As perfect worlds at the Creator's will.

(1–7)

In the nine months after Byron's arrival. Shelley produced only ten or so lyrics, some fragmentary translations from Calderon and Goethe, the 'Fragments of an Unfinished Drama', and the unfinished *Triumph of Life*, which he was able to begin writing only after he left Byron and Pisa and moved up the coast to San Terenzo on the Bay of Lerici. There was also *Charles I*, his only major ambition during that winter, but that went very haltingly. 'Lord Byron is established now, [& gives a weekly dinner *deleted*] & we are constant companions,' he wrote to Peacock in January 1822; 'I have been long idle,— & as far as writing goes, despondent—but I am now engaged in Charles the 1st & a devil of a nut it is to crack' (*Letters*, II, 373). Subsequent letters make it clear that Shelley's imaginative dryness and despondency arose mainly from his measuring his own achievement and public success against Byron's. Having told Leigh Hunt that 'particular dispositions in Lord B's character render the close & exclusive intimacy with him in which I find myself, intolerable to me,' he goes on to say: 'Indeed I have written nothing for this last two months. . . . What motives have I to write.—I *had* motives . . . but what are *those* motives now?' (2 March 1822; *Letters*, II, 393–4).

The complex tension and rivalry between Shelley and Byron, the sources of which were by no means exclusively literary, have been most recently and fully detailed by Charles E. Robinson and Richard Holmes. Holmes's account of their favorite pastime, target practice with pistols, is symbolically suggestive at almost every level:

> The shooting gradually changed from a casual exercise into a shared obsession. Byron rode out on a Hussar saddle slung with several pistols in decorated leather holsters; Shelley spent several hours a week preparing his own targets and carried them round in his pockets. . . . he and Byron seemed to have been by far the best shots among the party and there was a certain rivalry between the two. Tom Medwin noted their different styles of shooting: Byron drew a long aim, with a hand that visibly trembled, yet usually produced a high standard of hits. Shelley, on the contrary, took a sudden, rapid aim, with a rock-steady hand—'all firmness [Medwin's phrase]—and also produced regularly good shooting. Of the two, one has the impression from Williams's journal that Byron had the edge.

Another anecdote reconstructed by Holmes evokes the drama of Shelley and Byron's literary talks and is more pointedly relevant to Byron's impact on Shelley's poetic self-confidence:

Byron . . . always appeared to submit to Shelley's critical judgement on literary matters (it being understood that he regarded *Don Juan* and *Cain* as very great poems). Medwin was immensely impressed by this fact when one morning Byron handed Shelley the manuscript of a poem 'The Deformed Transformed'. Shelley took it over to the window to read, and having read it carefully, returned to where Byron leaned against the mantelpiece and announced that 'he liked it the least of all his works; that it smelt too strongly of "Faust"; and besides, that there were two lines in it, word for word from Southey.' Medwin quailed inwardly at the cool frankness of this judgement, but '. . . Byron turned deadly pale, seized the MS., and committed it to the flames, seeming to take a savage delight in seeing it consume'. Yet in part, this too was a stage device. Byron had another copy safely in his desk, and a revised version was published two years later by Murray.

Robinson's discussion of *The Deformed Transformed* adds a new dimension to Shelley's criticism of the manuscript and to Byron's 'savage delight' in apparently committing it to the flames. Byron's play contains a double transformation suggested to him, Robinson argues, by Shelley, who told Byron about a scene involving a similar device in Calderon's *El Purgatorio de San Patricio*. Unable to go forward with *Charles I*, Shelley had 'at the same time inadvertently given Byron the idea for a new drama' of his own.

    Shelley could not win with Byron, and he seems to have known it. His very openness to Byron's ruthless efficacy was bound to erode what confidence he had in, what ambitions he had for, his own major projects. In the 1822 lyrics we can see Shelley turning away from any direct competition with Byron—away from ambitious works on the scale of *Don Juan* and *Cain*, or *Prometheus Unbound* and *Adonais*—towards a more modest and intimate mode that he knew he was good at. But this does not mean that in these lyrics Shelley was able to write free of the pressure of Byron's success, any more than he could have written them without thinking of Mary's unhappiness, or of Claire's continuing dependence on his support and affection, or of his own dependence on their dependence on him. Just how Shelley's last lyrics contend with and accommodate anxieties they often seem to be trying to avoid is one of the questions I now want to pursue.

II

It may have been to try to get away from Byron and the established round of pistol-shooting and talking about each other's poetry that Shelley went for a day-long walk on 2 February with Jane Williams and Mary Shelley in the Cascine pine forest just outside Pisa. He drafted a 116-line poem about this occasion; he then revised the draft, split it into two poems, and gave them to Jane under the titles 'To Jane. The Invitation' and 'To Jane. The Recollection'. It has often been pointed out about both the draft and the revised poems that Mary is nowhere to be seen. True—and yet she haunts every line of these lyrics, which are the most important poems Shelley worked to completion in 1822. Less immediately, Byron haunts them too. The ways in which they are both there in Shelley's writing in spite of, or perhaps through, their apparent absence is part of what needs further consideration.

If we read 'The Invitation' and 'The Recollection' together, we find that Shelley has situated himself rhetorically on either side of the transient moment of lyrical intensity he attempts to define and sustain. One poem looks forward, the other backward, to a moment when he and Jane are together in the natural scene—but that moment itself is always out of reach, always either a wish or a memory. Shelley accentuated this sense of the inaccessibility of the moment of completion or fulfillment when he divided the original poem in two as he revised it. But the division is already there, strikingly, in the unified first draft. After an introductory quatrain, that draft moves through twenty-eight lines of tetrameter couplets that will eventually provide the foundation for 'The Invitation'. Then at line 33, before Jane has ever had a chance to accept the invitation and join the speaker in 'the wild woods and the plains' (25), we hear that 'the last day of many days' 'is dead' (33, 35). As the speaker calls upon 'Memory' to 'Rise . . . and write its praise!' (36), rhythms and rhyme-scheme undergo a subtle adjustment, and then settle into the ballad quatrain that becomes the new formal idiom for that part of the draft that will become 'The Recollection'. Although 'The Invitation' insists that 'To-day is for itself enough' (40), Shelley seems to have felt from the beginning that the moment with Jane could be articulated only as a prospective or retrospective construct of the imagination.

He develops the prospective movement of 'The Invitation' through a subtly muted variation on the *carpe diem* invitation genre that includes poems like Herrick's 'Corinna's going a Maying'. Where Herrick urges Corinna into a 'blooming morn' in May,

> Rise; and put on your Foliage, and be seene
> To come forth, like the Spring-time, fresh and greene,
>   (15–16)

Shelley invites Jane to join him on a winter morning that is prematurely and still only incipiently spring-like,

> The brightest hour of unborn spring
> Through the winter wandering
> Found, it seems, this halcyon morn
> To hoar February born.
>
> (7–10)

Shelley's speaker, like Herrick's, is already in the natural scene; rhetorically the invitation issues from a temporal sequence that is already underway (compositionally, of course, the invitation was written in retrospective anticipation of a past experience). The erotic impetus and wit of Herrick's poem are muted and displaced onto the landscape, where they work to release the scene's unobtrusive autobiographical symbolism:

> Bending from Heaven in azure mirth
> It kissed the forehead of the earth
> And smiled upon the silent sea,
> And bade the frozen streams be free
> And waked to music all their fountains.
>
> (11–15)

'Fairer far than this fair day' (2), Jane herself has been a prophetess of this 'prophetess of May' (17) who has warmed and freed a stream of song that had previously been frozen—almost entirely frozen, one could say, since Byron's arrival at the beginning of November. Characteristically, Shelley reverses the direction in which the basic figurative situation might be expected to move: it is not that Jane's effect on the speaker is like this morning's effect on the winter landscape, but—at the beginning and again at the end of the first verse paragraph—the other way around:

> Making the wintry world appear
> Like one on whom thou smilest, dear.
>
> (19–20)

Within the poem's rhetorical fiction, Jane is being invited to experience the natural enactment of a momentary imaginative reawakening she has already inspired.

Shelley's refined awareness of literary tradition is nowhere more apparent than in 'The Invitation', and it is not at all surprising that Donald Davie once paid it such handsome tribute in the chapter of *Purity of Diction in English Verse* he called 'Shelley's urbanity'. The poem, he wrote, is:

> a nonpareil, and one of Shelley's greatest achievements. It maintains the familiar tone, though in highly figured language, and contrives to be urbane about feelings which are novel and remote. . . . We can accept Jane as 'Radiant Sister of the Day', largely because the lyrical feeling has

already accommodated such seemingly unmanageable things as unpaid bills and unaccustomed visitors. It is an achievement of urbanity to move with such ease from financial and social entanglements to elated sympathy with a natural process; just as it is a mark of civilization to be able to hold these things together in one unflurried attitude.

If this were all there were to say about the poem, it would be enough to make it a poem worth caring about (in spite of Davie's sour and undetailed retraction of his tribute more than ten years later). But there is, I think, much more that needs to be said. If the poem is an instance of 'urbanity', then that term has to be able to accommodate forces which are darker and more deeply unsettling than unpaid bills and unwanted visitors (threatening though these were to Shelley in 1822). The larger structural pattern of Shelley's approach in 'The Invitation' and 'The Recollection', and in the draft from which they derive, should remind us of a famous stanza from 'To a Skylark':

> We look before and after,
>   And pine for what is not—
> Our sincerest laughter
>   With some pain is fraught—
> Our sweetest songs are those that tell of saddest thoughts.
> (86–90)

The prevailing tone of urbane romantic familiarity in "The Invitation' is shot through with references to a realm of sadness, anxiety and guilt which Shelley seems—and perhaps only seems—to be trying to set aside or banish.

Look at the second verse paragraph, all of which Shelley added in revision. With its inset 'notice on my door' (29) and wittily personified abstractions, this is the most eighteenth-century section of the poem and predictably the focus of much of Davie's praise. Yet from the beginning the paragraph evokes a world of frustration and disappointment from which it never manages fully to escape. Come away, the speaker says,

> To the silent wilderness
> Where the soul need not repress
> Its music lest it should not find
> An echo in another's mind.
> (23–6)

The fact that 'find' here does find an echo in the 'mind' that completes Shelley's fluent couplet may be appropriate to the anticipated meetings of minds with Jane, but it also throws into relief the memory of expectation of moments devoid both of music and of responsive echo. Reading a reference to Mary or Byron in these lines is possible but unnecessary to seeing how strongly the speaker's celebration of the moment he longs for with Jane is conditioned by an awareness of its opposite. One of the things Shelley wants to put on hold here is the echo of his own mind:

> Reflexion, you may come tomorrow,
> Sit by the fireside with Sorrow—
>
> (33–4)

But reflection will not stay at home until 'tomorrow' with 'Sorrow': in the final verse paragraph it is right there in the forest with the speaker as he waits for Jane, projected figuratively in:

> the pools where winter-rains
> Image all their roof of leaves,
> Where the pine its garland weaves
> Of sapless green and ivy dun
> Round stems that never kiss the Sun—
>
> (50–4)

This scene, beautifully and delicately articulated (the semantic antithesis in the rhyming of 'dun' with 'Sun' precisely condenses the tone of the passage), is potentially one of those arenas of reflexive self-involvement reaching all the way back through Shelley's career to *Alastor*. The image of 'stems that never kiss the Sun' momentarily reverses the opening image of the 'halcyon morn' as 'It kissed the forehead of the earth' (9, 12), and we may feel that Shelley has inadvertently found himself in a spot where Jane's and the spring-like morning's influence will be of no avail. The poem does not linger beside these embowered reflecting pools, however; it moves on to other vantage points, and to a climactic harmony in which the sun's unifying light and warmth prevail. At the end 'Sun' is bound in a couplet with 'one', not 'dun'. But we will return to those pools in 'The Recollection', and their figurative implications will be worked through to a very different conclusion.

'The Recollection' begins by acknowledging that the moment celebrated anticipatorily in 'The Invitation' was an 'evanescent visitation', a 'vanishing apparition' seemingly 'arrested' in advance in the previous poem through the artifice of a fictive invitation, but now traceable only by writing 'The epitaph of glory fled'(6). That rhyme-word 'trace' in line 5 suggests that Shelley may already be recalling his figure of inspiration as 'a wind over a sea' from the *Defence*; the 'epitaph of glory fled' indicates that Wordsworth has displaced Herrick as the text Shelley is now taking as a point of departure. 'The Recollection' has been less admired than 'The Invitation', mainly, I think, because the urbane familarity of the first poem is much less effective here in muting and disguising the underlying anxiety. Particular elements of the natural scene undergo dramatic transformations. The somber, embowering pines of 'The Invitation' are now seen as:

> the pines that stood
> The giants of the waste,
> Tortured by storms to shapes as rude
> As serpents interlaced.
> (21–4)

Even the day's paradisal calm, although it temporarily soothes the violent impulses now evident in the landscape, is latently threatening. This is precisely what bothered Leavis about the poem. Alert as he always was to Wordsworth's importance for Shelley, Leavis argued that the calm in section 3 of 'The Recollection':

> is the reverse of Wordsworthian; the peace is indeed momentary. What is bound is not the silence, but the impending violation—the chain will break; for 'inviolable' [37] suggests the opposite of what it says, and the characteristic leaning movement conveys the opposite of security. A Wordsworthian atmosphere is never filled with love, and love here is at the same time a sultry menace.

Often in his writing about Shelley, Leavis gets hold of the right point in the wrong way. In the midst of this crotchety denunciation he says just what needs to be said about 'inviolable quietness'. And while 'sultry menace' seems extreme for a passage with a 'busy woodpecker' in it (35), there is latent in the scene an element of erotic intensity that threatens to make the peace, as Shelley says in line 47, 'momentary'. Leavis goes on to object specifically to Shelley's having substituted 'thrilling silent life' (46) for the allegedly more Wordsworthian 'thinking about silent life' of the first draft (70). But 'thrilling', with its suggestions of intense arousal and its etymological implication of 'piercing' or 'penetrating', does something much more interesting to 'silent life' than does 'thinking'. Leavis is right about 'the characteristic leaning movement' of this passage: thirteen of the twenty lines lack end-stopping, and the verse accumulates a kind of energy that infuses with suspense the insistence on 'How calm it was!':

> The breath of peace we drew
> With its soft motion made not less
> The calm that round us grew.—
> (38–40)

There is a veiled tension or pressure in this intake of breath and in the calm 'that round us grew', much as there is in the prior reference to 'The inviolable quietness'. One feels that the 'leaning' Leavis perceives comes from an urgent striving to hold in check 'Our mortal nature's strife' (48).

The sense of erotic energy and personal anxiety under precarious and perhaps illusory control is important to what Shelley makes of those reflecting pools from 'The Invitiation' in the last two sections of 'The Recollection'. At first they may seem innocent enough as picturesque analogues for the idealizing imagination as it attempts to discover a transcendent realm represented there in the natural scene:

> We paused beside the pools that lie
>   Under the forest bough—
> Each seemed as 'twere, a little sky
>   Gulphed in a world below;
> A firmament of purple light
>   Which in the dark earth lay
> More boundless than the depth of night
>   And purer than the day,
> In which the lovely forests grew
>   As in the upper air,
> More perfect, both in shape and hue,
>   Than any spreading there.
>   (53–64)

But the illogically extravagant comparative rhetoric—'More boundless' and especially 'More perfect'—destabilizes the activity of idealizing reflection by making it seem driven, 'leaning'. 'More boundless' even threatens to undo that binding of 'Our mortal nature's strife' to 'momentary peace' in the previous section. What the process of idealizing reflection is being driven by is revealed in the poem's final section:

> Sweet views, which is our world above
>   Can never well be seen,
> Were imaged in the water's love
>   Of that fair forest green.
>   (69–72)

As Shelley draws out the implications of recognizing that love pervades the poem's 'inviolable quietness' and motivates its idealizing representation, the waters of the pool are darkly personified, the image they reflect becomes delusively untruthful, and the 'atmosphere without a breath' moves with the breath of envy:

> Like one beloved, the scene had lent
>   To the dark water's breast,
> Its every leaf and lineament
>   With more than truth exprest;

Until an envious wind crept by,
          Like an unwelcome thought
Which from the mind's too faithful eye
          Blots one dear image out.—
                              (77–84)

Shelley's revisions of and additions to the first draft are particularly revealing in this passage. Lines 77–80, with their darkening confirmation of what love's part in the experience may mean, are entirely new. 'Wandering wind' in the draft becomes 'envious wind' in the revision. Most commentators have identified this wind and the 'unwelcome thought' to which it is compared (in one of the most simply effective of Shelley's reversed similes) with Mary, who has been excluded from the poem but who makes her absence felt here at the end to a frustrated and perhaps guilty Shelley. The question of guilt is ambiguous: How are we to take 'too faithful'? 'Too faithful' to Mary (with an undertone of bitter resentment)? Or 'too faithful' to the actual circumstances of his life? If we are looking for biographical referents, the wind's envy might be Shelley's instead of (or as well as) Mary's, and refer to Shelley's worrying about Byron. After all, that 'Sonnet to Byron' had begun with the grim surmise that 'If I esteemed you less, Envy would kill / Pleasure.'

But no biographical reading alone is adequate to the way in which Shelley finally undoes the reflection imagery as it has evolved through the two poems by reworking the figure of inspiration as 'a wind over a sea' from the *Defence*. There it is the 'coming calm' that inevitably erases the wind's ephemeral imprint on the water's surface. Here the action is reversed: a moment of inspired calm within 'A magic circle traced', as Shelley says in line 44, does not 'erase' but is itself blotted out—the writing imagery is remarkably insistent—by a wind that mocks the breath of inspiration and brings the poem's writing, its activity of 'trac[ing] / The epitaph of glory fled' (5–6), to an end. If there is a way of squaring or reconciling these seemingly incongruous figures of wind and water, it is by recognizing that the 'envious wind' and the disturbing, unwelcome thoughts figured in it are in fact the poem's deep source of inspiration—that both 'The Invitation' and 'The Recollection' are defenses against, and in that antithetical sense are inspired by, thoughts which are only partly excluded from or bound within the 'magic circle' centered around Jane. To 'trace / The epitaph of glory fled' is to rewrite or re-record a death that has already been marked and inscribed. The epitaph traced in 'The Recollection' may be implicit in the elusive ephemerality of the moment described with fictive anticipation in 'The Invitation'.

III

The lyrics of 1822 transgress the boundary separating words from deeds. It is a deed, an act which springs from but also might be expected to cause suffering, for Shelley to make Jane Williams fill in the missing name at the end of 'The Recollection' when he gave the poems to her (this is how the last two lines appear in the British Library fair copy):

> Less oft is peace in ——'s mind
> Than calm in water seen.

Other lyrics too are deeds in that they were not only written for Jane but were shown or given to her as half-furtive, half-open acts of personal communication. Consider three poems also belonging to the early months of 1822. On 26 January, a week before the walk in the Cascine pine forest that occasioned 'The Invitation' and 'The Recollection', Shelley enclosed a seven-stanza poem entitled 'To ——' and beginning 'The serpent is shut out from Paradise' with the following note to 'My dear Williams':

> Looking over the portfolio in which my friend used to keep verses, & in which those I sent you the other day were found,—I have lit upon these; which as they are too dismal for *me* to keep I send them you [who can afford *deleted*].
>
> If any of the stanzas should please you, you may read them to Jane, but to no one else,—and yet on second thought I had rather you would not [*some six words scratched out*].
>
> (Letters, II, 384)

The blatantly transparent disguise ('my friend'), divided emotions, insinuatingly underscored pronoun and still legible deletions in this note are all gestures to be found in Shelley's poems of this period as well. 'The Magnetic Lady to Her Patient' can be dated to about the same time. At the top of the first page of the holograph Shelley wrote 'For Jane & Williams alone to see', and on an outer wrapping for the poem, 'To Jane. Not to be opened unless you are alone, or with Williams'. Like the titles of these poems, such inscriptions are hard to keep separate from the poetic texts to which they are attached. Somewhat later, probably in February or March, Shelley gave Jane a guitar accompanied by a beautifully written copy of the 'frightful scrawl' that Trelawny had found him working on in the woods outside Pisa. He now gave this poem the title 'With a Guitar. To Jane'.

These three poems adopt very different lyrical postures and tones of voice. 'The Serpent is Shut Out from Paradise', although the least successful and inventive of the three, presents some revealing difficulties.

Parts of it are openly self-pitying; there is little of what Davie would call urbanity in the almost Petrarchan sequence of images with which the poem opens:

> The serpent is shut out from Paradise—
>   The wounded deer must seek the herb no more
>   In which its heart's cure lies—
>   The widowed dove must cease to haunt a bower
> Like that from which its mate with feigned sighs
>   Fled in the April hour.—
>   I, too, must seldom seek again
> Near happy friends a mitigated pain.
>
> (1–8)

In the second stanza self-pity takes on a defiant, bitter edge and confronts the limitations of pity—although not, it seems, of self-pity:

> But not to speak of love, Pity alone
> Can break a spirit already more than bent.
> (12–13)

What really makes this poem so disturbed and disturbing is the furtive ambiguity of the emotional claims it makes on its immediate audience. As in the note he sent with the poem, Shelley shifts the focus of his attention from both Williams and Jane to just one of them—but to which one?

> Therefore, if now I see you seldomer,
>   Dear friends, dear *friend*, know that I only fly
>   Your looks, because they stir
> Griefs that should sleep, and hopes that cannot die.
> (17–20)

Given Shelley's note, we would expect Williams to see himself as the singular 'dear *friend*', but the lines that follow hardly make sense unless the narrowed reference is to Jane. For how long in the poem is this narrowed reference meant to apply? Does it still hold for the next stanza, where another added emphasis that looks like bold directness only heightens a sense of slippery indirection?

> *You* spoil me for the task
>   Of acting a forced part in life's dull scene.
> Of wearing on my brow the idle mask
>   Of author, great or mean,
>   In the world's carnival. I sought
> Peace thus, and but in you I found it not.
> (27–32)

The autobiographical reference to the role Shelley was forced to play in Byron's presence is obvious ('serpent' in line 1 alludes to Byron's favorite nickname for him). 'Idle mask' and the wavering of 'great or mean' seem to convey weary detachment from that role, but this itself may be a mask for defensive anxiety ('I have been long idle,' Shelley wrote to Peacock on 11 January 1822; *Letters*, II, 3740. Byron's influence on the poem may even be reflected in its *ottava rima* scheme, which Shelley complicates and partly disguises by varying the line lengths. But what effect do Jane and/or Williams have on Shelley's 'acting a forced part'? '*You* spoil me for the task' suggests that they made it more difficult; 'I sought / Peace thus, and but in you I found it not' suggests that they made it easier.

This poem dramatizes its own uncertainty in ways that complicate rather than clarify what it asks of its readers—of Jane and Edward Williams, but also of us. The flowers the speaker reads in stanza 5 yield an indeterminate message, yet he 'dread[s] / To speak' and his friends 'may know too well' one of its possible meanings. Is it this unspoken meaning or the indeterminacy itself that constitutes 'the truth in the sad oracle'? In the final stanza the vocal manner suddenly does become urbanely collo-quial; the speaker raises the question of resolution and confesses that he lacks it:

> I asked her yesterday if she believed
>   That I had resolution. One who *had*
>   Would ne'er thus have relieved
>   His heart with words, but what his judgment bade
> Would do, and leave the scorner unrelieved.—
>
> (49–53)

Does 'thus' in line 51 refer to the speaker's having 'asked her yesterday if she believed / That I had resolution'? Or does it refer to his present act of confessing his feelings in the poem itself? Either way, these lines are an act against 'her', against Mary: the third-person pronoun is no longer distanced from its biographical referent by being quoted in a folk saying, as in stanza 5. Perhaps it is this gesture, and not the hesitant allusion to 'Griefs that should sleep, and hopes that cannot die' (20) or to truths 'I dread / To speak' (38–9), that makes him feel that he has 'relieved / His heart with words.' What the poem's words leave the reader with is a sense of unrelieved, even unrelievable, frustration.

"The Magnetic Lady to Her Patient' stands between the con-sciously indulgent yet constructed self-absorption of 'The Serpent is Shut Out' and that elegant and ostensibly liberating 'ariette', 'With a Guitar. To Jane'. It is the only one of the 1822 lyrics written for more than one voice. Jane herself is made to speak the first four stanzas (she is named in stanza 5); what she says is rhythmically incantatory and, even in its demurrals, erotic:

> 'And from my fingers flow
> The powers of life, and like a sign
> Seal thee from thine hour of woe,
> And brood on thee, but may not blend
>   With thine.'
>
> (5–9)

Judith Chernaik may be right to say that the biographical 'explicitness of the poem . . . is part of its charm', but the charm is not without its painful equivocations:

> 'Sleep, sleep, sleep on—I love thee not—
>   Yet when I think that *he*
>   Who made and makes my lot
> As full of flowers, as thine of weeds,
>   Might have been lost like thee,—
> And that a hand which was not mine
> Might then have charmed his agony
> As I another's—my heart bleeds
>   For thine.
>
> (10–18)

Apparently Shelley could rely on Williams to take these words as the loyal compliment they seem to be and not to feel blamed for making his lot full of 'weeds', but the grammar is ambiguous and potentially makes Williams responsible for Shelley's unhappiness as well as for Jane's happiness. It is also troubling that while Jane's sympathy is made partly to depend on her imagining her husband in Shelley's unhappy situation, she stops short in the poem of imagining herself in Mary's, or of taking her explicitly into account at all. Jane's performance is contradictory: at the end of the third stanza she tells her patient to 'forget me, for I can never be thine' (26–7), but at the end of the fourth she claims 'Be mine thy being is to its deep / Possest' (35–6). Much of this veiled tension is momentarily released in the chatty dialogue at the beginning of the last stanza:

> 'The spell is done—how feel you now?'
>   'Better, quite well' replied
>   The sleeper
>
> (37–9)

But as the dialogue continues, the tone of relaxed intimacy takes on a tenser inflection:

> 'What would do
> You good when suffering and awake,
>   What cure your head and side?'
> 'What would cure that would kill me, Jane,
> And as I must on earth abide
> Awhile yet, tempt me not to break
>   My chain.'
>
>   (39–45)

Medwin's comment on these lines gives them a morbid medical gaiety: 'he made the same reply to an enquiry as to his disease, and its cure, as he had done to me,—"What would cure me would kill me."—meaning lithotomy' (the surgical removal of stones from the bladder—without anaesthesia, of course, in Shelley's day). What Medwin deliberately ignores—it is inconceivable that even he did not get it—is the sexual implication of these lines. 'The "chain" he must not break', Chernaik remarks, 'is the chain of life; also, undoubtedly, it is the chain of his marriage. Undoubtedly. Shelley gave the poem to Jane with instructions 'Not to be opened unless you are alone, or with Williams'. That Shelley could imagine, even desire, that Jane would read this poem in Edward's presence is the most disturbingly equivocal thing about it.

     In 'With a Guitar. To Jane' the frustrated desire, alienation and guilt of those early months in 1822 for once seem to be brought under playfully sophisticated control. The fragility and vulnerability of that control are, however, the poem's most interesting features. 'With a Guitar. To Jane' introduces itself as a lyrical dramatic monologue—'Ariel to Miranda' (1). And in addition to casting himself, Jane and Williams in roles borrowed from Shakespeare, Shelley also revives the courtly Renaissance tradition, as Richard Cronin has recently pointed out, of writing a poem to accompany and explain a gift presented to the poet's mistress (Herrick is again a possible influence, along with Donne). Yet pain and sadness are not excluded from this archaizing artifice; they are instead suspended within and by it:

>   Take
> This slave of music for the sake
> Of him who is the slave of thee;
> And teach it all the harmony,
> In which thou can'st, and only thou,
> Make the delighted spirit glow,
> 'Till joy denies itself again
> And too intense is turned to pain.
>
>   (1–8)

Joy is inherently unstable and self-destroying by virtue of its very intensity: the idea is certainly familiar in Shelley's writing, but in extending it here to the joy inspired by Miranda's anticipated music, Shelley indirectly links this compliment-*cum*-warning to the patient's wry reply to the Magnetic Lady: 'What would cure that would kill me, Jane.' Death is a continuous motif in Ariel's song, even though here, as in *The Tempest*, it is made to seem dreamily fictitious by an elegantly deployed fantasy of reincarnation:

> When you die, the silent Moon
> In her interlunar swoon
> Is not sadder in her cell
> Than deserted Ariel;
> When you live again on Earth
> Like an unseen Star of birth
> Ariel guides you o'er the sea
> Of life from your nativity.
> (23–30)

For a reader who recalls the figure of the 'cold chaste Moon' in *Epipsychidion*, Ariel's comparing himself to the darkened and 'silent Moon' may seem the only instance in the poem where the biographical symbolism darkens as it does in the other lyrics. In *Epipsychidion* the speaker recalls a time when he was dominated by the influence of this 'Moon':

> And there I lay, within a chaste cold bed:
> Alas, I then was nor alive nor dead:
> For at her silver voice came Death and Life,
> Unmindful each of their accustomed strife.
> (299–302)

Ariel is not entirely free of this lunar influence; the illusory reconcilations of 'her silver voice' echo through his celebration of Miranda's warm, intense 'harmony'.

As it turns out this Ariel, unlike Shakespeare's 'airy spirit', is 'Imprisoned for some fault of his / In a body like a grave' (38–9). His transitory release from this living death must come from Miranda's smiles and from her music. It is this idea that provides the intricate link between the first part of the poem and the second, with its tender etiological account of the guitar's death as a tree and double rebirth through art:

> The artist who this idol wrought
> To echo all harmonious thought
> Felled a tree while on the steep
> The woods were in their winter sleep . . .
> —and so this tree—
> O that such our death may be—

Died in sleep, and felt no pain,
To live in happier form again,
From which, beneath Heaven's fairest star,
The artist wrought this loved guitar,
And taught it justly to reply
To all who question skilfully
In language gentle as thine own.
                                        (43–61)

In so far as it speaks 'In language gentle', art—the guitar-maker's and then
Miranda's—transfigures death into an illusion. But we already know that
this language may provoke joy so extreme that it 'denies itself again / And
too intense is turned to pain' (7–8). Miranda's guitar, like the poem that
accompanies it to explain its genesis and potential, speaks a double
language, for:

It talks according to the wit
Of its companions, and no more
Is heard than has been felt before
By those who tempt it to betray
These secrets of an elder day.
                                        (82–6)

The graceful wit of Shelley's octosyllabic couplets is almost, but not quite,
enough to fend off suspicions that 'tempt it to betray' may mean 'tempt it
to prove false to' as well as 'tempt it to reveal'. Such suspicions will be
particularly hard to banish for a reader with the conclusion of 'The
Magnetic Lady to Her Paitent' still in her or his mind: 'tempt me not to
break / My chain'. Shelley insists that it is not just a question of what 'has
been felt before' by the guitar in its antenatal dream of nature's 'harmonies' (62–78), but of what Ariel and Miranda, he and Jane, have felt of
'Our mortal nature's strife' ('The Recollection', 48). Without them the
guitar is a 'silent token', even though its music may express 'more than
ever can be spoken' (11–12); it can 'echo all harmonious thought' (44),
and presumably all dissonant thought as well. They both know that even
'its highest holiest tone' (89) can never be impervious to the strains of
desire and loss.

      It may seem contrary to emphasize the pessimistic interpretive
possibilities of a text which is so clearly crafted to tease its readers, imaginary and actual, out of thinking about them. But I think it essential to
recognize that the most urbanely playful writing in Shelley's last lyrics is
never proof against the kind of 'unwelcome thought' that blots that 'one
dear image out' at the end of 'The Recollection', or that stains all the
images in 'When the Lamp is Shattered'—another lyric (if G.M. Matthews

is right) that belongs to these early months of 1822. One sequence of images in this latter poem bears particularly on the undertones of vulnerable mortality and death in 'With a Guitar':

> When the lute is broken
> Sweet tones are remembered not—
> When the lips have spoken
> Loved accents are soon forgot.
>
> As music and splendour
> Survive not the lamp and the lute,
> The heart's echoes render
> No song when the spirit is mute—
> No song—but sad dirges
> Like the wind through a ruined cell
> Or the mournful surges
> That ring the dead seaman's knell.
>
> (5–16)

The last line of this passage somberly echoes the last line of Ariel's 'Full fathom five' song from *The Tempest*: 'Sea nymphs hourly ring his knell' (I.ii.405). Jane's guitar, though fashioned 'To echo all harmonious thought', is as subject to silence and dissonance as are the hearts of those that question it, however 'skilfully' (60). The same could be said of the poem itself: Cronin is right to argue that while 'The poem explains the history and qualities of the guitar . . . the guitar acts as a metaphor explaining the genesis and the distinctive qualities of poetry'. These last lyrics suggest that although poems may acquire their own separate existence as verbal forms and fictions, they are never entirely free of the vicissitudes of those who write and read them. Matthews claims that 'When the Lamp is Shattered' 'was undoubtedly written for the "Unfinished Drama" of early 1822' and insists that 'it is ludicrous to treat a song written for private theatricals as if it were the cry of Shelley's own soul'. But thinking of the poem as a piece of dramatic 'artifice, creative play', need not preclude our also thinking of it as a deed, as an act inevitably if indirectly linked to personal motives and consequences. What *if* the poem were written to be performed in private theatricals, possibly (Matthews suggests) by Jane and Mary together? Acting is acting, as Hamlet discovers, despite the interventions of art. And since Shelley never finished the drama and apparently gave Jane a copy of the poem separately, it is difficult not to imagine how it would have been read by the recipient of 'With a Guitar. To Jane'.

IV

'Unwelcome thought[s]' about living and writing continue to emerge in the lyrics Shelley wrote later in 1822, during the last two months of his life. Since early February Shelley and Williams had been planning to find a summer place on the coast above Pisa where they could sail whenever they wanted and be out from under the shadow of Byron and his entourage. They looked for a house in the fishing village of Lerici, but all they could find was a dilapidated building, originally a boat-house, right on the water about a mile from Lerici, near the tiny village of San Terenzo. They were eager to move, however, so on 27 April the four of them—with their children, two servants and, at Shelley's urging, Claire Clairmont—sailed up the coast and moved in.

Being away from Byron was good for Shelley's writing: he may have begun work on *The Triumph of Life* fairly soon after settling in at Casa Magni. But the spectacle of Byron's success continued to oppress him, even at long distance. In February he and Byron had both ordered boats for their summer sailing to be built at Genoa. Byron's was to be much the larger and would be called the *Bolivar*; Shelley, with the financial assistance of Williams and Trelawny, commissioned a sleek twenty-four-foot yacht. Trelawny suggested that the boat be called the *Don Juan*, and Shelley initially agreed. But he eventually decided to assume full ownership of the boat and intended to change its name to the *Ariel*. Yet when the boat finally arrived in Lerici harbor on 12 May, Shelley was appalled to see stenciled on the forward mainsail, in large black letters, the name *Don Juan*. Even if the boat was to have kept the name originally given to it, such a display would have been totally inappropriate. Shelley knew whom to blame, of course, but as he said in a letter to Trelawny of 16 May, there was very little he could do about it:

> The Don Juan is arrived, & nothing can exceed the admiration *she* has excited, for we must suppose the name to have [been] given her during the equivocation of sex which godfather suffered in the Harem. . . . [*Heavily scratched over:* I see Don Juan is written on the mainsail. This was due to] my noble friend, carrying the joke rather too far; much I suspect to the scandal of Roberts [the shipcaptain charged with getting the boat built to specifications], & even of yourself. . . . though I must repeat that I think the joke was carried too far: but do not mention this to Roberts, who of course could do nothing else than acquiesce in Lord Byron's request. Does he mean to write the Bolivar on his own mainsail?—
>
> (*Letters*, II, 421–2)

Shelley's allusion at the beginning of the letter to the fifth canto of *Don Juan*, where Juan is threatened with castration unless he agrees to disguise himself as a woman and become Juanna, is revealingly suggestive of the kind of threat he jokingly attributes to Byron's joke. To catch the full force of Shelley's indignant sarcasm, one needs to know that less than a year before, having heard Byron read the fifth canto of *Don Juan* to him on his visit to Ravenna, he wrote in a letter to Mary:

> It sets him not above but far above all the poets of the day: every word has the stamp of immortality.—I despair of rivalling Lord Byron, as well I may: and there is no other with whom it is worth contending.
>
> (8 August 1821; *Letters*, II, 323)

Shelley's admiration—even his words ('the stamp of immortality')—had once again come back to haunt him. Byron had stamped the name of his finest achievement on Shelley's boat: so much for 'Ariel'. The joke infuriated and frustrated him: he tried for hours to remove the letters from the sail with turpentine and all sorts of other substances, but it was no use. An entirely new section of sail had to be carefully sewn in to disguise the disfigurement. And after all the fuss, the name *Don Juan* stuck, and even came to be accepted by Shelley himself.

Just how much Shelley's affection for Jane Williams intensified during these two months is a matter of conjecture. But that matters had grown considerably worse between Shelley and Mary is evident from their letters and from Mary's and Edward Williams's journals. Mary was pregnant again, probably since the end of March or the beginning of April, and this in itself might have made her unhappy about living in a run-down boat-house near a remote fishing village, in late spring weather that was oppressively hot even for Italy. And as if the deaths of three previous children were not enough to give her forebodings, she, and Shelley too, had to contend with the fact that just two days before they left Pisa, Allegra died of typhus in the convent where Byron had taken her to live, away from her mother Claire. On many days in late May and early June Mary stayed in the house unwell, while Shelley worked on *The Triumph of Life* and sailed in the bay with Williams, and sometimes with Jane.

On 16 June Mary Shelley had a serious miscarriage and almost bled to death. It was hours before a doctor could be found, and Shelley probably saved her life by getting hold of some ice and making her sit in a tub of it until the bleeding stopped. Two days later he wrote to John Gisborne about the incident with relief and confidence: 'I succeeded in checking the hemorrhage and the fainting fits, so that when the physician arrived all danger was over, and he had nothing to do but to applaud me for my boldness. She is now doing well, and the sea-baths will restore her' (*Letters*, II, 434). But in fact Mary was slow to recover, and so, in a different way, was Shelley—the miscarriage must have disturbed him in ways that the letter to Gisborne does not reveal. A week after the miscarriage, in the middle of the night, he ran screaming into Mary's room (they had slept apart since coming to San Terenzo) claiming that he had been visited by two terrifying 'visions'—he insisted that they were not dreams. Here is Mary's account of what he had told her, in a letter to Maria Gisborne written more than a month after Shelley's death:

> He dreamt that lying as he did in bed Edward & Jane came into him, they were in the most horrible condition, their bodies lacerated—their bones starting through their skin, the faces pale yet stained with blood, they could hardly walk, but Edward was the weakest & Jane was support-ing him—Edward said—'Get up, Shelley, the sea is flooding the house & it is all coming down.' S. got up, he thought, & went to his [*sic*] window that looked on the terrace & the sea & thought he saw the sea rushing in. Suddenly his vision changed & he saw the figure of himself strangling me, that had made him rush into my room. . . . talking it over the next morning he told me that he had had many visions lately—he had seen the figure of himself which met him as he walked on the terrace & said to him—'How long do you mean to be content'.
> (14 August 1822; *Letters of Mary Wollstonecraft Shelley*, I, 245)

Even allowing for the effect Shelley's drowning had on Mary's emotions, for the possibility that his death activated her own fictionalizing powers, she gives us a text or scenario that disturbingly reflects what we know of Shelley's life and writing at Casa Magni. I want to use her narrative as both biographical and figurative context for looking selectively at the short poems Shelley wrote at this time.

Of the four or five lyrics generally thought to have been written during the last two months of Shelley's life, two may be dated with relative certainty because they appear in the midst of *The Triumph of Life* manuscript. The three parts of the lyric beginning 'The keen stars were twinkling' were originally drafted out of final sequence on widely separated pages of this manuscript. We know their final sequence because we also have Shelley's fair copy of the poem, which he left in Jane's room with a cryptic and apologetic note ending, 'I commit them to your secrecy and your mercy, and will try to do better another time' (*Letters*, II, 437). The poem celebrates and rhythmically evokes Jane's singing on an evening when 'The keen stars were twinkling / And the fair moon was rising among them' (1–2). Clearly some new pattern of association has momentarily eclipsed the figure of the cold, sad moon in *Epipsychidion* and 'With a Guitar. To Jane'. Once again Shelley's lyric perspectives straddle and place out of immediate reach the actual moment being celebrated. The first stanza, in the past tense, indicates that this moment is being recollected; the second stanza is in the present and also the future tense because it asks Jane to:

> Sing again, with your dear voice revealing
>   A tone
>   Of some world far from ours,
> Where music and moonlight and feeling
>   Are one.
>
>   (20–4)

The world of ideal lyric unity is explicitly recognized as being 'far from ours', even though Jane has previously evoked it and may do so again. The first draft of the last two lines reads 'Where moonlight & music & feeling / Are *won*' (my emphasis), suggesting that Shelley may have been initially less concerned with a nocturnal version of the unifying ideal we find at the end of 'To Jane. The Invitation', than with the thought of fully possessing, through a performance or exertion of the interpretive will, experiences which here in our world are always 'arising unforeseen and departing unbidden', as he says in *The Defence*.

The other, longer lyric drafted in *The Triumph of Life* manuscript but left unfinished is also a nocturne; it has come to be called 'Lines Written in the Bay of Lerici'. Its position in the manuscript, together with certain correspondences between its imagery and external circumstances worked out in detail by Matthews, suggests that it was written about a week after Mary's miscarriage. (If Matthews's dating is correct, it may even be based on an experience that happened earlier on the very evening when Shelley had his gruesome nightmares.) The first part of the poem, through line 32, works to sustain the memory of an intensely beautiful encounter, presumably with Jane, against a pervasive awareness that the moment has vanished and left the speaker with divided feelings. Until Matthews's work on the poem appeared in 1961, published texts began where the manuscript draft seems to begin, at line 7:

> She left me at the silent time
> When the moon had ceased to climb
> The azure dome of Heaven's steep,
> And like an albatross asleep,
> Balanced on her wings of light,
> Hovered in the purple night.
>
>   (7–12)

What Matthews noticed was that a group of lines crammed into the space at the top of the manuscript page and obviously written later—lines which before had always been published as a separate fragment—were in fact a new opening to the poem:

> Bright wanderer, fair coquette of Heaven,
> To whom alone it has been given
> To change and be adored for ever. . . .
> Envy not this dim world, for never
> But once within its shadow grew
> One fair as [thou], but far more true.
>
> (1–6)

No one had previously taken these lines to be part of the poem because they address the moon directly and seem to be written in a different key. But Matthews and Reiman agree on the textual status of the lines, and it is only reasonable to accept them as a revised beginning. Yet it is difficult to avoid thinking that they spoil one of Shelley's finest openings. The abrupt simplicity of 'She left me', followed by the image of the moon balanced and hovering at its zenith just before starting its descent, set the tone and direction of the first part of the poem deftly and movingly. Then why did Shelley add the new opening? Matthews says he wanted to parallel 'the fair but changeable and vanishing moon' with 'the fair, unchanging but vanished Jane'. This may be so, but a further effect of the new opening is to disturb or contaminate in advance the image of the moon momentarily hovering at its height. It is as if Shelley had become uncomfortable retrospectively with the suggestion that the moon's suspended balance could be anything other than the delusive display of a 'fair coquette'. Considering the way in which the poem ends, we may have here from a compositional point of view a revised and contrived beginning distorted by an initially unforeseen ending.

Shelley's speaker clings to the memory of Jane's presence by first 'Thinking over every tone' of what she said or sang, and then by extending those thoughts in a way that leaves totally ambiguous whether Jane touched him as well as her guitar:

> And feeling ever—O too much—
> The soft vibrations of her touch
> As if her gentle hand even now
> Lightly trembled on my brow;
> And thus although she absent were
> Memory gave me all of her
> That even fancy dares to claim.
>
> (21–7)

The difference between 'Memory' and 'fancy' is blurred here in a distinctively Shelleyan, un-Wordsworthian, un-Coleridgean way. The uncertainty continues in the next couplet: 'Her presence had made weak and tame / All passions' (28–9) could mean that when he was with Jane he felt no passion, or that having spent his passion in her presence he no longer felt it. The uncertainty is not resolved, and may even be compounded, by our knowing that Shelley first wrote 'Desire & fear' in line 29, then cancelled it in favor of 'passions'. The critical question to ask is what to make of the ambiguity in this part of the poem. It might simply be said that we are dealing with an unfinished, incompletely revised text about which it is inappropriate to make decisive interpretive judgements. But the reader may still wonder whether the ambiguity is not there to disguise or veil the kind of intimacy Shelley's speaker remembers having experienced, the kind of passion he thinks he felt. One may even want to ask whether or not the poem is fundamentally uncertain or confused in its representations of intimacy and passion. Are the evasive insinuations of what 'even fancy dares to claim' and the blurring of 'Memory' and 'fancy' gestures of discretion or of protective self-deception, or of both?

Tentative answers to these questions begin to suggest themselves as the poem turns, dramatically, at line 33:

> But soon, the guardian angel gone,
> The demon reassumed his throne
> In my faint heart . . . I dare not speak
> My thoughts; but thus disturbed and weak
> I sate.
>
> (33–7)

Those who always complain when Shelley's speakers say that they are weak or faint rarely make clear whether they are objecting to these emotions *per se*, or to Shelley's way of writing about them. Judith Chernaik is on the right track when she compares this poem to the 'Stanzas Written in Dejection—Near Naples'. But the way in which self-pity is dramatized in that poem—'I could lie down like a tired child / And weep away the life of care / Which I have borne and yet must bear' (30–2)—is essentially different from this turn in 'Lines Written in the Bay of Lerici'. Here Shelley is 'disturbed' by emotional and imaginative exhaustion, not just 'weak' with it; 'I dare not speak / My thoughts' confesses an unwillingness, perhaps too an inability, to come fully to terms with the 'demon' in his heart.

In the midst of this critical moment of emotional and expressive failure—and also, the reader may feel, as a way of escaping from it—

Shelley returns in mid-sentence to the natural scene, and we get another passage of arresting lyric serenity that throws into relief the agitation he has just confessed. He remembers the boats out in the bay and imagines them sailing 'to some Elusian star':

> for drink to medicine
> Such sweet and bitter pain as mine.
>   (43–4)

'Sweet and bitter pain' sounds Petrarchan: could Shelley have been using sonnet 164 from Petrarch's *Rime*, a sonnet beautifully translated by Surrey, as a way of trying to formalize or stabilize the poem's emotional turmoil at this point? The poem moves towards its close through yet another sequence of delicately rhymed idyllic images:

> And the wind that winged their flight
> From the land came fresh and light,
> And the scent of sleeping flowers
> And of the coolness of the hours
> Of dew, and the sweet warmth of day
> Was scattered o'er the twinkling bay.
>   (45–50)

The graceful swing of these couplets, with their repeating 'And'-clauses, may lull us into thinking that the 'demon' has again been banished, this time without Jane's presence or even an explicit memory of her. But then we turn one last corner on 'And' and find him waiting in ambush:

> And the fisher with his lamp
> And spear, about the low rocks damp
> Crept, and struck the fish who came
> To worship the delusive flame.
>   (52–4)

The way in which the predatory violence of this image emerges so unexpectedly from the delicately observed seascape, and through the same syntactic pattern as that of the preceding lines, is like nothing else in Shelley, or in English Romantic poetry. Line 51 is syntactically extended and enjambed much like line 48—'And the coolness of the hours / Of dew'—only now the initial phrase after the line-ending, 'And spear', marks a lethal addition to the scene. Then the cadence of the octosyllabic line is disrupted and distorted in 'about the low rocks damp / Crept': notice how the first strongly stressed syllable has crept forward in each line from 'And the fisher' to 'And spear' to 'Crept'. One effect of the passage is to give the reader a sense of having been lured into a beautiful but deadly situation. To say that, however, is to see Shelley not as most commentators have seen him here, in the role of the helpless fish lured to destruction by the 'delusive flame' (a refiguring of the coquettish moon from the beginning of the poem, as well as a variation on the opening image from 'When the Lamp is Shattered'), but rather as the 'fisher with his lamp / And spear'—or perhaps as both fisher and fish—luring the reader, Jane and himself towards a grim ending.

The poem itself ends with a kind of moral—sardonic, obscure and unfinished:

> Too happy, they whose pleasure sought
> Extinguishes all sense and thought
> Of the regret that pleasure . . .
> Destroying [or Seeking] life alone not peace.
> (55–8)

Shelley changed his mind about the first word of the last line, and editors disagree about how it ought to read. Matthews, who reads 'Seeking life alone not peace', says that '*Destroying* is firmly cancelled in MS., with a space before the next word, and probably had no connexion with the rest of the line as it stands.' He paraphrases the entire conclusion: 'They are enviably happy who, in exchanging mere placid existence ("peace") for active sensuous enjoyment ("life"), can remain blind to the price they must pay for it (the spear).' Reiman reads 'Destroying life alone not peace', arguing that although 'It is true that the first seven letters of "Destroying" are firmly cancelled,' 'Seeking' is written a good distance below 'Destroying' as if it were to have been the first word of a new line. But 'even if one accepts Matthews' reading "Seeking" for "Destroying," ' Reiman concludes, 'the basic implications of the figure are not drastically altered.' This seems an astonishing claim to make—and yet in the context of Shelley's deeply unsettled stylistic performance in this poem, I think that Reiman is right. On one reading ('Seeking'), those who die in the instinctive, unreflective pursuit of pleasure are interested only in living, not in living peacefully; on the other reading ('Destroying'), these same creatures, when they die, lose only their life and not a peacefulness of which they were never aware. In either case, the bitter contrast with what Shelley has to lose is clear. It is nevertheless a remarkable thing to be able to say about a poem that its ending is not 'drastically altered' by the difference between 'Seeking life' and 'Destroying life'. No wonder Shelley left this poem without being able to find the rhyme he wanted for its last word, 'peace'.

Like several of the 1822 lyrics but in a more radically self-questioning way, 'Lines Written in the Bay of Lerici' couples an agitated uncertainty about desire and personal relationships with an agitated uncertainty about writing, about verbal representation. The coupling is important to Shelley's entire career: his writing is often most compelling when it questions, explicitly and implicitly, its own empirical origins and linguistic resources. It is also important to his last great piece of writing, *The Triumph of Life*. The draft of 'Lines Written in the Bay of Lerici' along with a draft of lines 11–18 of 'The Keen Stars Were Twinkling' and other fragments, cancellations and notes, appears at that very point in the manuscript of the ongoing poem where Rousseau claims:

> I
> Have suffered what I wrote, or viler pain!—
>
> 'And so my words were seeds of misery

Here *The Triumph of Life* draft appears to break off in the midst of a tercet, the lyric drafts and other scraps of writing intervene, and then Rousseau's speech is completed nine manuscript-pages later:

> Even as the deeds of others.'
> (278–81)

Even if the order of materials in the manuscript does not reflect the exact order of their composition, it is strikingly suggestive that 'Lines Written in the Bay of Lerici' should be framed by Rousseau's arresting internal rhyme: words as 'seeds', words as 'deeds'. Shelley uses Rousseau to make himself and his readers think about the mutual entanglements of writing and living. He might also have used Byron. But he did not dare.

If Shelley had somehow been able to seal off his last lyrics from sexual, domestic and personal literary perturbations, they would be less important demonstrations of his distinctive, unsettled brilliance. Their stylistic range and deftness, their often masterful inventions of voice and rhythm and stanzaic or couplet arrangement, are the workmanship of an artist instinctively wilful yet profoundly unresolved about writing, and about living.

Chronology

1792	Percy Bysshe Shelley born on August 4 at Field Place, Horsham, Sussex, the son of a prosperous landowner and Whig MP.
1802–04	Attends Sion Academy.
1804–10	Studied at Eton.
1810	Publishes *Zastrozzi*, a Gothic novel, in March, followed by *Original Poetry by Victor and Cazire* (Shelley and his sister) in September, and the publication of 'Posthumous Fragments of Margaret Nicholson' in November. Takes up residence at University College, Oxford.
1811	Expelled from Oxford on March 25 for writing pamphlet *The Necessity of Atheism*, with T. J. Hogg, who is also expelled. Elopes in August with Harriet Westbrook and they marry in Edinburgh.
1812	From February to April Shelley goes to Ireland to take part in political agitation on the radical side. In October he meets William Godwin, whose *Political Justice* he had read at Oxford, and with whom he had corresponded.
1813	*Queen Mab* is published in May, and a daughter, Ianthe, is born in June.
1814	On July 28 Shelley elopes to continent with Mary Godwin and returns in September.
1815	In January, Shelley's grandfather, Sir Bysshe Shelley, dies leaving Shelley an income.
1816	William is born to Mary Godwin in January, and "Alastor" is published during that summer. Shelley, Mary, and Mary's half-sister Claire join Byron in Geneva (Claire had seen Byron in London), and they leave for England on August 29. In December the body of Harriet Shelley is found in a pond in Hyde Park. Shelley marries Mary Godwin.
1817	Clara is born in September, and "Laon and Cythna" is printed in December.
1818	The *Revolt of Islam* is published in January, and Shelley moves to Italy in March. In September Clara dies, and Shelley begins *Prometheus Unbound* that Autumn.

1819   William dies in June, and Shelley writes "Ode to the West Wind" in October. He begins A *Philosophical View of Reform* (published 1920) in November. Percy Florence is born.

1820   *The Cenci* is published in the Spring, and Shelley writes "To A Skylark" in June. *Prometheus Unbound* is published during the summer. From August 14–16 Shelley writes "Witch of Atlas."

1821   "A Defence of Poetry" is written between February–March. *Adonais* and *Epipsychidion* is published that summer.

1822   From May–June Shelley works on *Triumph of Life*. On July 8 Shelley drowns at sea.

Contributors

HAROLD BLOOM, Sterling Professor of the Humanities at Yale University, is the author of *The Anxiety of Influence, Poetry and Repression* and many other volumes of literary criticism. His forthcoming study, *Freud: Transference and Authority*, attempts a full-scale reading of all of Freud's major writings. He is the general editor of *The Chelsea House Library of Literary Criticism*.

C. E. PULOS was Professor of English at the University of Nebraska. Besides *The Deep Truth: A Study of Shelley's Scepticism*, he wrote *The New Critics and the Language of Poetry*.

FREDERICK A. POTTLE is Sterling Professor Emeritus of English at Yale. He is renowned for his lifetime's labor of editing the papers of James Boswell and for his writings on Boswell and on Romantic poetry.

JAMES RIEGER is Professor of English at the University of Rochester.

STUART CURRAN is Professor of English at the University of Pennsylvania. His work on Shelley, in addition to his book on *The Cenci*, includes *Shelley's Annus Mirabilis*.

LESLIE BRISMAN is Professor of English at Yale, and the author of *Milton's Poetry of Choice and its Romantic Heirs* and *Romantic Origins*.

The late PAUL DE MAN was Sterling Professor of Comparative Literature at Yale University. His influential theoretical studies are gathered together in *Blindness and Insight, Allegories of Reading* and *The Rhetoric of Romanticism*.

JEAN HALL is Professor of English at California State University at Fullerton.

PAUL FRY is Associate Professor of English at Yale University. He is the author of *The Poet's Calling in the English Ode* and *The Reach of Criticism*.

WILLIAM KEACH is Professor of English at Rutgers University. In addition to his book on Shelley, he is the author of *Elizabethan Erotic Narratives*.

Bibliography

Baker, Carlos. *Shelley's Major Poetry.* New York: Russell and Russell, 1961.
———, ed. *The Selected Poetry and Prose of Percy Bysshe Shelley.* New York: Random House, 1951.
Barcus, James E. *Shelley: The Critical Heritage.* London and Boston: Routledge and Kegan Paul, Ltd., 1975.
Barnard, Ellsworth, ed. *Shelley: Selected Poems, Essays and Letters.* New York: Odyssey Press, 1944.
Barrell, Joseph. *Shelley and the Thought of His Time: A Study in the History of Ideas.* Hamden, Conn.: Archon Books, 1967.
Bloom, Harold. *Shelley's Mythmaking.* New Haven: Yale University Press, 1959.
———, ed. *The Selected Poetry of Shelley.* New York: Signet, 1966.
Brailsford, H.N. *Shelley, Godwin and Their Circle.* Hamden, Conn.: Archon Books, 1969.
Brown, Nathaniel. *Sexuality and Feminism in Shelley.* Cambridge: Cambridge University Press, 1979.
Butter, Peter. *Shelley's Idols of the Cave.* Edinburgh: University Press, 1954.
Cameron, Kenneth Neill. *Romantic Rebels: Essays on Shelley and His Circle.* Cambridge: Harvard University Press, 1973.
———. *Shelley: The Golden Years.* Cambridge: Harvard University Press, 1974.
———, ed. *The Esdaile Notebook: A Volume of Early Poems.* New York: Knopf, 1964.
———. *The Young Shelley: Genesis of a Radical.* London: Victor Gollancz, Ltd., 1951.
Campbell, Olwen Ward. *Shelley and the Unromantics.* London: Methuen & Co., Ltd., 1924.
Chernaik, Judith. *The Lyrics of Shelley.* Cleveland: Case Western Reserve University Press, 1972.
Clark, David Lee, ed. *Shelley's Prose or The Trumpet of a Prophecy.* Albuquerque: University of New Mexico Press, 1954.
Crampton, Margaret. *Shelley's Dream Women.* New York: A.S. Barnes & Co., 1967.
Cronin, Richard. *Shelley's Poetic Thoughts.* London: Macmillan, 1981.
Curran, Stuart. *Shelley's Annus Mirabilis: The Maturing of an Epic Vision.* San Marino, Calif.: Huntington Library, 1975.
———. *Shelley's Cenci: Scorpions Ringed with Fire.* Princeton: Princeton University Press, 1970.
Dawson, P.M.S. *The Unacknowledged Translator: Shelley and Politics.* Oxford: Clarendon Press, 1980.

Dowden, Edward. *The Life of Percy Bysshe Shelley.* London: Routledge and Kegan Paul, Ltd., 1951.

Duerksen, Roland A., ed. *The Cenci.* New York: The Bobbs-Merrill Co., Inc., 1970.

Grabo, Carl. *The Magic Plant: The Growth of Shelley's Thought.* Chapel Hill: University of North Carolina Press, 1936.

——. *A Newton Among Poets: Shelley's Use of Science in Prometheus Unbound.* Chapel Hill: University of North Carolina Press, 1930.

——. *Prometheus Unbound and Interpretation.* Chapel Hill: University of North Carolina Press, 1935.

——. *The Meaning of the Witch of Atlas.* Chapel Hill: University of North Carolina Press, 1935.

Grabo, Carl, and Freeman, Martin, eds. *The Reader's Shelley.* New York: American Book Co., 1942.

Hall, Jean. *The Transforming Image: A Study of Shelley's Major Poetry.* Chicago: University of Illinois Press, 1980.

Hoffman, Harold Leroy. *An Odyssey of the Soul: Shelley's "Alastor."* New York: Columbia University Press, 1933.

Hogg, Thomas Jefferson. *The Life of Percy Bysshe Shelley.* 2 vols. New York: E.P. Dutton & Co., 1933.

Jones, Frederick L., ed. *The Letters of Percy Bysshe Shelley.* Oxford: Clarendon Press, 1964.

Keach, William. *Shelley's Style.* London: Methuen, 1984.

King-Hele, Desmond. *Shelley: His Thought and Work.* 3rd ed. London: Macmillan, 1984.

Leighton, Angela. *Shelley and the Sublime: An Interpretation of the Major Poems.* London: Cambridge University Press, 1984.

Maurois, Andre. *Ariel: The Life of Shelley.* Translated by Ella d'Arcy. New York: D. Appleton & Co., 1924.

Norman, Sylva. *Flight of the Skylark: The Development of Shelley's Reputation.* Norman: University of Oklahoma Press, 1954.

Notopoulos, James A. *The Platonism of Shelley.* Durham, North Carolina: Duke University Press, 1949.

Peck, Walter Edwin. *Shelley: His Life and Work.* 2 vols. Boston: Houghton Mifflin Co., 1927.

Power, Julia. *Shelley in America in the 19th Century.* New York: Gordian Press, 1969.

Pulos, C.E. *The Deep Truth: A Study of Shelley's Skepticism.* Lincoln: The University of Nebraska Press, 1962.

Reiter, Seymour. *A Study of Shelley's Poetry.* Albuquerque: University of New Mexico Press, 1967.

Ridenour, George M. *Shelley: A Collection of Critical Essays.* Englewood Cliffs, New Jersey: Prentice-Hall, Inc., 1965.

Rieger, James. *The Mutiny Within: The Heresies of Percy Bysshe Shelley.* New York: George Braziller, 1967.

Rieman, Donald. *Percy Bysshe Shelley.* New York: Twayne Publishers, Inc., 1969.

Robinson, Charles E. *Shelley and Byron: The Snake and the Eagle Wreathed in Flight.* Baltimore: Johns Hopkins University Press, 1971.

Roe, Ivan. *Shelley: The Last Phase.* London: Hutchinson, 1953.

Rogers, Neville, ed. *The Complete Poetical Works of Percy Bysshe Shelley.* 4 vols. Oxford: Clarendon Press, 1972.

Rolleston, T.W., ed. *A Philosophical View of Reform.* London: Oxford University Press, 1920.

Shawcross, John, ed. *Shelley's Literary and Philosophical Criticism.* Folcroft Library Editions, 1976.

Shepard, Richard Herne, ed. *The Prose Works of Percy Bysshe Shelley.* 2 vols. London: Chatto and Windus, 1906.

Wasserman, Earl R. *Shelley: A Critical Reading.* Baltimore: Johns Hopkins University Press, 1971.

Webb, Timothy. *Shelley: A Voice Not Understood.* Manchester: Manchester University Press, 1977.

White, Newman Ivey. *Shelley.* 2 vols. New York: Knopf, 1959.

Woodman, Ross Greig. *The Apocalyptic Vision in the Poetry of Shelley.* Toronto: University of Toronto Press, 1964.

Zillman, Lawrence John, ed. *Shelley's Prometheus Unbound, A Variorum Edition.* Seattle: University of Washington Press, 1959.

———, ed. *Shelley's Prometheus Unbound: the Text and the Drafts, Toward a Modern Definitive Edition.* New Haven: Yale University Press, 1968.

Acknowledgments

"Introduction" by Harold Bloom from *The Ringers in the Tower* by Harold Bloom, copyright © 1971 by University of Chicago Press. Reprinted by permission.

"Skepticism and Platonism" by C.E. Pulos from *The Deep Truth: A Study of Shelley's Skepticism* by C.E. Pulos, copyright © 1954 by University of Nebraska Press. Reprinted by permission.

"The Role of Asia in the Dramatic Action of Shelley's *Prometheus Unbound*" by Frederick A. Pottle, from *Shelley: A Collection of Critical Essays*, edited by George M. Ridenour, copyright © 1965 by Frederick A. Pottle. Reprinted by permission.

"Orpheus and the West Wind" by James Rieger from *The Mutiny Within* by James Rieger, copyright © 1967 by James Rieger. Reprinted by permission of George Braziller, Inc.

"*The Cenci*: The Tragic Resolution" by Stuart Curran from *Shelley's Cenci: Scorpions Ringed with Fire* by Stuart Curran, copyright © 1970 by Princeton University Press. Reprinted by permission.

"Shelley and His Precursors" by Harold Bloom from *Poetry and Repression* by Harold Bloom, copyright © 1976 by Yale University Press. Reprinted by permission.

"*Epipsychidion*" by Leslie Brisman from *Romantic Origins* by Leslie Brisman, copyright © 1978 by Cornell University Press. Reprinted by permission.

"Shelley Disfigured: *The Triumph of Life*" by Paul de Man from *Deconstruction and Criticism* by Paul de Man, copyright © 1979 by Harold Bloom. Reprinted by permission of The Continuum Publishing Company.

"*Adonais*" by Jean Hall from *The Transforming Image: A Study of Shelley's Major Poetry* by Jean Hall, copyright © 1980 by University of Illinois. Reprinted by permission.

"Shelley's *Defence of Poetry* in Our Time" by Paul H. Fry from *The Reach of Criticism* by Paul H. Fry, copyright © 1983 by Yale University Press. Reprinted by permission.

"Shelley's Last Lyrics" by William Keach from *Shelley's Style* by William Keach, copyright © 1984 by Methuen Co. Reprinted by permission.

Index

A

Adonais (essay), 145–47
Adonais, 3, 9, 22–24, 59, 145–57
  aggression and, 150–51
  apocalyptic nature of, 24
  "Byzantium" poems compared to, 23, 24
  Coleridge and, 105–06
  concept of beauty in, 43, 44
  cycles of nature in, 148
  fire metaphor in, 107, 108
  heaven in, 152, 154
  immortality, concept in, 151, 152, 155
  Keats and, 22, 23, 24, 105
  materialism of, 24
  model for poem, 145
  poetic existence and, 23
  splendours of, 147
  "stranger" in, 150
  temporal elements of, 147–48
  transformational sections of, 145
  turning point in, 151
  Urania in, 146, 148–49, 153
  Wordsworth and, 105–06
aesthetic experience
  Shelley and, 9
Alastor, 5–6, 87, 98
  compared to *Epipsychidion*, 114–16
  concept of beauty in, 40–41
  hero of, 5
  idealized beloved in, 113
  imagination, concept in, 5
allegory
  Prometheus Unbound as, 47, 55
  Shelley's concept of, 174
Amphisbaena, 20
apocalyptic elements
  in *Adonais*, 24
  "Ode to the West Wind," 14
Apology Against a Pamphlet, An, 96
Apophrades, 104, 108
apotheosis, 23–24
a priori concepts, 36, 37

Ariel, 203–06
Aristotle, 125, 128, 160
Asia, 11–12, 13, 49–56
  Demogorgon's responses to, 51–53
  evil, concept of, 52
  passivity versus action of, 50, 51
  song of, 113
askesis, 103
Astrophel, 22
Auden, W. H., 111
Auerbach, Erich, 94, 95
"Ave Atque Vale," 22

B

Bagehot, Walter, 31
Barnard, Ellsworth, 32
beauty
  in *Adonais*, 43, 44
  in *Alastor*, 40–41, 42
  death and, 43–44
  in *Hymn to Intellectual Beauty*, 39, 41, 42
  in *Julian and Maddalo*, 42
  learning about beauty, stages of, 38–39
  Plato's position on, 38
  related to concept of knowledge, 38–39
  in *The Sensitive Plant*, 42, 86
  Shelley's mystical experience and, 38–39
  Shelley's position on, 38
  in *Speculations on Metaphysics*, 42
  in *The Triumph of Life*, 45
Bible, 91–95
  Book of Ezekiel, 91–94
  fire imagery in, 94, 98
  Revelation of St. John the Divine, 94
  visual representations in, 91–92
Biographia Literaria, 177
Bion, 145, 184
Blake, William, 2, 6, 10, 11, 17, 21, 92, 97
  concept of "the poet," 13
  religious aspects of, 12–13

Bloom, Harold, 91–112, 186
Borges, Jorge Luis, 9
Brisman, Leslie, 113–20
Bush, Douglas, 58–59, 170
Byron, George Gordon, Lord, 7, 61, 87,
    189–91, 198, 201
    Shelley's rivalry with, 190–91
    with Shelley in Pisa, 189–90
"Byzantium" poems
    compared to *Adonais*, 23, 24

C

carpe diem genre, 192
Casa Magni, 207–09
Cenci, Beatrice, 17, 18, 77–81
    compared to Prometheus, 79, 80
    father's sexual attack of, 79–80
    murder of father, 79–80
    view of the world, 74–75
Cenci, The, 16–18, 73–89
    aesthetic power of, 18
    Beatrice, 17, 18, 77–81
    characters, qualities of, 17
    compared to *Prometheus Unbound*,
        80–82
    Count Cenci, 17–18
    evil, concept in, 79–80, 84
    sexual union as metaphor, 81
    tragic aspects of, 17, 18
    warrant for Cenci, irony of, 81
    see also Cenci, Beatrice
"The Cenci: The Tragic Resolution,"
    73–89
chariot, 91, 92, 94, 95, 107, 110
    as image of transumption, 96–97, 98,
        108
    Chariot of Life in *The Triumph of Life*,
        138, 140, 142
    Chariot of Paternal Diety, 91, 96,
        100
    in *Prometheus Unbound*, 99
Charity, A. C., 94, 105
Charles I, 190, 191
Chernaik, Judith, 188, 202, 203, 212
Cicero, view of Plato, 35
Clairmont, Claire, 37, 88, 187, 188, 189,
    207
clinamen, 103
Coleridge, Samuel, 111, 159, 162, 177
    Adonais and, 105–06
"Corinna's going a Maying," 192

Count Cecil, 17–18
Cronin, Richard, 203, 206
"Crystal Cabinet, The," 6
Curran, Stuart, 73–89

D

Daemon of the World, The, 83, 98
daemonization, 103
Dante, 95, 105, 160
Davie, Donald, 7, 193, 194, 200
death
    concept of beauty and, 43–44
    Shelley's view of, 24
Deep Truth, The, 7
Defence of Poetry, A, 2, 34, 67, 159–84
    Bacon in, 163
    general signs in, 177
    imagination, Shelley's view of, 164,
        165, 167, 169
    language
        ancient and modern, 177–78
        Shelley's notion of, 172–74
    Longinus, similarities to, 160–61,
        180, 182
    mind in creation, 22
    Plato in, 163
    poets in, 110–11
    reason, Shelley's view of, 165–66,
        168–69
    signs, 178
    thoughts, Shelley's view of, 167–68
    veil-symbol, 175, 180
"Dejection" Ode, 106
De Man, Paul, 121–44
Demogorgon, 8, 49–50
    characteristics of, 12
    speaking to Asia, 51–53
devil, the, 78–79
Diotima, 38, 39
Diversions of Purley, 176
Dowden, Edward, 31
drama, as literary form, 57
Drummond, Sir William, 37, 168
Dryden, John, compared to Shelley,
    161–62

E

Eliot, T. S., 161, 173, 181
Endymion, 6
"England in 1819," rhyme scheme, 60
enjambment, 61–62

epipsyche, 6
Epipsychidion (essay), 113–20
Epipsychidion, 21–22, 59, 113–20
    cavern image in, 120
    compared to Alastor, 114–16
    concept of beauty in, 44
    concept of love in, 21
    dream-vision section, 117–18
    hope, 21
    idealized beloved and, 113, 114
    mind in creation, 21–22
"Essay on Christianity," 151, 180
"Essay on Life," 178
evil
    The Cenci, 79–80, 84
    Prometheus Unbound, 52, 53, 79, 84
    The Revolt of Islam, 82, 84
    Shelley's conception of, 82–88
Excursion, The, 5
Ezekiel, Book of, 91–94

F
Farrer, Austin, 94
figura, 94–97
    meaning of, 94–95
    Shelley's use of, 100–01
    Virgil as, 95
fire
    Hebraic image of, 94, 98
    as metaphor in Adonis, 107, 108
    as Romantic metaphor, 107–08
"Four Ages of Poetry," 163, 164, 167
Four Zoas, The
    compared to Prometheus Unbound, 10
"Fragment on Miracles," 165
French Revolution, The, 17
Fry, Paul, 159–84
Furies, the, 48

G
Giorgio, Francesco, 64
Godwin, William, 4, 82
Gosborne, John, 187
Grabo, Carlo, 32
Gray, Thomas, 97
Greek myth, 53

H
Hall, Jean, 145–57
Happner, Richard, 188
"Happner scandal," 188

Heaven, 152, 154
Hellas, 86
Hereford, C. H., 31
hermaphrodite, 21
Herrick, Richard, 192–93, 203
Hitchener, Elizabeth, 82
Holmes, Richard, 190
Homer, 125
hope, 21
Hume, David, 32, 36, 168, 173
    empirical concept of cause, 37
    innate passions, theory of, 37
    memory, view of, 175
"Hymn of Apollo," 2, 15
"Hymn to Intellectual Beauty," 26
    concept of beauty in, 39, 41, 42
    contradictory aspects of, 4
    weakness of, 4
"Hymn to Mercury," 7
    compared to The Witch of Atlas,
      19–20

I
Imagination
    concept of in Alastor, 5
    concept of tragedy and, 17
    Shelley's study of, 6
    Shelley's view of, 164, 165, 167, 169
    Wordsworth's definition of, 38
"Intimations" Ode, 102, 106, 108, 109,
    115
irony
    in The Cenci, 81
    in Shelley's poetry, 27
Italian stanza forms, 60–61

J
Job, 14
Johnson, Dr. Samuel, 13, 28
Julian and Maddalo, 7, 84
    concept of beauty in, 42
Jupiter, 11, 47, 52, 53, 55

K
Kabbalah, 92, 93, 94
Kant, Immanuel
    strict transcendentalism of, 36
Keach, William, 185–215
Keats, John, 27, 105
    Adonais and, 22, 23, 24, 105
"Keen Stars Were Twinkling, The," 215

kenosis, 10, 116, 117
Knight, G. Wilson, 20
knowledge
    concept of beauty and, 39–40
    Shelley's view of, 37

L
"Lament for Adonis" (Bion), 145, 148
language
    figuration, 138
    imposition, 140
    positing power of, 139–40
    Shelley's view of, 172–74, 177
    signs, 177–78
    in *The Triumph of Life*, 137–39
Laon and Cyntha, 6
"Letter to Maria Gisborne," 7, 28
Lewis, C. S., 27, 50, 161
"Lift not the painted veil"
    rhyme scheme, 60
light
    use in *The Triumph of Life*, 131, 133,
        142
"Lines . . . on . . . The Death of
    Napoleon," 15
"Lines Written in the Bay of Lerici," 7, 15,
    210–15
    revised beginning of, 211
    unfinished ending of, 214
    Jane Williams and, 210, 211, 212,
        213, 214
Locke, John, 176, 177
logic, 166–67
Longinus
    compared to Shelley, 159–61, 180,
        182
love
    destruction and, 3
    in *Epipsychidion*, 21
    in *Prometheus Unbound*, 48, 55, 56
Lycidas, 22, 24
lyrical poetry, 2–3
    Shelley's last poems, 185–215

M
Maddalo, Count, 185, 186
"Magnetic Lady to Her Patient, The,"
    199, 201–02
    Jane Williams in, 201–02
Mask of Anarchy, The, 28, 86
Matthews, G. M., 187, 210–11, 214

Medwin, Thomas, 23, 50, 187
memory, 175
Merkabah, 91, 92, 93, 97, 98, 100
metaphysics, 166–67
Milton, John, 22, 24, 96–97, 99, 100–01
    Prometheus Unbound and, 10–11
miracles, 165
Miranda, 203–06
misprision
    The Triumph of Life, 102, 103–04
"Mont Blanc," 22, 26
    contradictory aspects of, 3–4
    weakness of, 4
Montaigne, Michel
    view of Plato, 34
More, Paul Elmer, 31
mystical experiences
    concept of beauty and, 38–39

N
Narcissus (in *The Triumph of Life*),
    133–34, 138
nature, 148
"Notes on Sculptures in Rome and
    Florence," 179
Notopoulos, James A., 32
numerology, 64

O
"Ode to Liberty," 15, 68
"Ode to the West Wind"
    apocalyptic nature of, 14
    levels of myth in, 66
    rhyme scheme, 59–60, 61–62
    Roman art and, 67–68
    Rousseau and, 26
    stanzas, relationship to each other, 14
    voice of, 71
    wind, imagery of, 63
On a Passage in Crito, 33–34
"On the Devil and Devils," 78
On the Soul, 33
"Orpheus," 65–66, 68–71
"Orpheus and the West Wind," 57–71
Ottava rima, 20, 61
Ovid, 69–70
"Ozymandias," 60

P
Panthea, 49, 50, 51
    vision of, 100, 101

Paradise Lost
  relationship to *Prometheus Unbound*, 10
Peacock, T. L., 162–67
  concept of poetry, 163–64
Peck, Walter E., 187
Perfect Wagnerite, The, 11
Peter Bell the Third, 37, 85, 86
Phaedo, 39, 40
Philosophical View of Reform, A, 165, 181
Plato, 125, 129, 132
  admired by Shelley, 34
  beauty, concept of, 38–45
  differences from Shelley, 9
  doctrine of reminiscence, 36, 39, 40, 45
  eighteenth century view of, 32
  Montaigne's view of, 34
  as poetic dreamer, 32–33
  references to, 32–33
  revaluation by Shelley, 33–35, 45
  reveries of, 33
  Shelley's criticism of, 33
  as skeptic, 35
  sophisms of, 33–34
  strict transcendentalism and, 35–36
Platonism, 31–45
  absence of in Shelley, 8–9
  critic's positions about Shelley's, 31–32
  Neoplatonism of Shelley, 32
  skepticism of Shelley and, 32, 33, 34–35, 45
poet
  in *A Defence of Poetry*, 110–11
  Blake's conception of, 13
  Johnson's conception of, 13
  Shelley's view of, 183–84
poetry
  Peacock's concept of, 163–64
  Shelley's view of, 178–83
Pottle, Frederick A., 13, 47–56
Price, Martin, 12
Prince Athanase, 6
Progress of Poesy, The, 97
Prometheus Unbound, 7–8, 10–13, 47–56
  action of, 47, 48, 51, 54–55
  aesthetic achievement of, 13
  Asia, 11–12, 13
    role of, 49–56
    as symbol, 55

chariot, image of, 99
  compared to *The Cenci*, 80–82
  contradictory nature of, 7–8
  Demogorgon, 8, 12
  evil, concept of, 52, 53, 79, 84
  human mind, concept in, 13
  Jupiter, 11
    as symbol, 55
  love in, 48, 55, 56
  Milton and, 10–11
  Prometheus, 11
    as symbol, 55
  religious aspects of, 12
  sexual union as metaphor, 81
  spirits in, 48, 49–50
  tone of, 7
Pulos, C. E., 7, 8, 31–45
"pure reason," 36, 37–38
Putnam, Hilary, 170

Q
Queen Mab, 83, 86, 87, 98
  reference to Plato in, 32

R
reason
  Shelley's view of, 164, 165, 167, 169
regeneration, 85–86
Reiman, Donald, 123, 187
religion
  in Blake, 12–13
  in *Prometheus Unbound*, 12
  in Shelley's poetry, 2
reminiscence, doctrine of, 36, 39, 40, 45
reveries, of Plato, 33
Revolt of Islam, The, 6
  evil, concept in, 82, 84
rhyme scheme
  in "Lift not the painted veil," 60
  in "Ode to the West Wind," 59–60, 61–62
  in "Sonnet to Byron," 60
Richards, I. A., 166
Rieger, James, 57–71, 79
Robinson, Charles E., 190, 191
"Role of Asia in the Dramatic Action of Shelley's *Prometheus Unbound*, 47–56
Roman art, 67–68
Rousseau, Jean Jacques, 109
  characteristics of work, 127

Rousseau, Jean Jacques (*continued*)
  "Ode to the West Wind" and, 26
  self-knowledge of, 126, 128
  The Triumph of Life and, 25–26,
    123–32, 141
Ruin, 48, 49

S
Savella, 81
"Scepticism and Platonism, 31–45
science, Shelley's position on, 170–71
scorpion
  as symbol, 77–78
Sensitive Plant, The, 7, 18–19
  concept of beauty in, 42
  loss in, 19
  skepticism of, 19
  tone of, 19
"Serpent is Shut Out from Paradise, The,"
    199–201
  biographical referents, 201
  Byron's influence on, 201
  self-pitying tone of, 200
sexual union
  as metaphor, 81–82
Shaw, George Bernard, 11, 12
"Shelley and His Precursors," 91–112
"Shelley Disfigured: *The Triumph of Life*,
    121–44
Shelley, Mary, 188–89, 191–92, 200,
    201–02
  miscarriage of, 208–09
Shelley, Percy Bysshe
  Byron, relationship to, 189–91,
    207–08
  Casa Magni, 207–09
  chronological development of, 1–29
  compared to Dryden, 161–62
  compared to Longinus, 159–61
  critics of, 1, 16, 27, 28
  death of, 142
  death, view of, 24
  death, visions of, 209
  differences from Plato, 9
  evil, conception of, 82–88
  form of, 27–28
  growth as poet, 5, 6, 14, 15, 22
  Humean temperament of, 8, 9, 26
  intellectual transformation of, 4
  irony in poetry, 27
  lyrics of 1822, 185–215

  Ovid, compared to, 70
  Platonism of, 31–45
  poet, view of, 181, 183–84
  poetry, view of, 178–83
  regeneration, view of, 85–86
  as renovationist, 28
  Mary Shelley and, 188–89, 191–92,
    200, 201–02, 208–09
  skepticism of, 5, 7, 8–9, 19,
    22
  urbane style of, 7
  Jane Williams, relationship to,
    187–88, 208
  workmanship of, 15–16
"Shelley's *Defence of Poetry* in Our Time,"
    159–84
"Shelley's Last Lyrics," 185–215
skepticism
  of Shelley, 5, 7, 8–9, 22
  of *The Sensitive Plant*, 19
  Shelley's Platonism and, 32, 33,
    34–35, 45
Socrates, as skeptic, 35
"Sonnet to Byron," 60
sophism, of Plato, 33–34
soul
  Shelley's view of, 114–15
Speculations on Metaphysics
  concept of beauty in, 42
Speculations on Morals, 83
stanza, Italian forms, 60–61
"Stanzas Written in Dejection—Near
    Naples," 212
Statues, The, 123
Stevens, Wallace, 8, 14, 28, 175
strict transcendentalism
  of Kant, 36
  of Plato, 36
  of Shelley, 35, 37–38
Symposium, The, 38, 39
  references to Plato, 33

T
Taafe, John, 147
Temple, William, 38
terza rima, 59, 62, 68–69
tessera, 103, 115
Thyrsis, 22
Tikkun, 115
"To a Skylark," 194
  misinterpretation of, 15

"To Jane: The Invitation," 7, 15, 192–94
  carpe diem genre and, 192
  literary tradition in, 193–94
"To Jane: The Recollection," 15, 192, 194–99
  biographical referents, 198
  calm section of, 196–97
  reflection imagery in, 197–98
tone, 57, 58
Tooke, Horne, 176–77
transumption, 96–97, 98
  chariot as image of, 96–97, 98, 108, 110
Treatise on Morals, 166, 168, 179
  criticism of Tooke in, 176
Triumph of Life, The, 2, 3, 4, 6, 25–27, 87, 102–105, 121–44
  action of, gliding to trampling, 135–37
  as an antithetical work, 102
  beauty, concept in, 45
  Chariot of Life in, 108, 138, 140, 142
  disfiguration and, 141–43
  earlier versions of, 123
  figuration in, 138–39
  fire metaphor of, 107–08
  forgetting, metaphor of, 129–31, 132, 141
  Greek philosophers in, 124
  language of, 137–39
  light, use of image, 131, 133, 142
  map of misprision of, 102, 103–04
  message of, 26
  metamorphosis of Rousseau, 126–27
  Narcissus, 133–34, 138
  peace/aggression theme, 127
  positing power of language in, 139–40
  questions, structure of text, 125, 140–41
  Rousseau and, 25–26, 123–32, 141
  shape in, 131, 132–34, 136, 137, 138–39, 141–42
  sun as image, 134–35, 139–40
  tone of, 25
  waking/sleeping metaphor, 130
  water symbol, 132–33, 135
  Wordsworth and, 123–24

"Two Spirits: An Allegory, The," 15
Tyger, The,
  Hebraic influence in, 92

U
"Unfinished Drama," 206
Urania, 146, 148–49, 153
urbane style
  of Shelley, 7

V
veil, symbol of, 175, 180
Venus, 21
Virgil, as a figura, 95
Vision, A, 20
Visions of the Daughters of Albion, 17, 21
Vita Nuova, 44
Viviani, Emilia, 21, 44, 188
voice, Biblical, 94
Voltaire, 123, 124, 128

W
"When the Lamp is Shattered," 15, 205, 206
White, Newman Ivey, 188
Williams, Edward, 187, 200, 201
Williams, Jane, 15, 191–92, 199, 200, 201–02, 210, 211
  relationship with Shelley, 187–88, 208
Williams, William Carlos, 28
Winstanley, Lillian, 31
Witch of Atlas, The, 7, 19–21
  compared to "Hymn to Mercury," 19–20
  hermaphrodite, 20
  witch, behavior of, 20
"With a Guitar, to Jane," 15, 199, 203–06
  mortality and death in, 206
Wordsworth, William, 4, 5, 15, 102, 108–09, 110–11, 118, 177
  Adonais and, 105–06
  Triumph of Life and, 123–24, 132

Y
Yeats, W. B., 12, 20, 122, 130

Z
"Zeale," 96–97

Modern Critical Views

Continued from front of book

Gabriel García Márquez
Andrew Marvell
Carson McCullers
Herman Melville
George Meredith
James Merrill
John Stuart Mill
Arthur Miller
Henry Miller
John Milton
Yukio Mishima
Molière
Michel de Montaigne
Eugenio Montale
Marianne Moore
Alberto Moravia
Toni Morrison
Alice Munro
Iris Murdoch
Robert Musil
Vladimir Nabokov
V. S. Naipaul
R. K. Narayan
Pablo Neruda
John Henry, Cardinal
    Newman
Friedrich Nietzsche
Frank Norris
Joyce Carol Oates
Sean O'Casey
Flannery O'Connor
Christopher Okigbo
Charles Olson
Eugene O'Neill
José Ortega y Gasset
Joe Orton
George Orwell
Ovid
Wilfred Owen
Amos Oz
Cynthia Ozick
Grace Paley
Blaise Pascal
Walter Pater
Octavio Paz
Walker Percy
Petrarch
Pindar
Harold Pinter
Luigi Pirandello
Sylvia Plath
Plato

Plautus
Edgar Allan Poe
Poets of Sensibility & the
    Sublime
Poets of the Nineties
Alexander Pope
Katherine Anne Porter
Ezra Pound
Anthony Powell
Pre-Raphaelite Poets
Marcel Proust
Manuel Puig
Alexander Pushkin
Thomas Pynchon
Francisco de Quevedo
François Rabelais
Jean Racine
Ishmael Reed
Adrienne Rich
Samuel Richardson
Mordecai Richler
Rainer Maria Rilke
Arthur Rimbaud
Edwin Arlington Robinson
Theodore Roethke
Philip Roth
Jean-Jacques Rousseau
John Ruskin
J. D. Salinger
Jean-Paul Sartre
Gershom Scholem
Sir Walter Scott
William Shakespeare
    (3 vols.)
    Histories & Poems
    Comedies & Romances
    Tragedies
George Bernard Shaw
Mary Wollstonecraft
    Shelley
Percy Bysshe Shelley
Sam Shepard
Richard Brinsley Sheridan
Sir Philip Sidney
Isaac Bashevis Singer
Tobias Smollett
Alexander Solzhenitsyn
Sophocles
Wole Soyinka
Edmund Spenser
Gertrude Stein
John Steinbeck

Stendhal
Laurence Sterne
Wallace Stevens
Robert Louis Stevenson
Tom Stoppard
August Strindberg
Jonathan Swift
John Millington Synge
Alfred, Lord Tennyson
William Makepeace
    Thackeray
Dylan Thomas
Henry David Thoreau
James Thurber and S. J.
    Perelman
J. R. R. Tolkien
Leo Tolstoy
Jean Toomer
Lionel Trilling
Anthony Trollope
Ivan Turgenev
Mark Twain
Miguel de Unamuno
John Updike
Paul Valéry
Cesar Vallejo
Lope de Vega
Gore Vidal
Virgil
Voltaire
Kurt Vonnegut
Derek Walcott
Alice Walker
Robert Penn Warren
Evelyn Waugh
H. G. Wells
Eudora Welty
Nathanael West
Edith Wharton
Patrick White
Walt Whitman
Oscar Wilde
Tennessee Williams
William Carlos Williams
Thomas Wolfe
Virginia Woolf
William Wordsworth
Jay Wright
Richard Wright
William Butler Yeats
A. B. Yehoshua
Emile Zola